Sport Policy

WITHDRAWN

D0322122

Barrie Houlihan is Professor of Sport Policy at Loughborough University and also Visiting Professor at the Norwegian School of Sport Sciences, Oslo

Iain Lindsey is Senior Lecturer in Sports Development at Edge Hill University

Routledge Research in Sport, Culture and Society

Sport Policy in Britain

Barrie Houlihan and Iain Lindsey

Routledge
Taylor & Francis Group
NEW YORK   LONDON

First published 2013
by Routledge
711 Third Avenue, New York, NY 10017

Simultaneously published in the UK
by Routledge
2 Park Square, Milton Park, Abingdon, Oxfordshire OX14 4RN

First issued in paperback 2014

Routledge is an imprint of the Taylor and Francis Group,
an informa business

Library of Congress Cataloging-in-Publication Data
Houlihan, Barrie.
  Sport policy in Britain / Barrie Houlihan, Iain Lindsey.
    p. cm. — (Routledge research in sport, culture and society ; 18)
  Includes bibliographical references and index.
  1. Sports and state—Great Britain. 2. Sports—Political aspects—
Great Britain. 3. Sports administration—Great Britain. 4. Sports—
Social aspects—Great Britain. I. Lindsey, Iain. II. Title.
  GV706.35.H689 2012
  306.4'830941—dc23
  2012013300

ISBN 978-0-415-87483-0 (hbk)
ISBN 978-1-138-92060-6 (pbk)
ISBN 978-0-203-09427-3 (ebk)

Typeset in Sabon
by IBT Global.

Iain would like to dedicate this book to his father who, with his love of sport and ongoing thirst for knowledge, was and continues to be a wonderful role model and guiding influence.

Contents

Figures

Tables

1   The Framework for Analysis

The period since 1990 has been one of the most significant for British sport since government began to take a sustained interest in the policy area in the mid-1960s. What was, in the late 1980s, a largely neglected backwater of public policy has experienced a rapid increase in political attention leading to a plethora of policy initiatives and a substantial increase in public funding. The purpose of this book is to provide an analysis of the nature and extent of change in the fortunes of British sport. It is argued that since the early 1990s there has been significant change across a range of dimensions of sport policy and especially in relation to: the salience of sport to government; the allocation of government resources associated with sport; the machinery of government concerned with sport; and the distribution of power in the policy sub-sector.

The analysis in this book is focused on developments in policy related to community, elite and school sport, but is concerned mainly with the non-commercial providers and aspects. While it is acknowledged that the government has a significant role in regulating elite sport within the commercial sector (professional football, rugby, tennis et cetera) and in shaping the business environment of the commercial fitness sector, the activities of the government or the state more broadly in these areas of sport provision are not the central concerns of this study. As regards the geographic focus of the book, it is acknowledged that much of the substantive focus is on sport policy which operates at the UK level (mainly elite athlete development) and at the England level (for example, in the chapters that deal with local government and with youth sport). However, the impact of devolution is a theme that runs through the study and is dealt with explicitly in Chapter 4.

THE SIGNIFICANCE OF 1990

Nineteen ninety was an important year in British politics in general and, as would soon become clear, for sport policy. Margaret Thatcher, who had been prime minister for over eleven years and who had resigned in

November 1990, had had a profound impact on British politics and on the role of government. Her successor, John Major, shared many of her principles, especially in relation to the role of government and public expenditure (which should both be limited). However, where he differed significantly from his predecessor was in relation to his view of the relationship between the individual and society and in his attitude towards sport. Whereas Margaret Thatcher adopted an atomistic view of 'society' as comprising a collection of utility maximising rational actors, John Major took a view which was closer to 'one-nation' Conservatism and its acknowledgement of national and local community. More significantly for this study, he was passionate about sport and, although a reluctant interventionist, he successfully placed sport back on the public policy agenda.

In the early 1990s sport was a policy sub-sector which was underresourced, lacking in strategic leadership and on the margin of the government's agenda. When sport forced itself to the attention of government it was often through crisis. Yet by the end of the decade sport was being promoted by a number of senior politicians as a source of social capital and national pride. Given this history of relative neglect during Margaret Thatcher's time as prime minister, it is not surprising that there was a lack of clarity within public organisations, especially the Sports Council, about the public policy objectives of sport. Writing of the time, David Pickup, the Sports Council's director-general, commented that 'we were constantly vexed by the studied lack of any specific endorsement—or even rejection— by the government of those earlier strategies [*Sport in the Community: The Next Ten Years*, published in 1982, and *Into the Nineties: A Strategy for Sport 1988–1993*, published in 1988] . . . It has regrettably to be added that the corporate plans were no more productive of a specific Departmental endorsement' (1996, p. 53). While the Sports Council was busy formulating policy (in relation to important issues such as equity of access to sport and the nature of the sport development continuum), their internal discussions were taking place in a public policy vacuum.

As regards the machinery of government associated with sport, the picture was one of competing agencies, overlapping jurisdictions and role confusion. Not only did the GB Sports Council have a confusing dual remit for UK-wide issues and for English issues, but also the division of responsibility between the GB Sports Council and the three 'home country' sports councils was very unclear. There was also a degree of role confusion insofar as the GB Sports Council, at times, acted as though it were an advocate on behalf of sport rather than an agent of government (albeit masked by the fiction of a Royal Charter). Pickup again captures accurately the lack of clarity within government in this period over the roles and responsibilities of the agencies:

> As far as functions are concerned, [Minister for Sport] Iain Sproat's statement of 8 July 1994 shed little light upon the matter [of reform

of the GB Sports Council]; replete with ambiguities and confusion, it sought to present any future English Sport Council's involvement with 'mass participation' as unnecessary whilst encouraging it to promote 'grassroots' activity. He also envisaged both the planned UK Sports Council and all four Home Country Councils as having some responsibilities for promoting sporting excellence, but was impenetrably vague as to how the UKSC might, in practice, achieve any sensible co-ordination of effort (1996, pp. 209–210).

Other sport organisations operated within a broader sports landscape which was fragmented and resource-poor with the consequence that they were routinely excluded from policy debates. National governing bodies (NGBs) retained a high degree of autonomy from the state due in part to their preference, but also in part due to their lack of capacity to lobby effectively and to the state's lack of interest in hearing their opinions. Local authorities had proved ineffective in resisting privatisation of the management of sport and leisure centres and were generally considered to be an impediment to the ambitions of the Thatcherite wing of the Conservative party to reduce the size of the state. Schools were grappling with the implementation of the National Curriculum for Physical Education (NCPE) and still recovering from the damaging consequences of the introduction of local financial management of schools and the teachers' dispute with the government in the mid-1980s, both of which had significantly reduced the extent of extracurricular sport.

John Major's appointment as prime minister came at a time when the sport sub-sector was underresourced and fragmented, characterised by ineffective leadership and little sense of purpose and direction. The few indicators of effectiveness of sport policy that were available at the time painted a mixed picture. Somewhat ironically, 1990 marked the high point of sport participation (48 per cent of adults participated in sport—walking excluded—in the previous four weeks). However, this was more likely the result of the release of latent demand made possible by the building of facilities in the late 1970s and early 1980s than successful activity by sport development staff. Less positive were the differences in participation levels between genders (19 percentage point gap between men and women's participation), social classes (37 percentage point gap between professional and unskilled manual) and age groups (a 44 percentage point gap between the 20–24 years age group and the 60–69 years age group). As regards indicators of success at the high performance level, the British team at the summer Olympics in 1992 achieved a modest 13th place in the medal table before a disastrous 36th place in Atlanta four years later.

In the intervening period it would appear that this rather bleak picture of sport policy, provision and impact has been radically changed with sport having established ministerial representation in the Cabinet, having also benefited significantly from almost 15 years of national lottery funding,

Table 1.1 Dimensions of Change

Dimension	1980s	Mid-1990s	Early 2010s
Salience of sport to government	Low	Increasing following John Major's appointment as PM	Consistently and significantly higher than in the 1980s
Public policy objectives for sport (direct and indirect)	Vague, except in response to specific problems (e.g. football hooliganism) when they were confused	Emerging strong focus on school and elite level sport	Reasonably firmly established around youth participation, elite success, event hosting and sport's contribution to health improvement and improved educational standards
Machinery of government concerned with sport	Neglected and with limited resources; confused overlapping remits	Reduction in overlapping remits (due to establishment of UK Sport); appointment of a Minister for Sport and establishment of a ministry responsible for sport. Still very complex	Still complex
Broader national landscape of sport	Fragmented and labyrinthine; only limited contact between public, not-for-profit and commercial sectors	Fragmented and labyrinthine; only limited contact between public, not-for-profit and commercial sectors	Much closer integration between the public and not-for-profit sectors
Distribution of power in the policy sub-sector	Lobbying capacity weak in both the not-for-profit and commercial sectors	Increasing lobbying activity by Central Council for Physical Recreation, national governing bodies of sport and BISL (Business in Sport and Leisure)	A more vigorous policy network with more effectively organised interests especially in relation to elite sport and youth/school sport.
Sport policy outcomes	Limited connection between public policy inputs and sport outcomes	Significant increase in resources available to central government to shape sport (via the national lottery)	Tighter integration between public and not-for-profit sectors; NGBs increasingly the agents of government policy; substantial success in increasing participation in school sport and also in winning Olympic and Paralympic medals

being able to point to a significant increase in participation among school-children and having achieved considerable success at the Beijing Olympic and Paralympic Games in 2008. However, progress had not been uniformly positive as sport organisations still operated within a complex (and often fractious) organisational landscape and participation levels remained stubbornly static and variable by class, gender and age. Table 1.1 provides a summary of the contrast.

In the period since 1990 there has arguably been a significant transformation in the status and impact of sport policy. The primary aim of this book is to analyse the character and significance of the changes that have taken place in relation to the government's policy towards, and forms of intervention in, sport. A necessary complementary aim is to identify, assess and utilise a set of concepts and analytic frameworks which will help in fulfilling the book's primary aim. With these two aims in mind, this chapter continues with a review of concepts and frameworks which have proved to have the greatest utility in previous analyses of sport policy or which have been developed in the general discipline of policy analysis and which are considered to have the potential to make a contribution to the examination of sport policy. It is argued that effective analysis of policy is only possible through the application of concepts and analytic frameworks which offer not only the opportunity to recognise patterns and processes in policy development, but which also provide a rigorous challenge to the conventional wisdom and easy empiricism. With these concerns in mind, the final chapter will provide both conclusions regarding the nature, extent and process of policy change in sport and also an examination of the utility of the concepts and frameworks introduced in the remaining sections of this chapter and the degree to which they provided insights into the policy process.

ANALYSING CHANGE IN SPORT POLICY

The study of policy change involves the search for, and analysis of, pattern, trends, key events, continuities and breaks with the past with the aim of giving meaning to a collection of events and policy decisions in a particular time period: in other words, to move beyond the mere cataloguing of events through descriptive research to an understanding of the deployment of power and the protection and promotion of interests. In order to obtain an accurate perspective on the scale and nature of change in a particular policy area, it has been argued that a period of at least ten years is required (Sabatier 2007). However, even a period of ten years may not be sufficient to identify policy trends or watersheds that mark significant policy transitions. Uncertainty about the temporal parameters of policy analysis arises, in part, from uncertainty regarding the nature of policy itself and particularly what constitutes significant policy change.

Policy may be defined in a number distinct ways, for example, as aspiration and symbolism or as action and process. Contemporary sport policy in the United Kingdom (UK) is replete with aspirational statements and symbolic flourishes. Recent examples of aspirational statements include that from UK Sport, which identified one of its three 'corporate themes' as being to promote 'UK Sport to win and maintain the respect, trust and engagement of everyone with whom we interact' (UK Sport 2010, p. 10). In Game Plan, one of the recommendations was 'To encourage a mass participation culture . . . A benchmark for this could be Finland' (DCMS/Strategy Unit 2002, p. 80). More recently, Sport England stated that it aspired to 'create a world-leading community sport environment, as part of the legacy of the 2012 Olympic and Paralympic Games [and to establish] a lifelong sporting culture in this country [which] will change sport from a minority to a majority pastime' (Sport England 2010, p. 9). Sport Northern Ireland's stated vision is to develop ' . . . a culture of lifelong enjoyment and success in sport . . . ' (Sport Northern Ireland 2009b, p. 7). While many would question whether these aspirations were feasible, few would argue that they were not laudable. More importantly, in relation to all of these organisations a strong case could be made that even if their mission statements and goals were overambitious the sentiments that they incorporated have been supported, even if only modestly, by the commitment of resources—that is, policy as action and process.

Unfortunately, identifying action (the commitment of resources such as time, money, expertise, personnel and political support to the achievement of realistic objectives) is not always straightforward. The outputs of the political system can take a range of forms only some of which would meet this definition of action. Indeed, in sport there are many examples of policy outputs which are simply policy re-branding or organisational tinkering such as the establishment of the Sports Cabinet and the proposed merger of UK Sport and Sport England.

In relation to policy change, the acceptance in the mid-1960s that sport fell legitimately within the remit of government was equivocal rather than wholehearted and policy interventions were sporadic and generally disconnected rather than continuous and strategic. In the period immediately prior to Major's appointment as prime minister, the governments of Margaret Thatcher displayed little interest in sport apart from the obligatory photo opportunities (being kissed by Kevin Keegan before the departure of the England team for the 1982 World Cup finals was probably the prime minister's most intense sporting experience). When sport did intrude into the consciousness of the prime minister, it was almost always in a negative context, as two of the most prominent sports issues of the 1980s were football spectator violence both at home and abroad involving the supporters of English football clubs and stadium safety (a fire at Bradford City FC stadium in 1985 and a crowd surge at Hillsborough stadium in 1989, both of which resulted in substantial loss of life). Apart from the attempt to tackle the issues of spectator violence and stadium safety, the government's most significant impact on sport was as a consequence of its general commitment to privatisation of public services which affected public sport facilities due to the requirement that local authorities should put the management of their facilities out to competitive tender.

The appointment of John Major as prime minister in November 1990 appeared to mark an important break with the past. In addition to very different levels of personal interest in sport, the period of John Major's premiership contrasted sharply with that of his predecessor most notably in terms of financial investment (which increased considerably due to the introduction of the national lottery), administrative reform (for example, the establishment of sportscoach UK, UK Sport and the Department of National Heritage) and strategy development (a significant policy document in 1995, the first in 20 years). However, the apparent clarity of the break with the past needs to be put in perspective. First, it is important to note that increased public investment, administrative reform and publication of strategy documents were evident across most areas of public policy, certainly from the mid-1990s. In education, for example, Chitty (2004) notes that between 1944 and 1979 there were only three significant education acts, but between 1979 and 2000 there were over 30 separate education acts. The last 20 years or so has not only witnessed an increase in legislative output by government but also an increase in administrative tinkering.

Caution in accepting 1990 as a watershed in sport policy is required for a second reason, which is the methodological problem in identifying specific periods. Debates concerning historical periodisation warn against the premature identification of periods and emphasise that period identification depends on the historical characteristics or variables that are considered significant. Attempts at periodisation invariably bear the imprint of their time of origin. More importantly, the erroneous imposition of a period on a series of events or policy developments can obscure analysis as the researcher attempts to make the data fit the defining characteristics. The historian Fernand Braudel warned against 'scholars who . . . first create these signs and then glue them on their precious bottles, to end by giving the signs authority over their content' (quoted in Gerhard 1956).

In this respect it is valuable to adopt a metaphor of levels of change in relation to sport policy, as this alerts the researcher to the danger of ascribing significance and 'period' status on the basis of relatively superficial or epiphenomenal events. For example, at the superficial level one might point to actions by the state which affect the distribution of resources, the establishment of new, or the reform of existing, administration structures, the change in the use of national lottery funding or change in the criteria for allowing national governing bodies of sport access to world class performance funding for their elite athletes. At a deeper level, change would be located in actions by the state which altered its long established relationships with civil society sport organisations such as national governing bodies or the place of physical education in the school curriculum. At a much more profound level are the changes in societal values which directly or indirectly impact on sport. Change at this deep societal level would include public acceptance that intervention in sport was a proper concern of government or that women or those with disabilities have the same right to participate in sport at the elite level as male able-bodied athletes. It would be possible to identify periods at each of these levels with the length of the period increasing with depth of change.

A number of writers have utilised a metaphor of levels in policy analysis with the work of Sabatier and colleagues being particularly useful. A central aspect of their advocacy coalition framework (ACF) is the role played by ideas in shaping the direction, nature and pace of policy change. The ACF conceptualises a three-tiered structure of beliefs: deep core beliefs; policy core beliefs; and secondary beliefs. Deep core beliefs are 'very general normative and ontological assumptions about human nature, the relative priority of fundamental values such as liberty and equality, the relative priority of welfare of different groups. The proper role of government versus markets in general, and about who should participate in governmental decision making' (Sabatier and Weible 2007, p. 194). At a slightly less profound level are a set of policy core beliefs which affect a whole subsystem and are the application or operationalisation of deep core beliefs. Policy core beliefs would indicate, for example, 'the priority of different policy-related values, whose welfare counts, the relative authority of government and markets, the proper roles of the general public, elected officials, civil servants, experts, and the relative seriousness and causes of policy problems in the subsystem' (Sabatier and Weible 2007, p. 195). At the final level are secondary beliefs which are 'relatively narrow in scope (less than subsystem wide) and address, for example, detailed rules and budgetary applications within a specific programme, the seriousness and causes of problems in a specific locale . . . ' (Sabatier and Weible 2007, p. 196). Secondary beliefs are more flexible and open to change. Table 1.2 provides examples of how the concept of a hierarchy of beliefs and levels of policy might be illustrated in relation to sport.

As the foregoing discussion indicates, it is important to take a sceptical approach to claims that a particular event or policy represents a watershed in the development of public policy in a specific subsystem. It is important to bear in mind that what might appear a profound shift in policy might, with the sharper perspective that temporal distance gives, appear as more incremental and part of a longer term pattern in policy development. For example, it is open to debate whether the sharp shift in sport policy following the resignation of Margaret Thatcher and the appointment of John Major marked the beginning of a new period in the history of government involvement or whether the Thatcher years should be seen as a relatively short break in the longer term trend of increasing government involvement

Table 1.2 Levels of Beliefs and Policy

Level	Examples of beliefs related to sport	Examples of policy
Secondary beliefs/ surface level policy	• Hosting major sports events reflects positively on a country • All Olympic gold medals are of equal value irrespective of the sport in which they were won	• Allocating responsibility and resources to a government department/agency • The identification of sports where a country has some relative advantage
Policy core beliefs/ substantive policy	• International sporting success projects a positive image of a country • Young people's participation in sport builds positive personal characteristics	• Allocation of resources in pursuit of Olympic medals • Investment by government in school sport provision and in competitive sport
Deep core beliefs/ profound policy underpinnings	• Sport participation is appropriate/ inappropriate for women • Sport is a frivolous/serious pastime/career	• Introduction of regulations/ processes to require funded sport organisations to increase sports opportunities for women • Regulations which determine the status (compulsory or optional) of sport/physical education in the school curriculum

in sport. Thus it could be argued that John Major's increasing interventionism picked up where the previous Labour government sports minister, Denis Howell, left off in 1979 rather than marking a break with the past. With regard to the related example of modernisation, one could argue that the strong association between the Blair government and the modernisation of the institutions of government and civil society was a distinctive New Labour policy and marked a break with the more ideologically driven reforms of the previous administration. Indeed, as will be discussed below, both UK Sport and Sport England were tasked with promoting the modernisation of national governing bodies of sport and their constituent clubs. However, a contrary interpretation would be that rather than modernisation being a New Labour innovation, a strong case can be made that New Labour was continuing a process championed by the previous Conservative governments under the banner of new public management. Indeed, it is also arguable that the modernisation of the civil service has a much longer history which can be traced back to the Northcote-Trevelyan report published in 1854 (Burnham and Pyper 2008).

In summary, while periodisation is attractive as a way of organising empirical data about a policy area, it is a concept that should be used with caution as continuity has the habit of breaking through the most determined attempts to change policy direction. With this admonition in mind, the time span which is the focus for this study should be treated at this point in the analysis as having no significance beyond the fact that it marked the end of the time as prime minister of a particularly dominant personality in twentieth-century British politics and also that 1991 was the date when one of the present authors published his previous analysis of British sport policy (Houlihan 1991). Whether the span covered by this study deserves the definition as a distinct policy period will be discussed in the conclusion.

A related approach to assessing policy change is through a closer analysis of the particular instruments or resources used to effect change. A number of authors have proposed either directly or indirectly typologies of policy instruments (Lowi 1964, 1972; Hogwood 1987; Hood and Margetts 2007). Many of them are variations or expansions of the basic trio of policy instruments, namely inducements, threats and marketing. Lowi, for example, although referring to types of policy issues, provides a typology of responses to issues, suggesting that governments respond to issues in one or more of the following ways: distribution, redistribution, regulation and changes to administrative arrangements. Hood and Margetts provide a different typology, but one that has substantial overlaps with that of Lowi insofar as it identifies the resources that underpin the selection and deployment of particular instruments or combination of instruments. For them there are four basic resources available to government: nodality (the fact that government tends to hold a central strategic position in terms of flow of information); authority (to make and enforce regulations and laws); treasure (money which can be distributed or exchanged for other resources); and organisation (administrative capacity and expertise).

In order to develop a clearer understanding of the significance of instrument design and deployment, it is important to relate them to the intended policy change. Hall (1986) provides a valuable typology identifying three levels or 'orders' of policy change. First-order changes are alterations to the intensity or scale of an existing policy instrument, an example of which in relation to funding would be the decision in March 2006 by the UK government to provide an additional £200m to help prepare athletes for the 2012 London Olympic Games. Second-order changes are those that introduce new policy instruments designed to achieve existing policy objectives: examples of which would include the designation of some secondary schools as specialist sports colleges as a way of improving the quality of physical education teaching and increasing opportunities for participation in sport. Finally, third-order changes are those that involve a change in policy goals of which the short-lived decision by the government in the early 2000s to prioritise increased physical activity rather than more narrowly defined sport would be an example.

Table 1.3 Policy Change and Policy Instruments

	Nodality—Authority—Treasure—Organisation			
	Inducement/ rewards—Sanctions—Information/education/social marketing			
	Distribution of resources	Redistribution of resources	Regulation	Administrative (re)design
Underpinning resources which				
enable the selection from clusters of instruments ...				
... which engineer change through ...	... and thus deliver different orders of change, for example, in relation to elite sport			
Change to existing instruments	Increasing the level of Exchequer funding or increasing the share of national lottery funding	Diverting resources from other government budgets, such as school sport or community sport, to the elite sport budget	Relaxing the tax regulations to make corporate donations to elite sport projects more attractive	Establishing a committee to coordinate the activities of the agencies concerned with elite sport development
Introduction of new instruments	Introducing new sources of funding such as new lottery games	Decision to import excellent coaches rather than develop home-grown coaches	Introduce criteria (regulations) which determine access to elite sport funding	Establishing a specialist administrative agency to oversee elite sport investment
Adoption of new policy goals	Direct funding to a country's best medal prospects	Diverting funds to a country's best medal prospects and away from a country's best athletes (if the latter are competing in sports where the quality of competition is especially high)	Relaxing the tax regulations to make corporate donations to specific summer Olympic sports more attractive	Establishing a specialist unit/agency to pursue new policy objectives such as improved elite level coaching, talent identification or children's play

Table 1.3 combines these typologies of resources and instruments and illustrates their potential application in relation to elite sport. The important aspect of the table is the dimension of depth derived from Hall's notion of orders of change. What Hall's conceptualisation suggests is that watersheds in policy are far less likely to be defined by doing more of the same (that is, simply adjusting existing patterns of resources, regulation and administration intended to better achieve the same set of policy goals). The break with the previous period is more likely to be defined by a significant change in policy goals.

FRAMEWORKS FOR ANALYSING POLICY CHANGE

Although this study utilises frameworks developed for meso-level analysis, that is, frameworks intended to analyse policy at the sectoral or subsystem level, it is important to bear in mind that each meso-level framework or approach has its roots in assumptions at the macro level, which include, inter alia, those about the distribution of power at the societal level, the significance of the pursuit and protection of sectional interests, the significance of ideas (whether as myths, evidence or ideology, for example) and the relationship between the state and civil society. In addition, each of the major macro-level theories sensitises the researcher to different aspects of the policy process as illustrated in Table 1.4.

While it is not within the scope of the present study to articulate and explore in detail the implications for policy analysis of macro-level theories, it is important to bear in mind that meso-level analytical frameworks are not value free and are derived from the often highly contentious and ideological theorisations at the societal level. There are a number of excellent summaries and examinations of macro-level theory which can be consulted for a more detailed engagement with this level of analysis. Parsons (1995) and Howlett and Ramesh (2003) provide valuable reviews of the main elements of a selection of the major theories, while Dryzek and Dunleavy (2009) and Hay, Lister and Marsh (2006) provide more sustained explorations of contemporary macro-level theorising. There is also a substantial body of work which explores the application of macro-level theorising to sport, including Giulianotti (2004), Morgan (1994), Carrington and McDonald (2009), Hargreaves (1986a), Horne, Tomlinson and Whannel (1999) and Jarvie and Maguire (1994).

The number of studies which have explicitly utilised meso-level frameworks to inform the analysis of aspects of UK sport policy is growing, but is still small. For example, Parrish (2003) and Green and Houlihan (2004, 2005) have drawn upon the advocacy coalition framework in their studies of the emergence of European Union sports law and elite sport policy change, respectively; Houlihan and Green (2006) have utilised the multiple-streams framework in relation to the development of school sport in England; and

Table 1.4 Selected Major Macro-Level Theories and Sport Policy

Dimension	Neo-Marxism	Governance	Neo-pluralism	Market liberalism
Unit of analysis	Social classes	Policy networks and subsystems	Interest groups	Markets and individuals
Role of the state	Under Marxism the state is an instrument of the ruling capitalist class: Under neo-Marxism the position and role of the state is less clear with some arguing that the state's role is to manage capitalism which might involve short-term actions which go against the interests of capital accumulation, e.g. provide welfare services through taxation to enhance legitimation.	Due to increasing complexity of social issues, governments seek to act in partnership with civil society organisations. Rhodes (1994) sees this as a loss of power (the hollowing out of the state), whereas Rose (1999) argues that we are witnessing an extension of state power, i.e. a 'rolling out' of state power.	The state is an active participant in making policy, partly mediating between rival groups, but also protecting and promoting its own interests (especially in relation to problem definition and preferred solutions). The state has a bias towards business interests.	Argued that markets maximise social welfare and that individuals are rational utility maximisers. The role of the state is to enable markets to operate effectively (with as little regulation as possible). Market liberals, especially rational-choice theorists, have a deep suspicion of state action and argue that politicians and state officials will act rationally and consequently seek to maximise their budgets (through taxation) to secure organisational growth and therefore larger personal rewards. The role of the state should be limited to activities such as protecting property rights, defence, providing basic infrastructure and services (in cases of market failure) and regulating monopolies.

(continued)

Table 1.4 (continued)

Dimension	Neo-Marxism	Governance	Neo-pluralism	Market liberalism
Dynamic for policymaking	Class conflict and/or the inherent instability of capitalism (e.g. the 2008 European and North American banking crisis).	Accumulation of evidence and/or external events (e.g. financial crisis).	Interaction between groups with unequal influence.	Market competition and the pursuit, by individuals, of personal interest.
Associated meso-level frameworks and approaches	None clearly, but elements of network theory in which business-dominated or business-oriented networks would manage policy subsystems; and institutionalism in which dominant power relations become institutionalised in the state.	Policy communities; institutionalism.	Advocacy coalition framework; punctuated-equilibrium theory; institutionalism.	Multiple streams.
Primary focus for the study of sport policy	Sport as a form of social control (i.e. diverting attention from the ills of capitalism) or sport as a source of profit (e.g. through broadcasting and commodification).	Sport policy networks/community and their membership, values and decision processes.	Existence and influence of advocacy coalitions for interests such as elite, women, youth and community sport.	The regulatory role of the state. The relationship between the state, the market and the not-for-profit sector.
Orientation/key questions	How is the tension between sport as a 'new industry' and as an element of welfare provision managed?	What are the dominant values in the community? How is the membership of the community decided? How insulated is the community from other policy subsectors?	To what extent do advocacy coalitions exist in sport? If they do, what is their relative strength and what is their relationship to government?	Is the state competing with the commercial sector by providing sports facilities? Is the expansion of state involvement in sport evidence in support of the public choice critique of public officials (seeking personal benefits, such as increased salaries, rather than social welfare)?
References	Offe (1984), Brohm (1978), Jessop (1990), Morgan (1994), Girginov and Sandanski (2011)	Pierre and Peters (2000), Houlihan and Groeneveld (2011), Rose (1999)	Lindblom (1977), van den Berg and Janoski (2005), Green and Houlihan (2004)	Friedman and Friedman (1962), Niskanen (1971)

Houlihan (1991) drew on network theory in his study of British sport. The volume of applications of meso-level frameworks is certainly too small to suggest that one framework provides the most accurate description of the sport policy process or is the most effective tool of analysis. It is also still not clear whether particular frameworks provide insights only into specific issues within the sport subsystem (whether defined geographically, by scope or by pattern of activity) or whether it is possible to refer to the sport policy subsystem exhibiting a set of policymaking characteristics which are not only stable over time, but which also correspond reasonably closely to one particular framework. Due to the relative paucity of theoretically informed empirical studies, four meso-level analytical frameworks, which have the greatest potential explanatory value, will be examined briefly. The basis for selecting analytical frameworks has been discussed elsewhere (Houlihan 2005), but in summary the criteria are as follows: They should be internally consistent; have been applied empirically to sport; they should offer a reasonably comprehensive analysis of the policy process that is not over-focused on one aspect of the policy process such as implementation; and are intellectually robust, having been subject to sustained critical evaluation. More specifically, a useful framework should have the capacity to explain both policy stability and change (John 1998; Sabatier 1999); have the capacity to illuminate a range of aspects of the policy process; and facilitate at least a medium-term (five- to ten-year) analysis of policy change. The four frameworks reviewed are punctuated equilibrium, institutional analysis, multiple streams and advocacy coalitions.

Punctuated Equilibrium

One significant criticism of a number of meso-level frameworks is that they tend to be better at explaining stability *or* change, but rarely stability *and* change. One exception to this criticism is Baumgartner and Jones's punctuated-equilibrium model, which suggests that policy sectors are characterised by long periods of relative policy stability typified by conservative incremental movement in policy which are then punctuated by intense periods of policy instability and change (Baumgartner and Jones 1993, 2002; True et al. 2007). The punctuated-equilibrium model is concerned to explain the factors that cause a shift in the rate of policy change. Periods of relative policy stability are explained by the institutionalisation of a dominant set of ideas (about the nature of the policy area and the acceptable responses to issues) which are reinforced by powerful interests, the media and public opinion. Instability and rapid policy change are the result of the emergence of new issues, the accumulation of evidence challenging the status quo through feedback and changes in the broader government agenda which spill over into the macro-politics subsystem. 'Macropolitics is the politics of punctuation—the politics of large-scale change, competing policy images, political manipulation, and positive feedback. Positive

feedback exacerbates impulses for change; it overcomes inertia and pro-
duces explosions or implosions from former states' (True et al. 2007, p.
162). Baumgartner and Jones (1993) explained that these intense bursts of
change—punctuations—are caused by the interaction of image (the way
in which a policy is characterised and understood by the public and the
media, for example) and institutions (the institutional context of issues/the
arenas in which policy is discussed). 'Institutions . . . freeze a set of political
participants into the policy process and exclude others. Institutions help
ensure that problems are defined in a particular manner and not in another.
They set the agenda' (John 1998, p. 179).

The punctuated-equilibrium model is firmly located within a set of pluralist assumptions which views policy subsystems as fragile and vulnerable
rather than institutionalising, on a long-term basis, bias towards particular interests on a semi-permanent basis. While Baumgartner and Jones
do acknowledge that 'middle class interests' do seem to fare better in the
American political system than those of the economically and politically
weak, they nonetheless concluded that 'Rather than being controlled by
any single group, institutions, or individual these forces are the result of
complex interconnection of many institutions in society' (Baumgartner and
Jones 1993, p. 237).

In some respects the model has potential utility in analysing sport policy
in the UK, but there are elements of the model which might be difficult to
support with evidence. On the positive side there are a number of occasions when macro politics has conflicted with the institutionalisation of a
particular definition of sport policy priorities—for example, the large-scale
government-wide priorities such as privatisation under Margaret Thatcher,
social inclusion under the Blair government and, potentially at least, 'Big
Society' under the coalition administration. Each of these government-
wide initiatives disrupted the settled pattern of the sport policy agenda,
the institutional arrangements, the allocation of responsibility and funding arrangements. However, it is debatable whether sport has experienced
sustained periods of equilibrium which are then available for punctuation.
Some areas of sport policy, such as community sport, experienced periods
of sustained instability with any periods of equilibrium arguably being the
consequence of neglect. However, other areas such as youth/school sport
and elite sport can be characterised as having periods of equilibrium and
evidence of incremental policy change during those periods.

Institutional Analysis

Overlapping with the punctuated-equilibrium model is a group of policy
analysts who give even greater emphasis to the role of institutions in shaping policy. According to Thelen and Steinmo, institutions 'shape how
political actors define their interests and . . . structure their relations of
power to other groups' (1992, p. 2) and are seen as significant constraints

and mediating factors in politics. Although the institutionalist literature is diverse, there are two broad orientations, one emphasising the significance of institutions as organisational entities (local authorities, national semi-autonomous agencies, departments et cetera) and the other, cultural institutionalism, which highlights shared values, norms and beliefs and can be seen as the routinisation of individual agency. Institutions constrain choice through their capacity to shape actors' perception of both problems and acceptable solutions. As such, the emphasis on institutions is a valuable corrective to the tendency of much pluralist theory to treat organisations (Sport England, the Sports Council for Wales and the Department for Culture, Media and Sport, for example) as arenas in which politics takes place rather than as independent or intervening variables in the process. Cultural institutionalism, with its emphasis on values, norms and beliefs, draws attention to the social construction of meaning and 'how interest groups, politicians, and administrators decide their policy preferences' (Fischer 2003, p. 29). It is also at odds with the rhetoric of 'evidence-based policy' so frequently used by the Blair government and thus adds weight to Coalter's argument regarding the mythopoeic nature of sport (Coalter 2007). Coalter (2011) sees mythopoeic concepts as based on popular and often idealistic beliefs which are generated and maintained largely independent of a robust evidence base and which consequently 'isolate a particular relationship between variables to the exclusion of others and without a sound basis for doing so' (Glasner 1977, pp. 2–3, quoted in Coalter 2011). However, the relevance of institutionalism for sport policy analysis extends beyond the support it provides for the capacity of sport to shroud itself in a supportive mythology. Houlihan and White (2002), Pickup (1996), Roche (1993), and Henry (2001) all identify the organisational infrastructure of UK sport as a significant variable in shaping policy. Allocation of functional responsibility for sport among central government departments, the role of devolved assemblies, the use of 'arm's-length' agencies, and the presence of a minister for sport are all seen as having a noticeable impact on sport policy and its implementation.

One of the key strengths of institutionalism (as it relates to organisational arrangements and structures) is that it is a powerful corrective to those who are too ready to ignore the significance of state institutions in the policy process. However, this insight, that state institutions matter, is in many ways self-evident and leaves largely unanswered the more important questions such as 'To what extent and in what circumstances do institutions matter?' In many respects the distinctive contribution of institutionalism lies in the attention that it gives to ideas in the policy process and the extent to which ideas (whether based on evidence or on myth) can become an institutionalised constraint on policy choice. As such, institutional theorising resonates with the concept of path dependency, which suggests that 'the trajectory of change up to a certain point constrains the trajectory after that point' (Kay 2005, p. 553), and the notion that institutions 'leave their own imprint' (Thelen and Steinmo 1992, p. 8) by being significant mediating factors in the policy process. Whether the emphasis is on institutions as organisations or as sets of values and beliefs (culture), they constitute 'unique patterns of historical development and [impose] constraints . . . on future choices' (Howlett and Ramesh 1995, p. 27). Past decisions need to be seen as institutions in relation to subsequent policy choices with path dependency capturing the insight that 'policy decisions accumulate over time; a process of accretion can occur in a policy area that restricts options for future policy-makers' (Kay 2005, p. 558). In a narrow application of the concept of path dependency one would argue that early decisions in a policy area result in current policy being locked on to a particular policy trajectory. A broader application of the concept would suggest that rather than the next policy choice being inevitable it is more accurate to suggest that early decisions significantly constrain subsequent policy options and make policy reversal or termination progressively more difficult.

In relation to the broader conceptualisation of path dependency it has been argued very persuasively that the welfare regimes in countries in Western and Northern Europe can be divided according to historic political traditions associated with Christian conservatism, social democracy and neoliberalism (Esping-Andersen 1990). The strength of these traditions explains, partly at least, the persistence of distinct approaches to welfare at a time of intense global pressures to reduce the tax burden on business. However, recent comparative research by Bergsgard et al. (2007) suggests that caution is needed in assuming that welfare regime type imposes significant constraints on policy choice and the role of the state in relation to sport. Based on a study of countries considered to be exemplars of Esping-Andersen's three welfare types, the authors found only a loose association, with the anomalies being more striking than the indicators of consistency.

> The overall impression with regard to welfare state regimes and variations is that our assumptions need to be modified. In all four countries voluntary sports organisations . . . still play prominent roles as organisers of sports activities. However, in all four cases we also find that government is strongly involved with sport. This is not only the case in the "state friendly" social democratic welfare state of Norway. Public policies are important for sport in the conservative welfare regime of Germany and the liberal welfare regimes of Canada and England (Bergsgard et al. 2007, pp. 244–245).

Attractive though the literature on the broad version of path dependency is, the relationship between regime type and policy outputs is apparently far from consistent in relation to sport and suggests that sport policy is not and should not be defined solely in terms of those elements that are associated with welfare. The case can be made that, more than other aspects of welfare provision (such as personal social services, education, health and housing), the dominant rationale for government intervention is as much business as it is welfare and that the commercial elements of the sector (sports broadcasting, sponsorship, sports events et cetera) are much more influential in shaping policy direction than the private schools or hospitals are in shaping policy in their respective fields. In addition, one could argue that broad sport policy is also influenced by international-relations objectives (Olympic medal success and increased UK influence in key international sports organisations) than other welfare sectors.

The links between institutional theory and macro-level analyses are far less direct than with the other three frameworks that are considered. Apart from market liberalism, institutional analysis could fit comfortably within any of the other three macro-level theories. Neo-pluralism, for example, is distinguished from pluralism by the acceptance of the institutionalised influence of business in the policy process. Marxism and neo-Marxism similarly argue that the state is, to a greater or lesser extent, subordinated to the interests of capital, while one version of governance theory assumes governance structures to reflect the institutionalisation of particular interests.

The Multiple-Streams Framework

At first sight the multiple-streams framework (Kingdon 1984) would seem inappropriate for the study of sport policy in a country which has a relatively centralised policy system and where points of entry to the decision process, for example, at regional or local government levels, are limited. Yet Houlihan and Green (2006, p. 89) in their study of the school sport policy process concluded that 'while the evidence from this study provides some support for the ACF [advocacy coalition framework] it is the multiple-streams framework that offers a more plausible explanation of policy change'. The framework takes as its organising metaphor for policy choice the 'garbage can' where 'various kinds of problems and solutions are dumped by participants as they are generated' (Cohen et al. 1972, p. 2). Giving stress to the extent of ambiguity, complexity and residual randomness in the policymaking process, Kingdon identifies three distinct streams: problems, policies and politics. Problems are 'conditions that come to be defined as problems, depending on who is paying attention at the time, the values and beliefs of the individuals concerned, and the magnitude of the change in the conditions' (Zahariadis 2003, p. 7). Governments are often prompted to 'recognise' a problem as a result of crisis (sexual abuse of children by sports coaches [Brackenridge and Telfer, 2011], declining standards of fitness among the young [Green, 2006]) or the accumulation of evidence, regarding sport participation, for example, from the routine collection of information such as the School Sport Survey, the Active People Survey or the General Household Survey. The second stream comprises policies or ideas which are normally developed within specialist policy communities and which relate to specific problems or classes of problems and are thus distinct from macro-level ideological orientations such as market liberalism. Policies which are deemed easier to implement and which are able to attract a higher level of support within a policy community from key actors, such as public officials and pressure groups, are more likely to be adopted. The third stream is politics, which is independent of the other two streams and comprises a number of elements including the national mood (sentiment towards issues among voters), organised political forces (political parties and interest groups, for example), and turnover within government (for example, a change of sports or education minister).

A central aspect of the multiple-streams framework is the notion of 'coupling', which refers to the process by which issues achieve political recognition and attract policies (solutions). The coincidence of the three streams, for example, as a result of a crisis and/or the activities of policy entrepreneurs, can provide a 'launch window' where 'a problem is recognized, a solution is developed and available in the policy community, a political change makes the time right for policy change, and potential constraints are not severe' (Kingdon 1984, p. 174). However, windows of opportunity might also be the result of routine aspects of policy cycles such as the annual budget-setting process or an election. To some degree Kingdon's framework is a significant challenge to rational models of decision making, but as Zahariadis points, out multiple streams does not suggest randomness in policy selection, but rather highlights 'the importance of context and politics' (2003, p. 9).

There is much in the multiple-streams framework that is attractive in addition to it being a corrective to the rationalist assumptions of other frameworks. The capacity of the framework to be integrated with the more firmly established and empirically founded literature on policy communities provides a rich conceptual language for analysis. Furthermore, the concept of spillover is valuable, as it suggests that the successful implementation of a policy in one area (for example, marketisation, privatisation, 'naming and shaming') 'may spill over to another, facilitating the adoption of the same solution in a seemingly unrelated area' (Zahariadis 2003, p. 154).

However, while the framework does not neglect the significance of context, it plays down too strongly the importance of structural factors and institutionalised power, perhaps due to its roots in pluralist macro-level theory. The weakness in the framework's underlying theory of power is especially important due to the prominence given to ideas in the policy process, where the significance of ideas in relation to interests and power is under-theorised.

The Advocacy Coalition Framework

It is in the light of the inadequacies of the frameworks reviewed so far that consideration is now given to the advocacy coalition framework (ACF), which, in recent years, has emerged as a highly regarded basis for policy analysis, both in its own right and in combination with other frameworks. According to Sabatier and Weible (2007, pp. 191–192), there are three 'foundation stones' to the framework: '(1) a macro-level assumption that most policymaking occurs among specialists within a policy subsystem but that their behaviour is affected by factors in the broader political and socio-economic system; (2) a micro-level "model of the individual" that is drawn heavily from social psychology; and (3) a meso-level conviction that the best way to deal with the multiplicity of actors in a policy subsystem is to aggregate them into "advocacy coalitions" '. The dynamic of policy change is based on policy-oriented learning and external perturbations.

The ACF suggests that policy subsystems normally comprise between two and five coalitions each united by shared normative and causal beliefs and competing for influence. As mentioned above, belief systems are hierarchically structured with the first level being 'deep core' beliefs, which cover fundamental norms and values and which span a number of policy subsystems. Second-level values comprise 'policy core' beliefs, which are the basic normative commitments that span the whole policy subsystem. Sabatier and Jenkins-Smith (1999) identify eleven categories of policy core belief including perceptions of the causes and severity of system-wide problems, the effectiveness of policy instruments, and the appropriate division of responsibility between the market and the public sector. At the third level are secondary policy beliefs, which are narrower beliefs related, for example, to the seriousness of particular issues or to geographically specific issues, and are much more susceptible to change.

Exogenous factors, such as conflict between coalitions or external shocks such as scandal (e.g. a doping violation by a leading UK athlete) or crisis (the fire at Bradford City FC in 1985), often mediated by a 'policy broker', are sources of policy outputs and policy change, although change can occur as a result of 'policy-oriented learning' (Sabatier 1998, p. 104). Policy-oriented learning describes relatively long-term changes in beliefs that result from 'experience and/or new information' (Sabatier 1998, p. 104) and reflects the underlying assumption of rational behaviour in decision making, at least in the long term. However, learning may take some time to affect policy as 'individuals face cognitive constraints and filter or avoid belief-conflicting information' (Weible 2007, p. 7).

The ACF is an attractive analytical framework not least because it has been so widely tested empirically. The framework also addresses the challenge of explaining both stability and change, although it is more persuasive in explaining the persistence of stability than in explaining the dynamics of policy change which rely on the combination of rational learning and external perturbations. Perhaps of greater concern is the lack of a sustained discussion of power and how institutionalised power (mobilisation of bias) affects individual behaviour with regard to problem perception and policy choice.

The foregoing discussion of policy theory and concepts is an essential exercise prior to the analysis of UK sport policy. Kurt Lewin's (1951, p.

169) often quoted remark that there is 'nothing so practical as a good theory' is a succinct reminder that making sense of the policy process requires not only robust empirical data but also an equally robust set of concepts and theoretical frameworks for their interpretation.

Meso-level frameworks such as the four discussed above fulfil two important functions for the researcher. The first is that they offer a framework for the conduct of research insofar as they direct the researcher's attention (or sensitise the researcher) to particular aspects of the policy process (for example, agenda-setting or policy learning and transfer) and particular relationships (such as the role of policy brokers) and themes (such as the influence of business or other organised interests). The use of a particular meso-level framework works best when the testing of its appropriateness is the central research question or when the previous research in the field suggests strongly that one framework is more appropriate than the alternatives. Testing a particular framework is not the central concern of this study and, as mentioned previously, there is no consensus on the most appropriate framework for the analysis of sport policy. Hence, the four frameworks will be used to sensitise the researchers to aspects of the policy process and the relationships and patterns of influence that underpin the process.

The second function of meso-level frameworks is as tools for the analysis of empirical data—a guide to the interpretation of research findings. This function is best fulfilled through an iterative process by which, during the conduct of the research and particularly at the conclusion of the research, there is reflection on the data collected and how it can be illuminated and refined by reference to particular analytic frameworks. This second function of the frameworks is one that will be adopted for this study.

THE STRUCTURE OF THE ANALYSIS

An understanding of the developments in sport since 1990 requires analysis across a range of dimensions which include changes in government motives for involvement in sport, changes in the range of instruments used to effect the implementation of sport policy, shifts in the pattern of power relations between policy actors, changes in the organisational landscape and the implications for the configuration of networks and the balance between policymaking and policy taking. These five dimensions provide the thematic structure for the subsequent analysis.

First we need to explore the motives for government involvement in sport not only in terms of the breadth of motivating factors but also in terms of shifts in the salience of sport to government. At this stage it would appear that over the last 20 years or so the salience of sport, particularly elite sport and to an extent school sport, to government has increased while that of community sport has remained largely on the margins of political agendas. As regards changes to the range of instruments available to the government to effect policy implementation, such changes would include the introduction of the national lottery and the expansion (though recent contraction) of specialist agencies such as UK Sport, the English Institute of Sport and School Sport Partnerships. The analysis of power relations is always a challenge as the voluminous literature on the concept attests, but an assessment of the nature, deployment and impact of power is at the heart of policy analysis, as is a theme that runs through all the meso-level frameworks discussed above.

The fourth dimension concerns changes in the configuration of networks and whether the nascent policy community identified by Houlihan in 1991 has materialised or whether other metaphors such as coalitions or loose issue networks are more apt descriptions. The final dimension recognises that in many policy sectors interests and policy actors are forced to adopt a reactive stance in relation to policy initiatives. Dery provides a useful distinction between policymaking and policy taking. Policymaking 'implicitly presumes control over key variables that shape policy in a given area' whereas policy taking 'denotes the pursuit of a given set of policy objectives, which is primarily or entirely shaped by the pursuit of other objectives . . . the resulting policy . . . [is] . . . the by-product of policies that are made and implemented to pursue objectives other than those of the policy in question' (Dery 1999, pp. 165–166). The conceptualisation of policy taking would seem to have considerable relevance to the study of sport, given the long history of the instrumental use of sport to achieve a wide range of non-sport policy objectives.

In order to explore these dimensions, the research relied heavily on two sources of data—documents and a series of semi-structured interviews. The analysis included documents produced by a wide range of national and subnational-level policy actors, for example, central and local government, national governmental sports agencies and national interest/lobbying organisations. Documents were collected and selected through systematic searches of the published output of organisations either available in paper copy or available on official Web sites. Access was also provided by some interviewees to internal documents. Documentary sources were augmented by the conduct of a series of semi-structured interviews with policy actors who were selected on the basis that they had been or were still involved in policy at a strategic level; they were, in broad terms, representative of a particular group of policy actors; and that they had been involved, either directly or indirectly, in the sports policy subsector for at least five years.

The book is divided into eight chapters. Chapters 2 and 3 provide an analysis of the change in national government policy from the late 1980s through to the early phase of the coalition government elected in 2010. Chapter 4 explores the impact of devolution on the development of sport policy in the four home countries. While a detailed analysis of the policy process for sport in Scotland, Wales and Northern Ireland is beyond the scope of this study, the chapter will focus on the significance of devolution for two aspects of sport policy: first the extent to which home-country policies in relation to youth/school sport and community sport have diverged and second the impact of devolution on UK-wide policy for elite athlete development.

Chapter 5 explores the relationship between community sport and elite athlete development. The chapter will examine the tension between these two sets of objectives and the problems that the governments have had and continue to experience in establishing consistent and stable objectives in both these areas, but especially in relation to community sport. Chapter 6 develops some of the issues and themes identified in Chapter 5 and focuses on the role and significance of local government for the delivery of sport policy objectives. The chapter traces the reintegration of local government into the delivery framework for Labour's sport policy which followed the long period of neglect by the governments of Margaret Thatcher and John Major. Chapter 7 focuses on school and youth sport and examines the changing salience of school sport to governments, the particular role of national organisations, such as the Youth Sport Trust, and the way in which school sport policy frameworks such as the PE and Sport Strategy for Young People integrated school sport into a broader youth sport development programme. The final chapter explores the pattern and nature of policy continuity and change through the application of the various concepts and analytical frameworks introduced in this chapter.

2 John Major's Conservative Governments

Chapter 1 advocated caution in identifying particular historical moments as watersheds at which a significant policy change can be identified. Nevertheless, the period of John Major's premiership from 1990 to 1997 was certainly significant in terms of many sport policy developments. In some ways this was surprising given that, more generally, the period of the John Major governments is widely recognised as one in which there was little change in the substantive policy agendas inherited from the previous Conservative administrations led by Margaret Thatcher. Taylor (2006) suggested that Major, in fact, cemented much of the legacy of the Thatcher years. Moreover, partially due Major's more pragmatic style and the political pressures facing him (Kavanagh 1994), the overall approach to policy was 'ad-hoc, fragmented and piecemeal' (Taylor 2006, p. 119). In the particularly relevant area of welfare policy, assessments of policy under the Major government were of 'stagnation' (Alcock 1997) or 'drifting' (Atkinson and Savage 1994).

However, in at least in two respects, John Major's personal values differed significantly from the ideology promoted by his predecessor Margaret Thatcher. First, Major was less ideologically opposed to state provision than Thatcher. While Thatcher favoured the singular mechanism of privatisation, Major sought to improve public service provision through a variety of means including policies such as the Citizen's Charter, which sought to empower and offer greater choice to individuals (Kavanagh 1994). Second, Major himself was also 'intensely traditionalist' (Young 1994a, p. 22) in keeping with the one-nation strand of Conservatism. Major wished to preserve 'continuity, community and stability' (Kavanagh 1994, p. 13), a view which placed him in opposition to Thatcher's lack of belief in society itself (Young 1994a). As will be demonstrated, it is certainly the case that these values influenced the distinctive approach to sport and sport policy pursued by John Major in government.

This chapter will examine the distinctive sport policy turn that emerged during the period of John Major's premiership. In so doing, the chapter will examine the reasons for sport becoming a policy concern of some salience for government and the distinctive sport policy themes that emerged as a result. Furthermore, the chapter will examine the changing manner in which control was exercised within the sport policy sector and the way in which this control was associated with changing institutional and funding arrangements. In order to contextualise these developments, it is necessary to commence the chapter with an examination of the sport policy legacy left to John Major in 1990 by the outgoing premier, Margaret Thatcher.

MARGARET THATCHER'S LEGACY OF NEGLECT

Government intervention in sport during the period of Margaret Thatcher's premiership was framed by the broader, and largely ideological, agendas pursued by her governments. While the nomenclature of 'Thatcherism' implies a degree of coherence within these broader agendas, more careful examination allows identification of contradictory elements (Atkinson and Savage 1994). The neoliberal, free-market economic policies enacted represented a major retrenchment of the role of government combined with support for the private sector and its supposedly more efficient practices. Privatisation of publicly owned industries, the introduction of private sector provision of local government services and the introduction of market-based management of services such as the NHS were all exemplars of the neoliberal approach (Wilding 1997). However, this 'hollowing out' of the state was accompanied by increasing centralisation of power through the expansion of centrally controlled quangos and increased regulation of many areas, including the privatised industries, during the period of the Thatcher premiership.

Similar trends can be seen in terms of the welfare and social policies enacted by the Thatcher governments. There was consistency in terms of the attack on the collectivist approach that had largely predominated since the Second World War. Instead, welfare and social policies emphasised individualistic self-support designed to enable people to function within the market-based economy (McCarthy 1989). Although these policies were again designed to reduce the role of the state, in reality broader economic conditions led to an increase of government spending (Hills 1998). Moreover, the focus on individual liberty was balanced by a more traditionally conservative desire to maintain the role of the family (Atkinson and Savage 1994) and a 'vigorous' emphasis on law and order (Monnington 1993).

As with broader policy agendas, the period of the Thatcher government witnessed a breakdown of the previously broad consensus regarding sport policy (Roche 1993). Given the broader attack on aspects of the welfare state, it was unsurprising that sport was not seen as an important function of government. Oakley and Green (2001, p. 76) characterised the Thatcher governments' view of state intervention in sport as representing 'encouragement of inefficiency and the suppression of individual initiative'. Added to this broad, ideological view was Margaret Thatcher's personal lack of affinity with, or indeed antipathy towards, sport (Monnington 1993; Houli-han 2000). Thus, sport lacked any great status either within the machinery of central government or in terms of national public spending (Pickup 1990; Gilroy and Clarke 1997). This is not to say that sport never encroached on the agenda of the Thatcher governments. However, as will be identified in the following paragraphs, exceptions to the broader neglect of sport by the Thatcher governments were only evident when it could be used as a politi-cised tool to further other policy agendas or when it was associated with a perceived social problem (Hargreaves 1996; Coghlan 1990).

Government intervention in sport during Thatcher's premiership was often triggered by specific incidents or events. One of the first examples of such intervention was Thatcher's strong personal advocacy for a boycott of the 1980 Moscow Olympics. Clearly an intervention aligned with the prime minister's own ideologically orientated foreign policy, Coghlan (1990, p. 245) stated that, in pursuing a boycott, Thatcher sidelined the minister for sport and 'lectured rather than listened' to sports organisations. The fact that calls for a boycott were ignored was something of a personal embar-rassment for Thatcher (Monnington 1993). Nevertheless, the government's approach to elite sport continued to be premised on its potential contribu-tion to international prestige and broader foreign policy goals. This was highlighted by the Sports Council itself in its 1988 policy document, *Into the Nineties: A Strategy for Sport 1988–1993*, which identified that 'public support of excellence in sport . . . is primarily defined in terms of external goals, several as an adjunct of foreign policy' with 'the objective of helping the elite performer to develop their personal potential last [in terms of pri-ority] after a series of foreign policy goals' (Sports Council 1988, p. 48).

Government intervention in domestic sport followed a similar pattern to international sport. Riots in inner-city areas in the early 1980s acted as a trigger for investment in programmes, such as Action Sport, intended to counter social problems in deprived areas. Views on such programmes varied. Hargreaves (1986b, p. 259) viewed the use of sport in this way as a reactive 'focus on the symptoms rather than the causes of deprivation and disorder'. Coalter et al. (1986, p. 37) went further, suggesting 'sport and sporting provision was in danger of being turned into a "dustbin of social policy"—a cheap, cost-effective and immediate response to social problems'. Alternatively, for Lentell (1993), the riots opened a 'window of opportunity' exploited by the Sports Council at a time when it was other-wise weakened by the government's more general objective of 'rolling back' the public sector (Houlihan and White 2002). Although Action Sport and associated projects launched by the Sports Council were relatively short-lived (Coghlan 1990), their long-term policy impact was perhaps signifi-cantly greater. The start of government appropriation of sport as a form of 'benign policing' (Green 2006, p. 225) represented a significant change from the preceding policies which valued sport and leisure as a human need (Monnington 1993). Although Sports Council spending on Action Sport programmes was a small part of its overall budget (Coalter 2007), the need to justify the contribution of sport to wider policy agendas was evident in Sports Council policies (e.g. Sports Council 1982, 1988) throughout the period of the Thatcher government and beyond.

Inconsistent with the use of sport as a tool for social control, government intervention was also prompted by Thatcher's recognition of sport, and in particular football, as a site for social deviance. Hargreaves (1996b, p. 249) noted that Thatcher spoke about regular outbreaks of hooliganism at both domestic and international football matches in the 1980s 'in much the same vocabulary and tones as those reserved for terrorism, street crime, strikers and demonstrators, and other perceived enemies within'. That outbreaks of hooliganism occurred at the same time as Thatcher was conducting important negotiations on Britain's future in Europe only served to heighten her political embarrassment (Monnington 1993). Believing that self-regulation of the problem had failed (Roche 1993), Thatcher sought to circumvent sport authorities and even her own sports minister to introduce legislation that would require spectators to hold identity cards (Monnington 1993; Pickup 1996). Ultimately, however, plans for this extension of repressive state control were abandoned by the subsequent Major government as a result of the Taylor report into the 1991 Hillsborough disaster.

A final area of government intervention, with significant long-term implications, was in the system of national sport governance. As the examples of the Olympic boycott and football hooliganism signify, successive ministers for sport were largely marginalised within the Thatcher governments (Houlihan 2000), although they increasingly displayed an alignment with Thatcher's own New Right ideology. It was perhaps of greater importance that the government started to utilise its power of appointment to place individuals of similar political persuasion to board and chair positions within the Sports Council (Henry 2001). Furthermore, in a trend that has subsequently been extended, government increasingly began to specify projects to which the Sports Council were to direct funds (Hargreaves 1996b). While the exertion of such powers of influence were recognised by the then deputy director-general of the Sports Council as counter to its Royal Charter, increasingly they became seen as the norm (Coghlan 1990). Moreover, these trends in the relationship between the national government and the Sports Council were reflective of the increasing central control over quangos more generally, despite being somewhat contradictory to governmental rhetoric regarding rolling back state influence (Henry 2001).

Besides the implicit repositioning of the Sports Council that came from increasing governmental control, there were also more explicit attempts on the part of government to redefine the role of the Sports Council. In 1986, the government tasked the Rossi Committee with considering the rationale for, and the role of, the Sports Council (Green 2004). Subsequently, one of the most active ministers for sport during the period of the Thatcher governments,

Colin Moynihan, suggested that the Sports Council's role, especially in relation to elite sport, be reduced (Henry and Bramham 1993). Although significant changes to the Sports Council were not enacted until the end of John Major's period in office, the cumulative effect of government intervention was to create instability within the Sports Council throughout much of the 1980s. Moreover, in the fragmented and sometimes fractious national sport policy sector (Roche 1993), the Sports Council was unable to effectively advocate within government either for sport or for itself as an organisation (Green 2004). This weakness of the sport policy sector was implicitly recognised by the Sports Council itself, stating in 1988 (p. 67) that

> Whilst the Council clearly has a role to play in ensuring greater co-ordination among sporting interests it cannot, as an adviser to Government, simultaneously be the prime organiser of a lobby, though there will be many occasions to share and proclaim identical views.

These limitations and weaknesses of the Sports Council did not impede it setting its own policy agenda for sport in the 1980s. During this period, the Sport Council published two major policy documents: *Sport in the Community: The Next Ten Years* (1982) and *Into the Nineties: A Strategy for Sport 1988–1993* (1988). Based on a significant body of evidence, both policies were wide-ranging and comprehensive in covering all elements of the 'sports development continuum' that was introduced in the later document (Sports Council 1988). In so doing, the policies sat somewhat in contradiction to limited sport policy aims of the government and, in the later document, the neoliberal-orientated focus of the chairman's own introduction (Smith 1988). It was perhaps partially for these reasons that the deputy director general himself recognised that the government paid little heed to either document (Coghlan 1990).

Nevertheless, it is useful to briefly consider the details of these policy documents in order to inform understanding of future developments. Initially, in preparing *Sport in the Community* (1982), the Sports Council had agreed that school sport was the responsibility of the Department of Education and Science. However, by 1988, there was an identified decline in extracurricular school sport due in part to the government's wider education policies (Holt and Tomlinson 1994), and the Sports Council (1988, p. 61) recognised a 'need to give further impetus to work with young people in view of the relative lack of success in the past five years'. Young people, alongside women, became one of the two main target groups for encouragement of mass participation in *Into the Nineties* (1988). The adoption of these and other target groups represented recognition that there were insufficient resources to continue the generalist 'sport for all' campaigns of the 1970s (Sports Council 1982) although the desire for widespread participation remained:

Most important of all, there are . . . major inequalities in participation. To use an analogy, the sports franchise has been greatly extended but the suffrage is far from universal. (Sports Council 1988)

Besides the focus on participation amongst target groups, the Sports Council remained committed to developing performance and excellence (Holt and Mason 2000). However, in these areas, despite some learning from international contexts (Coghlan 1990), the Sports Council was explicit in its desire not to follow Eastern European models of elite sport success (Sports Council 1982; Green 2004). Incremental improvement in approaches to developing excellence were promoted rather than any radical change to existing systems in the United Kingdom (Sports Council 1982).

The implementation of both Sports Council strategies was recognised to be dependent on additional government funding, which was largely not forthcoming (Sports Council 1982, 1988). For the deputy director-general, this represented 'a sad commentary on the power and influence of the Minister for Sport, Colin Moynihan' (Coghlan 1990, p. 224). Instead, the drive from the minister of sport, in line with Thatcherite ideology, was for the Sports Council to attract greater private sector investment especially in elite sport (Moynihan 1990). Moreover, central government controls and cuts in local government finance further limited the funds available for sport and leisure provision (Coghlan 1990; Coalter 2007). The weakness of the funding position of sport was explicitly recognised by the Sports Council in *Into the Nineties* and NGBs were urged to 'avoid becoming over-dependent on grant aid from Government' (1988, p. 6). An acknowledgement of the lack of funding was perhaps responsible for the Sports Council promoting 'an overriding theme of . . . better co-ordination and co-operation' (1988, p. 69) rather than an expansion of existing provision.

JOHN MAJOR AND THE RE-EMERGENCE OF SPORT

That the approach adopted by John Major's governments towards sport was significantly different to that of the preceding administrations is unquestionable. Besides representing a break with the past, the changes in government policy and approach towards sport begun under Major were to have influence beyond the lifetime of his governments (Houlihan and White 2002). As stated earlier, that is not to say that there was necessarily a single point or event during the seven years of Major's premiership that could be represented as a 'watershed moment'. In fact, within two years of Major's appointment as prime minister the government department then responsible for sport published a policy statement, *Sport and Active Recreation* (Department of Education and Science 1991), which was a fairly unremarkable document that only hinted at some of the more significant changes to come. More important were three developments instigated after Major's re-election in 1992. A new Department of National Heritage was created in 1992; the National Lottery commenced in 1994 and 1995 saw the publication of a second policy document, *Sport: Raising the Game* (DNH 1995). These three developments signalled a significant increase in the salience of sport for government. Furthermore, as shall be discussed in subsequent sections, collectively they had a degree of coherence that enabled them to 'lay the foundations for sport policy development and governance into the twenty-first century' (Green 2009, p. 127). However, before examining these developments in greater detail, it is important to examine the broad thrust of the sport policy agenda developed by John Major and, subsequently, the political factors that enabled this agenda to be promoted.

Just as the broad policy agenda pursued by John Major's government represented an accommodation between his predecessor's brand of neo-liberal ideology and his own one-nation Conservatism, so these two different aspects were evident in the overall thrust of the sport policy agenda (Henry 2001). John Major's beliefs regarding the qualities of sport were strongly shaped by its influence on his own life starting from childhood during which he described himself as being happiest while playing team sports, spending his spare time at the Oval Cricket Ground and reading cricket literature (Major 1999). His empathy with cricket in particular was strongly linked with his one-nation Conservatism, as is demonstrated in the following passage from his autobiography:

> It is difficult to capture the special fascination of cricket. It is unique. It has grace and charm and athleticism. . . . Above all, with occasional lapses, cricket is played with a generosity of spirit that is refreshing, as it is unfashionable. It is, I think, a very English game, that still encapsulates old values. (Major 1999, p. 23)

Given the strength of John Major's personal passion and belief, it was hardly surprising that these values shaped the increasing intervention in sport undertaken by his governments (Holt and Mason 2000). Rhetorically, this influence was evident in early statements regarding sport made by ministers for sport. For example, in a debate on sport in the House of Commons, the then minister for sport argued that the government should nurture

> the great British tradition of sport, which makes Britain envied throughout the world, is that it is amateur and local. That access to sport makes the sporting tradition of this country so unique. (Key 1992)

The strongest examples of John Major's own personal advocacy for government intervention based on a peculiarly traditional image of sport all came in his forward to *Sport: Raising the Game*. Highlighting the nomenclature of the government department created to promote his agenda in sport, Major (1995, p. ii), for example, eulogised that

Sport is a central part of Britain's National Heritage. We invented the majority of the world's great sports. And most of those we did not invent, we codified and helped to popularise throughout the world.

Part of the government's agenda for sport was thus orientated towards its potential to contribute to a somewhat homogenous (Gilroy and Clarke 1997) vision of national identity. Again, this was espoused in John Major's forward (1995, p. ii):

Sport is a binding force between generations and across borders. But, by a miraculous paradox, it is at the same time one of the defining characteristics of nationhood and of local pride.

John Major's belief in the communal potential of sport stood in stark contrast to the individualism that underpinned Thatcher's ideology, as did his support for government intervention in sport and other cultural activities based on the supposed benefits it could bring to participants. In fact, in the forward to *Sport: Raising the Game,* Major placed himself in direct opposition to Thatcher's prioritisation of economic development as the sole contributor to individual welfare:

I have never believed that the quality of life in Britain should revolve simply around material success. Of equal importance, for most people, is the availability of those things that can enrich and elevate daily life in the worlds of the arts, leisure and sport. All too often in the past these areas have been overlooked. It is time for change. (Major 1995, p. i)

John Major and other government ministers (e.g. Sproat 1995c) were especially keen to laud the contribution that sport could make to the social and moral development of children and young people (Gilroy and Clarke 1997). It was in so doing that elements of the competitive individualism that was central to the neoliberal ideology came to the fore to a greater extent in Major's rhetoric regarding sport. Perhaps in a desire to relate to the particular audience, the following passage from Major's speech to the Conservative Party Central Council Meeting in 1994 is a prime example that demonstrates some of the values he felt sport could instil in young people:

And I also hope we'll see more team sport back in our schools. I have no time for those Left-wing ideologues who oppose competitive sport. Put children together and what do you see. They run. They jump. They fight. They compete. It is their natural instinct. We don't help them by hiding that away from them. Life can be tough. They need to know victory and defeat. And the sooner they learn it, the better equipped they will be for life. (Major 1994)

A similarly neoliberal view that sport could help to produce citizens capable of fitting into and contributing to the national economy was espoused by the then minister of sport, Ian Sproat (1995c), who spoke of the utility of sport in creating young people suitable for recruitment to the armed forces and fire service. As shall be discussed further in the following sections, neoliberal aspects were also especially prominent in the approach enacted to achieve the government's desired sporting objectives (Henry 2001).

From the preceding discussion, it is evident that the policy agenda set for sport was an intensely personal one for John Major. It is notable that besides advocating his desired agenda, Major also took an unusual interest in the detail of policy as suggested by Seldon's (1997) description of his intimate involvement in the drafting of *Sport: Raising the Game*. That this degree of prime ministerial involvement was required was in part due to the political context in which sport policy was developed at the time. Previous statements have demonstrated the support of ministers of sport for Major's sporting agenda and, perhaps more significantly and fortuitously, senior members of his cabinet, such as Ken Clarke, David Mellor and Peter Brooke, shared Major's affinity with sport (Major 1999; Henry 2001; Houlihan and White 2002). However, as Major himself recognised, his interest in pursuing a sporting agenda was 'thought to be rather quirky by some colleagues' (Major 1999, p. 412). His official biographer also identified that Major's cabinet colleagues were 'variously indifferent to, amused or irritated by, his passion for sport' (Seldon 1997, p. 594). Importantly, Seldon (1997, p. 594) also quoted a senior member of the civil service who described sport as 'one of those areas where the Whitehall machine is rather resistant and regards it as somewhat frivolous'. Evidence for this resistance was also provided by the minister for sport who indicated the 'terrible battle to get [*Sport: Raising the Game*] through the treacle of Whitehall . . . [as it] trespasses on other Departments' (Sproat 1995c). It is a measure of the powerful forces supporting the government's sporting agenda that the recalcitrant Departments 'eventually saw the wisdom of our ways' (Sproat 1995c).

Despite the need for prime ministerial impetus to drive the sport agenda forward within an unsupportive governmental apparatus, other aspects of the political context were supportive of John Major's initiative, especially around the time that *Sport: Raising the Game* was published. At that time, public support for the Conservative government was low and John Major was struggling to retain control of a party that was significantly divided, especially over Europe. John Major was therefore able to present his sporting vision strongly, and unusually, at the Conservative conference in 1994 (Hargreaves 1995) as something with which the broader party could empathise (Houlihan 2000). Furthermore, in terms of a broader audience, Major's advocacy for sport was seen as a 'clever attempt to gain popularity for a flagging government by appealing to an aspect of popular culture that most people see as innocent and beneficial' (Hargreaves 1995, p. 39). This view is supported by Gilroy and Clarke (1997, p. 22), who suggested that Major's 'focus on sport was a palliative to help draw attention away from other more fundamentally problematic areas'. What was also notable was the lack of opposition to the vision presented in *Sport: Raising the Game*. As noted by the minister for sport himself (Sproat 1995a), the Labour party raised little objection when the policy was discussed in parliament. Amongst the broader sport policy community, used to the disdain with which sport had been treated by the Thatcher government, any positive governmental impetus for sport would have been welcomed. Although Sports Council policy was different in a number of ways from that presented in *Sport: Raising the Game*, as shall be explored in the following section, for the organisation to have voiced any objection would have been 'political suicide' (Gilroy and Clarke 1997, p. 35).

SPORT POLICY THEMES 1990–1997

Largely fitting within the broader agendas examined in the previous section, sport policies during the period of John Major's premiership increasingly focused on specific aspects of sport. One such significant policy focus was school sport, an issue that rose to prominence due, in large part, to perceptions that it had been in a period of decline. As noted earlier in the chapter, the Sports Council had begun to raise concerns regarding sport for young people while Margaret Thatcher remained in power. Nevertheless, in *Sport and Active Recreation*, the Department of Education and Science (1991) remained somewhat equivocal regarding youth sport, noting that a decline in extracurricular activities was balanced by an increase in opportunities for young people within the community. However, the 'perception that something needed to be done' (Houlihan and Green 2006, p. 81) about school sport increased to the point where the narrative about decline became a significant rationale for the policy focus accorded to school sport in *Sport: Raising the Game*. This narrative was highlighted at the beginning of the section of *Sport: Raising the Game* which was devoted to school sport:

> It is serious cause for concern that sport no longer commands the place it once did in school life. Sport has had to compete for time in an increasingly crowded school day. . . . We are determined to reverse the decline . . . and put sport back at the heart of school life. (DNH 1995, pp. 6–7)

Moreover, in Commons debates on *Sport: Raising the Game,* the minister for sport justified the need to reinvigorate school sport in terms of the need to increase health amongst young people and as a contributor to overcome the failure of the home nations to qualify for the 1994 FIFA World Cup (Sproat 1995b).

The somewhat bizarre nature of this last justification highlights an important issue regarding the availability and use of evidence in the policy process. While Roche's analysis (1993) did support the case regarding the decline of school sport, both the minister for sport (Sproat 1995b) and, previously, the Sports Council had identified that evidence regarding school sport provision was lacking. Moreover, Gilroy and Clarke (1997) argued that what evidence was available was either ignored or used selectively, especially in relation to the pressures on curricular time for PE that resulted from implementation of the national curriculum. Instead, it was on the back of personal enthusiasm by John Major and other members of his government, reinforced by a widely accepted narrative, that school sport became 'the single most important element in the sporting continuum' (DNH 1995).

It was largely this personal enthusiasm that also underpinned the prioritisation of traditional competitive team sports over individual sports or other forms of physical education. The prioritisation of competitive team sports had initially emerged through the development of the National Curriculum for PE early in John Major's time in office (Houlihan and White 2002), but was made fully explicit in his forward to *Sport: Raising the Game* and by the minister for sport in the subsequent House of Commons debate (Sproat 1995c). Gilroy and Clarke (1997, p. 26) critiqued the focus on traditional team sports as representing a 'restorationalist discourse that school sport was better in some halcyon and romanticised bygone age'. Nevertheless, this discourse only served to strengthen the government's commitment to their agenda at a time when they were promoting a broader 'Back to Basics' campaign (Holt and Tomlinson 1994; Penney and Evans 1999). The Sports Council responded to the developing government agenda by similarly beginning to prioritise youth sport, as evidenced by publication of their own policy document *Young People and Sport* (1993a). However, it is notable that the Sports Councils agenda remained somewhat broader than that of the government through seeking to encourage 'basic movement skills' and developing 'positive attitudes to active recreation' (Sports Council 1993a, p. 18).

Implementation of the government's school sport agenda was to be achieved through a variety of mechanisms. As shall be discussed further in this chapter's penultimate section, John Major's government committed little or no new public funding to improve school sport (Holt and Tomlinson 1994; Taylor 2006). Any additional funding for school sport was to come through redirection of existing Sports Council and National Governing Body funding and, in alignment with a neoliberal agenda, through private sector sponsorship (DNH 1995). Of greater influence was the commitment in *Sport: Raising the Game* to the utilisation of more coercive governance techniques. Inspections by the Office for Standards in Education (OFSTED) were to examine both teacher training for sport and, most importantly, the provision of competitive team games in schools' curricular and extracurricular provision (DNH 1995). In addition, a new *Sportsmark* for schools was initiated which was to be awarded on the basis of government criteria including targets regarding the hours of available PE and extra-curricular sport. The public nature of such awards was, as in other areas of public services, envisaged as enabling enhanced parental choice which would in turn drive increased standards of provision (Sproat 1995c).

Besides school sport, the other major focus of sport policy was elite sport. That this was an especially strong feature in *Sport: Raising the Game* reflected not only the perceived contribution international success could make to national identify and cohesion but also the notable lack of success in the Atlanta Olympic Games in 1994. In at least one way the agenda promoted by the time *Sport: Raising the Game* was published in 1995 demonstrated the incremental change of government policy throughout John Major's period in office. The earlier policy document, *Sport and Active Recreation,* had pro-moted a non-interventionist and voluntaristic approach:

> The Government's role is to encourage and support what are largely voluntary efforts, not to direct and finance these activities which remain the responsibility of the British Olympic Association, the Com-monwealth Games Federation and the independent governing bodies of the sports concerned. (DES 1991, p. 27)

In the face of increasing international competition (Oakley and Green 2001), recognition developed within the sport policy community of the need for a more systematic and scientific approach to elite success (e.g. Sports Council 1993b). Visits to Australia and Canada by members of the Sports Council (Pickup 1996) and especially government ministers (Sproat 1995c) were influential in shaping a new policy approach towards achiev-ing elite sport success (Oakley and Green 2001). As a result, *Sport: Rais-ing the Game* included a proposal for the creation of British Academy of Sport, which mirrored the Australian Institute of Sport instigated fourteen years earlier in 1981. Alongside other developments, including the use of National Lottery funds examined later in the chapter, the policies of the Major government marked a 'watershed for the emergence of an organi-sational, administrative and funding framework for sport at the elite level' (Oakley and Green 2001, p. 371). Certainly, to use the words of Houlihan and White (2002, p. 74), 'John Major finally put the myth of the inspired British amateur to bed'.

Another developing area of elite sport policy was governmental support for bids to host international events. Again, the publication *Sport and Active Recreation* offered only lukewarm and indirect support in 'welcom[ing] initiatives to stage major sporting events in the UK' (DES 1991, p. 27). At the behest of John Major, however, there was a large government pres-ence including the prime minister himself at the Barcelona Olympic Games in 1992 (Pickup 1996). This 'reminder of [sport's] cultural and emotional power', alongside England's successful run in the 1990 World Cup, was credited by Holt and Mason (2000, p. 154) as encouraging Major and his government to pursue their sporting agenda. With Manchester undertaking a second successive bid to host the Olympic Games in 2000, Major's personal interest prompted the government to provide both financial and political support to the bid (Seldon 1997). Support was also offered by Deputy Prime Minister Michael Heseltine, who, despite lacking Major's personal enthusiasm for sport (Major 1999), saw the Games as potentially contributing to economic regeneration (Pickup 1996). Despite Manchester's bid being unsuccessful, the minister for sport reiterated that attracting the Olympic Games to Great Britain was a key priority (Sproat 1995c), although such an objective was not mentioned in *Sport: Raising the Game.*

It could be suggested that governmental support for elite sport and hosting major sporting events was not solely premised on the potential boost to national pride and identity, but also as a prominent tool of international relations. At the outset of his premiership, John Major was personally involved in negotiations with Nelson Mandela to lift the sporting ban on South Africa (Seldon 1997). Cricket also featured prominently in his first visit to South Africa in 1994 and it was notable that the minister for sport highlighted the positive role models presented by English cricketers when touring the country in 1995 (Sproat 1995c). Moreover, two of Major's early ministers for sport, Robert Atkins and Robert Key, both sought to highlight the leading role taken by Great Britain in international anti-doping efforts (Atkins 1991b; Key 1992). That the Sports Council (1993b) itself placed anti-doping at the centre of its attempts to retain ethics and fair play in sport again demonstrates the link between sport policy and John Major's tradition-orientated conservatism.

However, not all aspects of Sports Council policy fitted neatly with the government's sporting agenda. In the first instance, the publication of *Sport and Active Recreation* by the Department of Education and Skills in 1991 presented a dilemma for the Sports Council, who were in the process of preparing a third strategy to follow *Sport in the Community* (1982) and *Into the Nineties* (1988). Rather than abandon the work already undertaken to develop the strategy, the Sports Council decided to publish *Sport in the Nineties: New Horizons* although without the detail and evidence that was included in the previous policy documents (Sports Council 1993b). Elements of *Sport in the Nineties: New Horizons*, such as the focus on young people and excellence, were in line with the emerging government agenda (Houlihan and White 2002). However, especially in relation to aspects of mass participation, the Sports Council's strategy was rapidly superseded by *Sport: Raising the Game*. As part of continuing to support the philosophy of 'sport for all', *Sport in the Nineties: New Horizons* (1993b) reiterated the comprehensive approach of the Sports Council across the four elements of the 'sports development continuum': foundation, participation, performance and excellence. Damning the sports development continuum with faint praise as 'a word beloved by the Sports Council' (Sproat 1995c), the government tried to 'maintain the notion of a unified sports development policy' (Houlihan and White 2002, p. 67) whilst following a more limited agenda. Responsibility for the creation of pathways between the dual priorities of school sport and elite performance was placed, in *Sport: Raising the Game,* with sports clubs and further and higher education establishments (DNH 1995). While possibly offering some pathways, these organisations were unsuited and lacked the capacity to offer widespread sporting opportunities across the breadth of the population. Furthermore, the government envisaged that participation would naturally increase as a result of elite success (DNH 1995). Irrespective of the limited evidential legitimacy of these claims, it was inevitable that the government agenda would prevail, resulting in what Green (2004, p. 371) subsequently viewed as the 'withdrawal of central government and the Sports Councils from the provision of opportunities for mass participation'.

Similarly, the sporting agenda pursued by the government limited the impact, at least in the short term, of a series of Sports Council policy papers concerned with achieving equitable involvement in sport amongst particular groups, for example, women, people with disabilities and ethnic minorities (Sports Council 1993c, 1993d, 1994). These papers provided radical new perspectives on the institutional and organisational barriers affecting participation in sport (Houlihan and White 2002, p. 63). However, the government took a significantly different approach in *Sport: Raising the Game,* as explained by the minister for sport at the time:

> I want to make it clear that we did not mention the very important needs of the disabled in the paper for the same reason that we did not concentrate specifically on individual sports or matters of gender or race. The policy statement is for people of all abilities. (Sproat 1995c)

A particularly strong critique of the inclusivity of this approach was presented by Gilroy and Clarke (1997, p. 32), who argued that the 'traditional' sports that were the focus of *Sport: Raising the Game* were only viewed as such by a 'largely white, male and middle class section of the population'. The lack of consideration of gender was also highlighted for these authors by the rhetoric of 'sportsmen' and 'sportsmanship' used by John Major in his forward to *Sport: Raising the Game* (Gilroy and Clarke 1997). Nevertheless, it was only in time and with the election of the Labour government that issues of equity again became prominent as part of the sport policy agenda (Houlihan and White 2002).

ORGANISATIONAL REFORM AND SHIFTING BALANCES OF POWER

The organisational context of sport at the start of John Major's time in power was one that was recognised to be highly fragmented. In an assessment that was pessimistic about the existing situation and future prospects,

Roche (1993, p. 91) wrote that 'the structural disorganisation and internal conflict are at least longstanding and probably endemic in the British sport policy community'. The disjointed nature of sport policy processes was even identified in official documentation with the Sports Council (1993b, p. 8) recognising that 'the UK's sporting achievements have too often been secured in spite of the disparate goals having been set by our sporting community'. It was in this context that significant organisation reforms were enacted during the period of John Major's premiership. As shall be discussed later in this section, not all of these reforms contributed effectively to the desired objective of both the government and the Sports Council to achieve a greater degree of coherence within the country's sporting system (Sports Council 1993b; Taylor 1997).

Sport had long been relegated to a marginal place in political and departmental structures within Margaret Thatcher's governments. Before becoming prime minister, John Major (1999, p. 404) was himself aware that 'in the empires of Cabinet ministers [both sport and the arts] were regarded as lightweight responsibilities and something of an irrelevant diversion'. That this institutional weakness contributed to the neglect of sport within governmental policy meant that, for Major in particular, 'we were undervaluing a national asset and missing a political opportunity' (1999, p. 404). Nevertheless, prior to his re-election in 1992, the only organisational change enacted by Major was to transfer responsibility for sport from the Department of the Environment to the Department of Education and Skills. The implications of this change were to replicate the consequences of previous changes in departmental responsibility for sport that altered the balance of power between various organisations within the sporting community (Green and Houlihan 2005). On the one hand, the transfer of sport from the Department of the Environment 'weaken[ed] the link between sport and the other range of community-focused services' within the department (Houlihan and White 2002, p. 78) and, more generally, within local government itself (Lentell 1993). Murdoch (1993), on the other hand, viewed the transfer to the Department of Education and Skills as offering the potential for improving collaborative planning across PE and youth sport. That this potential was not realised was due to the Department of Education and Skills having an attitude towards sport which 'combined neglect, disdain and incomprehension in almost equal measure' (Houlihan and White 2002, p. 62).

After the re-election of the Conservatives in the 1992 general election, John Major was better placed to assert his own agendas and ideas within government. One almost immediate action was to create a Department of National Heritage (DNH) encompassing sport as well as the arts, broadcasting and tourism. While Henry (2001, p. 89) described it as 'an unexpected stroke', the creation of the DNH can be accounted for in terms of a number of supportive factors. Taylor (1997) credited David Mellor and Kenneth Baker with playing key roles in persuading John Major of the need for the new department and a minister for national heritage within the cabinet. Irrespective of the role of these individuals, John Major's personal support for the DNH was crucial. In order to give culture and sport the profile he felt that they 'deserved' in government, John Major described himself as 'convinced that this could only be done through establishing a new department of state to bring together all aspects of the arts, sport and heritage' (Major 1999, p. 405). In addition, wariness amongst the Conservative party regarding a new department (Taylor 1997) was allayed as the proposed name represented an 'appeal to One-National Conservatives of implying a unitary national heritage' (Henry 2001, p. 49). Taylor (1997) also indicated that factors within the arts community also contributed to the creation of the DNH. However, although the Sports Council (1993b, p. 16) had long 'argued that such an organ of central government was needed in the best interests of British sport', there is little indication that this advocacy had any impact either in the creation or operation of the DNH.

The aspirations of the Sports Council and others were, in part at least, realised by the creation of the DNH. Polley (1998, p. 24) recalls that 'the new designation [of the DNH] was important in terms of flagging sport's significance as part of national culture'. In this regard, the name of the department was certainly significant in pre-empting the subsequent direction of sport policy described earlier in the chapter (Henry 2001). Similarly, for Green (2009, p. 127) the creation of the DNH represented the first time that sport policy had been 'registered . . . as a serious national government responsibility'. As with most areas experiencing increased governmental interest, the creation of the DNH also engendered increasing central control over sport (Oakley and Green 2001). However, Taylor (1997) suggested that the way that central control was enacted by the DNH represented something of a significant departure for government more generally. Partly due to the preference of David Mellor, the first minister of state for national heritage, and partly due to the organisational complexity of sport and other policy areas overseen by the department, the DNH sought to achieve its policy goals more through steering networks of organisations rather than direct intervention (Taylor 1997). This approach was reaffirmed by the then minister for sport, who stated that the government did 'not believe in centrally imposed blueprints or day-to-day political interference in sport' (Key 1992). Instead, it was through the provision of policy direction, ministerial activism, scrutiny and arm's-length control of organisations such as the Sports Council that governmental policy objectives were pursued (Taylor 1997).

For the Sports Council itself, the period of John Major's premiership was largely one of uncertainty in terms of its role and organisational structure. Initial proposals published in *Sport and Active Recreation* (DES 1991) foresaw the splitting of the Great Britain Sports Council into a UK Sports Commission and an English Sports Council. Amongst the roles envisaged for the former were improved co-operation in planning of 'facilities and services to sustain excellence', to provide 'stronger representation of the UK in international deliberations on sport' and to, more generally, allow 'a more effective exchange of information and expertise; to concentrate activities in the fields of promotion and research which can better and more effectively be carried out at UK level' (DES 1991, p. 10). The remaining role of the English Sports Council was to focus to a greater extent on the promotion of 'participation and the development of sports foundation skills' as well as undertaking work in the relation to excellence when commissioned to do so by the UK Sports Commission (DES 1991).

There was some support for these proposals within the existing Great Britain Sports Council. Concerns regarding the ambiguity of the Sports Council's role in relation to the Sports Councils for Scotland, Wales and Northern Ireland were addressed in the proposals (Sports Council 1993b), which were also seen as an opportunity for improved co-operation across the four home countries (Hart and McInnes 1993). Nevertheless, the lack of immediate action to enact these proposals created a hiatus for the Sports Council which contributed to the limited impact of its *Sport in the Nineties: New Horizons* policy published in 1993 (Houlihan and White 2002). Later that year, the newly installed minister for sport announced the government's intention to withdraw the original proposals as he considered that creating the UK Sports Commission would represent 'another vast bureaucracy' with no 'proper job to do' (Sproat 1993a). The 'delay and prevarication' on behalf of government (Houlihan and White 2002, p. 70) was merely confirmed one year later when the same minister for sport announced plans for the creation of separate UK and England Sports Councils which were distinctly similar to those that had recently been abandoned.

Contradicting his previous statements, these latest plans were justified by the minister for sport on the basis of the 'grotesque and illogical inconsistency' of representation of Scotland and Wales on the Great Britain Sports Council, which itself had responsibility for English sport (Sproat 1995c). To a large extent, the division of roles between the UK and English organisations initially proposed in 1991 was reaffirmed by the minister for sport in 1994. However, maintaining a neoliberal focus on the reduction of state bureaucracy (Henry 2001), the minister wished to re-orientate the new organisations away from spending on the 'publications, pamphlets, conferences and seminars' (Sproat 1994) that the Great Britain Sports Council (1993b) had viewed as important in fulfilling its advisory role. In another notable rhetorical flourish, the minister also disparaged the previous input of Sports Council 'bureaucrats' in the development of policy and instead called for members of the board, such as Ian Botham ('a man of strong and independent mind and strong character') to take a lead in setting a policy agenda for the new English Sports Council (Sproat 1995c). While most probably negligible in its actual influence, the tone of this statement was representative of the significant departure from the strongly evidenced policies produced by the Great British Sports Council in the 1980s.

Of more immediate influence was the amendment of the original proposals in order to reduce the size of both of the new organisations (Sproat

1994). The UK Sports Council was to have an initial staff of around 20 rather than the 180 that had been initially proposed (Sproat 1994). When the restructure was finally completed in 1996, the UK Sports Council was far smaller than the English Sports Council, having only 20 per cent of the combined financial and human resources (Houlihan and White 2002). As a result, Oakley and Green (2001, p. 82) viewed the emergent arrangements as 'far from satisfactory', particularly as the UK Sports Council also had no initial role in the distribution of National Lottery funds. Houlihan and White (2002) were similarly critical, describing the resultant division of responsibilities as a 'bifurcation of sports development' in which National Governing Bodies of Sport had to work with two national bodies rather than one as previously had been the case.

At national level, one final and notable development in the organisational context of sport while John Major was in power was the creation of the Youth Sport Trust. The trust was set up with funding from the businessman Sir John Beckwith in 1994 and, with its TOPS programme, initially focused on distributing sports equipment and activity cards in schools. Through the advocacy of the trust's chief executive, Sue Campbell, and its astute focus on promoting traditional sports (Penney and Evans 1999), the trust was quickly able to 'challenge the Sports Council for policy leadership in the increasingly politically salient area' of school and youth sport (Houlihan and White 2002). The trust soon attracted additional funding from the Department of Education and Employment and, faced with the difficulties of their own reorganisation, the Sports Councils became increasingly marginal to the delivery of school sport (Houlihan and Green 2006). In the broader context, therefore, the emergence of the trust can be viewed as a further consequence of the broader neoliberal programme of rolling back the state. At least in the short term, the addition of the trust to an already disjointed landscape did nothing to enhance coherence within the national sport policy community.

ADDITIONAL FUNDING AND ASSOCIATED NEW MECHANISMS OF CONTROL

From the outset, John Major realised that further funding was required if he was to realise his objectives for sport. In his only budget as Chancellor of the Exchequer in spring 1990, prior to becoming prime minister, he reduced tax on Football Pools revenue on the condition that the added revenue went to the Football Trust to fund improvement in football stadiums. That this proposal 'only survived against much scepticism in the Treasury' (Major 1999, p. 146) demonstrates that providing mainstream Exchequer funding for sport at that time was highly unlikely. Subsequently in 1991, after John Major's appointment to the post of prime minister, a further reduction of tax on the Football Pools companies led to the creation of the Foundation for Sports and Arts (FSA). For the Football Pools companies, who had initially suggested the creation of the foundation (Lamont 1991), this represented an attempt to pre-empt government moves to create a national lottery by providing their own funding for community-based sport projects (Evans 1995; Oakley and Green 2001). For the government, encouraging investment by private sector organisations into sport was very much in tune with the neoliberal ideology that remained strong within a significant proportion of the Conservative party. It was notable, given the organisational reforms identified in the previous section, that the Sports Council was 'kept on the margins of decision making' regarding the instigation of the FSA (Houlihan and White 2002, p. 71). Nevertheless, the Sports Council had little option but to welcome the £40m that the FSA provided annually for sport (Sports Council 1993b).

Given that the creation of the FSA only forestalled the creation of the National Lottery meant that its impact was only short-lived. In fact, one of the largest pools companies, Vernons, subsequently withdrew from the voluntary agreement to contribute 5p from every 105p spent on the pools to the FSA (Evans 1995). Nevertheless, the considerable significance of the FSA lay in its use as a template, and as a something of an unheeded warning, for the subsequent development of the National Lottery (Houlihan and White 2002). Not long after the instigation of the FSA, the Sports Council (1993b, p. 63) was already warning of their 'concern that the most effective use is not being made of the funds' provided by the FSA. This concern was on account of the lack of strategy underpinning the allocation of funds and was to be a lesson learned in the early years of the National Lottery. Furthermore, in another move to be followed by the National Lottery, the FSA in its early years focused on facility projects before subsequently changing tack to allow provision of revenue funding (Evans 1995).

Besides the FSA, a second mechanism created by the Major government to lever greater private sector funds into sport was the Sportsmatch scheme. Started a year after the FSA in 1992, Sportsmatch was designed to promote sponsorship of voluntary sector sport. The incentive to encourage this private sector investment was the potential for any funding to be 'matched' by a similar amount from a government fund of approximately £3m (Atkins 1991a). That the Sportsmatch scheme combined private sector involvement with support for the voluntary sector only enhanced its respective appeal to neoliberal and one-nation strands of the Conservative party (Oakley and Green 2001). Three years after it started, it was also notable that government began to utilise strategically the Sportsmatch scheme to further its own objectives with the minister for sport announcing that £1m of the government contribution would be earmarked solely for youth sport projects (Sproat 1995c).

While welcome for a chronically underfunded sport sector, the scale of funding provided by the FSA and Sportsmatch was limited and critics of the time started to suggest that John Major's support for sport was merely rhetorical (Holt and Tomlinson 1994; Talbot 1995). However, the creation of a National Lottery, signalled in the first Queen's speech after the 1992 election, was to provide substantial additional funds to support the government's sporting agenda. In many ways, the politics surrounding the creation of the National Lottery were similar to those that affected other sport policy developments of the period. Recognising the impact of national lotteries in other European countries (Houlihan and White 2002), the Sports Council had been supportive of the introduction of a similar scheme in the UK for some time. As prime minister, John Major's early openness to the idea of a national lottery differed significantly from the antipathy expressed by his predecessor (Pickup 1996). However, there was again hostility to the creation of a national lottery amongst ministers when it was first proposed within government in 1991 (Major 1999). Moreover, the Treasury was also unsupportive (Pickup 1996; Seldon 1997) perhaps because Major (1999, p. 405) saw the National Lottery as a way to protect funding for sport and the arts from the Treasury-dominated 'bunfight' for public money. That the National Lottery proposal proceeded despite this opposition was, in part at least, due to its fit with the ideological contradictions that continued to be evident within the Conservative party. For neoliberals, the National Lottery held the potential of increasing investment from a source that was not classified as public expenditure (Henry 2001; Houlihan and White 2002) and in parliament the government keenly emphasised the principle that National Lottery funds were to be 'additional' to core government funding (Moore 1997). In addition, there was consistency in the use of arm's-length organisations to distribute lottery funds, a mechanism which somewhat concealed the centralisation of power that had been continuing since the Thatcher government (Henry 2001; Houlihan and White 2002).

The National Lottery et cetera [*sic*] Bill was passed in 1993 with the first draw held in 1994. Approximately 28 per cent of the money spent on ticket sales was allocated to five 'good causes': sports, arts, heritage, charities and projects to mark the millennium. Distribution of these funds was the responsibility of eleven bodies, including the Sports Councils for each of the four home countries. On the one hand, Evans (1995, p. 234) suggested that the role of organisations such as the Sports Councils in the distribution of National Lottery funds gave 'these beleaguered institutions previously under attack from central government a new lease of life'. On the other, the original policy directions issued in June 1994 by the government to the sports, arts and heritage distributing bodies considerably restricted the freedom of these organisations as to the grants that could be awarded (Oakley and Green 2001). These directions specified that the distributing bodies should spend lottery funds mainly on capital projects that had a large element of partnership funding. Distributing bodies were also not allowed to solicit applications from particular organisations. The implications of these directions were central to many of the early criticisms of National Lottery funding for sport.

A first line of criticism arose from the strict interpretation of the requirement not to solicit applications on the part of lottery distributing bodies. White (1999) questions the extent to which such a strict interpretation was necessary in light of a letter from the government which stated that the initial direction did 'not prevent the distributing bodies from considering applications from particular types [of organisation], or in particular geographic or subject areas' (letter, 20 June 1994, cited in White 1999). Nevertheless, the direction hindered the Sports Councils from adopting a strategic or planned approach to the distribution of lottery funds (Evans 1995; Houlihan and White 2002). The direction also limited local authorities, as a significant potential beneficiary of lottery funding, to an ad hoc approach towards undertaking applications (White 1999). A second concern related to the restriction of funds solely to capital projects, an aspect which John Major himself had insisted on to 'to keep [individual projects] from being a long-term commitment and from treasury attempts to sequester' lottery funding (Major 1999, p. 409). Both Sports Councils and local authorities took a different viewpoint regarding the first of Major's rationales and, increasingly over the early years of the lottery, became concerned regarding the long-term future and strategy of facilities newly built with lottery funding (White 1999). Moreover, in another major criticism, the direction regarding capital funding meant that the Sports Councils were not able to fund feasibility studies or other up-front payments to architects or surveyors. While these conditions may not have been a significant hindrance for larger organisations, such as local authorities, White (1999, p. 83) suggested that they 'appeared to seriously disadvantage' community organisations in pursuing potential applications. This disadvantage was particularly felt amongst less affluent organisations, especially since they were also required to find and demonstrate significant amounts of partnership funding in order to be successful with any lottery application (Evans 1995). As a result, there were proportionately less applications from deprived areas in the first year of lottery funding (Oakley and Green 2001).

Subsequently, in 1996, a number of changes to distribution policies were made which sought to address some of the issues identified in the previous paragraph. In the House of Commons, the minister for sport claimed that the changes were part of a process of 'learning from experience' (Sproat 1996). A Priority Areas Initiative was launched by the English Sports Council that was designed to promote applications from deprived areas, for which the partnership funding requirement was reduced to 10 per cent of total costs. Similarly, a reduced requirement of 20 per cent partnership funding was placed on school and community-based projects. A third and hugely significant change was the easing of the restrictions on revenue funding to allow the Sports Councils to provide finance for elite athletes (Oakley and Green 2001).

Overall, Henry (2001) identified the National Lottery as the key 'lasting contribution' of John Major's government to sport and leisure. It was certainly an initiative of which Major himself was proud, describing it in his autobiography as 'the most successful innovation of any government for years' (Major 1999, p. 409). Lottery funding immediately dwarfed the money invested in sport by the government itself. In the financial year ending March 1996, the Sports Council received £244 million from the National Lottery compared to £47 million directly granted by the Department of National Heritage (Sports Council 1996). Houlihan and White (2002, p. 78) stated that the scale of lottery funding helped to 'alter the pattern of resource dependencies between the main organisations responsible for sports development'. Power over the criteria for distribution of National Lottery funds allowed the government greater scope to centrally determine sport policy. Moreover, distribution procedures and conditions for lottery funding enacted through the Sports Councils represented relatively new mechanisms by which national policy goals could be pursued. First heralded in *Sport: Raising the Game,* funding for National Governing Bodies became increasingly conditional on achieving government objectives and targets that were also written into business plans that NGBs had to agree with the Sports Councils (DNH 1995). Within other organisations, especially local authorities, a 'bidding culture' emerged whereby priorities were increasingly orientated towards opportunities to apply for National Lottery funding (Henry 2001). These trends, and the increasing centralisation of power over the sporting community that they represented, were to continue long after John Major had left office.

CONCLUSIONS

In the context of both this book and wider literature, it is not necessarily novel to identify the period of John Major's government as one in which sport became an increasingly salient issue for government. What is of more concern in the conclusion to this chapter are the processes that contributed to this increasing salience and the resultant implications, during this period and beyond, for the sport policy sector. In terms of sport policy itself, one key development was the bifurcation initiated by the Major government between policy concerns within the sector. The general lack of interest in sport on behalf of the Thatcher government meant that the Sports Council's advancement of an integrated and holistic approach to sport policy, as exemplified by the sports development continuum, had remained a strong feature of the policy sector. Part of the significance of the *Sport: Raising the Game* policy statement was, therefore, the instigation of a split between distinct sport policy agendas, primarily school and elite sport. Certainly, the continuation of these two sport policy agendas, and the concomitant weakening of community sport, represents something of a continuing legacy of the Major government. Furthermore, while there had previously been a fragmentation of interests within the sport policy sector, the development of coalitions of interest around both youth and elite sport (described further in subsequent chapters) may be traced back to the distinguishing of these policy priorities in *Sport: Raising the Game*.

That strong coalitions advocating for sport policy were not present during John Major's period in government highlights the impact of other factors and processes in contributing to the rise in salience of sport. Instead, as has been noted throughout this chapter, this rise in salience demonstrates the impact that powerful individuals, in this case John Major himself, can have in shaping sport policy. The malleability of sport, and its institutional structure, proved conducive to it being promoted and utilised by Major. For a politically weak prime minister, it was also advantageous that sport could be linked to various aspects of the different and inconsistent ideologies that, to differing extents, both he and his party subscribed to. Major viewed sport in such a way that he was able to align it both rhetorically and instrumentally with his own one-nation Conservatism. Conversely, many of the mechanisms by which sport was to be developed, such as delivery by non-governmental organisations like the Youth Sport Trust and garnering private sector funding, sat well with the neoliberal ideology prevalent within the Conservative party of the day. These influences on sport policy draw attention to the role that ideas and beliefs rather than scientific evidence may have on policy processes and this is again a theme that will be considered further in subsequent chapters. Furthermore, the lack of significant resistance to adoption of these ideological agendas demonstrates a willingness for 'policy taking' within a sport policy sector that had suffered years of neglect throughout the Thatcher governments.

Where Major did encounter resistance to his sporting agendas was from within his own government and its departmental structures. Despite the impetus given to sport by Major, it still remained marginal to the everyday concerns of much of government, a position that changed only to a limited extent in the subsequent period after the election of the Labour government. Some of the muddled implementation of the Major government's sport policies, for example, in respect of Sports Council restructuring and early National Lottery strategy, can potentially be attributed to the lack of governmental expertise in such matters. Again, as shall be examined in the next chapter, it was the subsequent modernisation programme of the Labour government that created a more structured sport policy implementation system.

If these aspects represent areas of continuity and progress from John Major's government to the subsequent Labour administrations, then a further trend that had continued resonance was the increasing central government control over the sport policy sector. In particular this period witnessed the marginalisation of the Sports Council as a policymaking agency. Despite attempts to continue to develop distinctive and evidence-based strategies, the influence of the Sports Council in shaping overarching sport policy was weakened both by the continued uncertainty over its structure as well as the instigation of the National Lottery, one of the distinguishing features of John Major's time in office. The increased funding provided by the National Lottery became a significant policy tool by which central government could increasingly direct support to specific sport policy goals and priorities. As a result, the Sports Council, and subsequently Sport England, was increasingly cast in the role of funding distributor on behalf of the government. The continuation of a number of these trends and themes will be a feature of the following chapter.

3 From New Labour's Modernisation to the Coalition's Big Society

Over the last 70 or so years there have been three periods of continuous government by one party which have, arguably at least, left a clearly identifiable legacy: the 1945 to 1951 Labour governments of Clement Atlee and a legacy of state intervention; the 1979 to 1990 governments of Margaret Thatcher and privatisation; and the Blair governments of 1997 to 2005 and modernisation. While the claims relating to the Atlee and Thatcher legacies have a considerable degree of credibility due to having 'stood the test of time', it is too soon to determine whether the Blair legacy will be re-evaluated and downgraded in the coming years and also whether the coalition government's promotion of the 'Big Society' will develop a sufficiently clear profile to deliver an impact that outlives the government. However, the rhetoric of the Labour governments of Tony Blair and to a lesser extent that of Gordon Brown was certainly ambitious and, importantly, the party was in power for 13 years, which gave it the opportunity to make fundamental changes to policy and administration. However, one of the conventional assumptions about British politics is that continuity between administrations is considerably greater than the rhetoric of day-to-day political debate might suggest (Rose 1984). New administrations tend to add to, or tinker with, what already exists rather than try to dismantle existing policies and procedures. Current opinion on the significance of New Labour's legacy is sharply divided (Gamble 2010). For some the defining quality of New Labour was the degree of continuity either with the preceding Conservative governments (Heffernan 2001) or with 'old' Labour (Fielding 2003), while for others New Labour marked a radical break with party history and a genuine 'Third Way' (Giddens 1998). A variant on the latter assessment of New Labour's legacy is that the impact was less on policy and more on electoral strategy—a successful change of style which made the Labour brand attractive to the electorate at three successive elections rather than a significant change of substance. Although the policy implications of the 'Third Way' can be somewhat elusive, if not illusive, it would be a mistake to dismiss the 13 years of Labour government as contentless—far from it. In a number of important policy areas Labour introduced policies which it is hard to believe the Conservatives would have considered and which have had a marked and arguably irreversible impact on Britain. The most notable policies concern devolution to the home countries and the incorporation of the European Convention on Human Rights into British law, the first of which had, as will be argued in Chapter 4, a limited impact on sport policy up to 2010, but has the potential to have a much greater impact on UK sport policy since the election of the coalition government. Two broader policy objectives of New Labour which were prominent during the prime ministership of Tony Blair were a commitment to greater social inclusion and the promotion of a modern government built around the principles of partnership and decentralisation (Blair 1998). Both these objectives had substantial implications for sport policy, although they were also controversial in interpretation and in realisation.

However, not only was sport affected by the Labour government's broader objectives but it was also significantly affected by policy developments in contiguous policy areas such as education and health. Consequently, this chapter identifies and reviews the government-wide principles and practices which characterised New Labour's period in office and their impact for public service provision in general and, in particular, for two subsectors—education and health—and the objective of social inclusion. The reason for examining these subsectors and the objective of social inclusion is that, as will be discussed more fully below, the sport policy subsector is less self-contained than most and far more liable to having 'sport' policy determined through spillover from other more powerful non-sport policy subsectors. From this review of the experience of these sectors and services we illustrate the themes, principles, technologies and narratives associated with modernisation. Modernisation is discussed as a refinement of/reaction to new public management (NPM) ideas, which were at their most prominent during the 1980s and early 1990s. Social inclusion and the associated concepts of stakeholding, evidence-based policy and partnership working are discussed in terms of their consequences for the organisation of the machinery of government, and the role of local authorities and government agencies. The chapter also identifies and explores the shifting sport-specific policy objectives since 1997 including: elite success; school sport; physical activity and health; and the hosting major sports events. The broad implications of both modernisation and social inclusion for sport policy are threaded through the chapter and provide the context for the discussion of the sport policy developed in the early years of the coalition government elected in May 2010.

As noted in Chapter 1, the adoption of a metaphor of levels is a useful heuristic device in the analysis of policy change. In recent decades governments have, at least during election campaigns, often promised fundamental change as a strategy for attracting votes. While most of these promises soon proved to be purely rhetorical, there have been occasions when governments could claim with greater confidence to have introduced policies which have had a lasting and significant impact. The governments with the most secure grounds for substantiating the claim to long-term legacy are those which deliver change across the broad sweep of government activity (across the policy core) rather than simply in one policy subsector. It is argued that 'modernisation' was one such policy and social inclusion perhaps another which, like Thatcher's privatisation/marketisation policy, left its imprint across government.

MAKING SENSE OF MODERNISATION
AND SOCIAL INCLUSION

According to Finlayson (2003, p. 66), 'If there is one word that might capture the essence of New Labour's social and political project then it is "modernisation". The jargon and rhetoric of modernisation abound within the Labour Party and government' (p. 66; see also Fairclough 2000). While Finlayson points to the imprecision associated with the use of the term, he also argued that, for Tony Blair, the change that modernisation was to bring about was to be progressive, emancipatory and imbued with a 'missionary zeal' (p. 74). In short, Blair's vision for guiding and shaping policy formation and implementation from 1997 had, at its heart, the aim of 'completely reforming the British state and society . . . the country is weighed down by out-dated habits and institutions that are no longer fit to fulfil their stipulated tasks because the world has changed' (Blair 1994, p. 1). The political significance of the reform agenda is captured by Michael Barber's account of his time as head of the prime minister's Delivery Unit between 2001 and 2005: 'From January 2004 onwards . . . he [Blair] gave more and more attention to radicalising public service reform, both because he believed it was essential and because he saw it as a means of dominating the political scene' (Barber 2008, p. 212). This ideological rationale amounted to much more than New Labour merely maintaining a Thatcherite agenda or capitulating to capital and the market.

Yet, inevitably, there are a number of competing interpretations of New Labour and its modernising reform agenda. Richards and Smith (2004, p. 124) argued that from 1997 there evolved 'a hybrid state that retains elements of the traditional Westminster model (a strong centre), Thatcherite reform (managerialism), social democracy (the welfare state) and New Labour (pluralising policy-making, policy advice and delivery)'. Hall (2007, p. 119) reaches a similar conclusion: 'New Labour is in fact a hybrid formation, combining neo-liberalism with a commitment to "active government", contracting out parts of the state while engaging in an excess of top-down state management and triangulating a marketisation strategy (in the leading position within its political repertoire) with a social-democratic strand (in a more subordinate place)'. However, whereas New Right Conservative ideology, at least in its mainstream rhetoric, promoted a minimal role for the state (cf. Le Grand 2007), Richards and Smith (2004, p. 124) suggest that probably one of the most striking aspects of the Blair modernisation agenda 'is a highly developed, progressive and modernist notion that the state has responsibility for improving the social conditions of groups in society: whether this is the reading ability of school children or the goal to abolish poverty'.

Indeed, in the early years of the Blair administration much was made of the government's concern to create a stakeholder society where decision making would be more decentralised and more participative with the aim of stimulating a more pluralist civil society and thus increasing the generation of social capital. There was some experimentation with different forms of service delivery, particularly various forms of local partnerships, which gave credence to the rhetoric of the enabling state, but progress was limited by the underlying tension between the desire for greater localism and the deep-rooted centralism of the British political tradition. Consequently, greater localism in service delivery was generally accompanied by increased central supervision to the extent that 'the enabling state increasingly came to resemble the old command state [which bred] resentment at increasing government interference—in particular the big extension of the techniques associated with the new public management, the target and audit culture, and performance indicators' (Gamble 2010, p. 647): while responsibility was devolved to partnerships power remained firmly with central government.

Yet the reference to plurality in policymaking—reflecting the arguments for a shift from government to governance—under New Labour is questionable. Shaw (2004, p. 67), for example, argues that the 'New Labour Party [exemplifies a] drift towards a more powerful central apparatus, greater organisational centralisation, more concentrated patterns of authority, and tauter discipline' mirroring the previously mentioned centralising tendencies within the wider political system. Prompted by a concern that the party should not return to the internal factionalism of the 1970s and early 1980s, there was thus a 'vital need', in Blair's words, to transform Labour into 'a modern, disciplined party with a strong centre' (*The Independent*, 20 November 1998, cited in Shaw 2004, p. 67). Within this context it is hardly surprising therefore that, given New Labour's retention of neoliberalism's advocacy of market solutions and individualism, people who are financially dependent on the state become the focus of policies and rhetoric designed to foster and encourage self-reliance and engagement in economically useful activity.

Such an analysis draws attention to the usefulness of the Foucauldian governmentality literature, and in particular the work of Miller and Rose (2008, p. 53), who investigate the notion of 'political power beyond the state'. Miller and Rose maintain that the political lexicon structured by oppositions between state and civil society, public and private, government and market, coercion and consent, sovereignty and autonomy does not sufficiently capture the complexity of governing in advanced liberal democracies. Contemporary political power is exercised through a plethora of shifting alliances or partnerships between diverse authorities in programmes to govern a multitude of areas of economic activity, social life and individual conduct. For Miller and Rose, then, '[political] power is not so much a matter of imposing constraints upon citizens as of "making up" citizens capable of bearing a kind of regulated freedom' (p. 53). The exercise of political power under this schema is characterised, in Foucauldian terms, by 'the conduct of conduct', where personal autonomy is a fundamental tenet in its exercise, 'the more so because most individuals are not merely the subjects of power but also play a part in its operations' (p. 54).

Four points are worthy of note at this stage. First, this linking of 'freedom' with 'responsibility', and the significance of governing through alliances and partnerships was reflected in many ministerial comments such as those made in 2008 by the then secretary of state for culture, media and sport, Andy Burnham, in his speech at Lords to launch the government's latest policy document, *Playing to Win* (DCMS 2008). The secretary of state stated that:

> In return for public money and the new freedom comes responsibility. Governing bodies will be expected to operate to high standards of internal organisation and democracy, ensuring that the voice of all levels and participant groups can be heard. This should be the standard of good governance for the modern governing bodies. School and youth sports centre stage, women and girls' games, and disability sport, not an optional extra, but a vital part of what governing bodies will be required to do. And if any sport does not wish to accept the challenge, funding will be switched to those that do. (p. 4)

Second, this perspective on the role and operation of NGBs fits well with the language of modernisation and the Third Way (Fairclough 2000; Finlayson 2003). New Labour's language, especially in relation to social inclusion, was imbued with a strong rhetoric about duty, rights and responsibilities which, at least for the party modernisers, created a vision of Labour that was not simply a veiled version of Thatcherism. Third, and related to the first two points, the political rationalities of modernisation 'seeks to apply policy mechanisms designed not to create the conditions for social inclusion but to create the sorts of citizens who will themselves create the conditions of their own inclusion' (Finlayson 2003, p. 154). In other words, in line with the organisation of advanced liberalism, New Labour was not attempting to create the 'good society' through direct intervention but through 'producing' the good citizens who can do so for themselves. Through a barrage of (largely performance management) technologies in areas such as education, health, and social welfare more generally, the aim of policy was to create a new subject: the good, self-governing citizen. New Labour had thus distanced itself from the 1980s and early 1990s and the New Right's exhortations for the creation of singular self-interested individuals: unlike Margaret Thatcher, society and community mattered to New Labour. But, somewhat paradoxically, New Labour's new social regulation, entangled as it was with the technologies of performance management, produced, or at least encouraged, an entrepreneurial individualism. In this respect, Rose (1999, p. 166) argued that:

> Within such rationalities, it appears that individuals can best fulfil their political obligations in relation to the wealth, health and happiness of the nation not when they are bound to relations of dependency and obligation, but when they seek to fulfil themselves as free individuals. Individuals are now to be linked into a society through acts of socially sanctioned consumption and responsible choice.

The fourth point may not come as much of a surprise; that is, the picture, and the practicalities, of 'freedom' running through the narrative of New Labour's modernising agenda was an illusory or, at best, a regulated freedom. It is not hard to find examples in different policy sectors. The sport policy sector is the primary concern of this study and the first example is the language used in 2008 by the secretary of state for culture, media and sport in the quotation mentioned earlier in this section. Another example, among many, taken from *Playing to Win* is just as pertinent:

> Most importantly, Sport England will strike a new partnership with each of the National Governing Bodies. In return for greater freedom and control over public funds, governing bodies will be challenged to expand participation and provide more quality coaching for more people. (DCMS 2008, p. 1)

Ironically, *Playing to Win* concludes with the statement that 'This is not a top down Government agenda, it puts the experts in charge, offering sports more freedom and control. We believe it goes with the grain of what people in sport want' (DCMS 2008, p. 21).

One further example relates to the *No Compromise* policy adopted by UK Sport in 2006. The *No Compromise* policy is unashamedly about maximising Olympic medals, and one crucial aspect of this strategy is to ensure that the organisations upon which UK Sport relies to deliver this success—NGBs—are modern, fit for purpose and professional. UK Sport made it very clear that in subsequent years its *No Compromise* investment strategy for Olympic sports would target resources exclusively at those athletes capable of delivering medal-winning performances (UK Sport 2006a, p. 1). This new funding strategy clearly epitomised a narrative or storyline constructed around a broader discourse of ensuring elite sport success in 2008 and in 2012 in particular. The shaping and guiding of the conduct of NGBs, and especially the threat of funding reappraisals if NGBs fell short of the high standards now required, drew attention to one of the central insights of governmentality research, which is that as a government agency, UK Sport's power does not rely 'upon the traditional Hobbesian means of sovereignty plus coercion' (Davies 2006, p. 254), but draws increasingly on a range of disciplinary techniques of manipulation.

As Finlayson (2003, p. 176) noted in his analysis of New Labour and modernisation, the DCMS 'does not directly interfere in the running of many cultural institutions [e.g. Sport England, UK Sport], yet it is in a position to act in ways that manifestly do alter them'. Moreover, the broader political context within which the *activity* of modernisation was focused was one where a fundamental concern was to change the ways in which government worked and public services were delivered. Set within this context, the technologies of *No Compromise*, performance management, target-setting and sanctions begin to make more sense. However, modernisation of sport institutions was intended to impact on the behaviour of the individual, and especially the elite athlete, who must now regard him or herself not as an object of state policy but more as a subject who must take on the responsibility for development, change, and ultimately winning medals and trophies for the (communal) 'glory' of the nation.

The interaction between New Labour's political vocabulary of modernisation, cooperation and partnership on the one hand, and the various practices of performance assessment on the other, illustrates well the interface between programmes and technologies, or mechanisms, of government (Kurunmäki and Miller 2006, p. 89). Programmes of government such as modernisation require technologies in order to be 'made' operable. In this respect, the rhetoric of *Modernising Government* promoted 'local solutions' and innovation (Cabinet Office 1999), yet combined this with a centralising agenda that increased the capacity of the centre to monitor and control local service provision. Performance measurement was one of the key technologies of government that ran through this centralising dimension, manifested in the 'avalanche of performance indicators, performance reviews, audits and inspections in the UK public sector' (Kurunmäki and Miller 2006, p. 97). Centralism and localism therefore went hand in hand in a performance culture that had one notable characteristic in the context of the *Modernising Government* agenda: 'the imperative to develop *joined-up performance measurement* to complement *joined-up working*' (p. 98). In this respect, New Labour's social welfare reform agenda, primarily in the fields of education, health and social inclusion more broadly, was in the vanguard of the party's modernisation project (Finlayson 2003; Newman 2001) and also had a considerable impact on sport due to the vulnerability of the sport policy subsector to spillover from contiguous policy areas.

In Chapter 1 the concept of spillover was identified as an element of both punctuated equilibrium theory and of the multiple streams model insofar as spillover from the wider government agenda (for example, privatisation or social inclusion) affected sport policy along with other substantive areas of government interest. However, spillover also refers to a situation where policies that are primarily focused on one service area spill over into others or where a number of different policy areas share a common focus on a particular constituency or client group. Far from being relatively self-contained, sport policy is often affected by policy decisions spilling over from a range of other policy subsectors including education (design of the National Curriculum for PE, for example), criminal justice (sports-based interventions for 'at-risk' youth), urban policy (regeneration through sport facility development) and health (strategy to tackle the consequences of a more sedentary lifestyle). One obvious consequence of vulnerability to spillover is that the profile of policy in the sport subsector is shaped as much, if not more, by policy taking than policymaking.

A recurring theme in discussion of sport policy is the extent to which it is used in an instrumental fashion by governments to address a range of non-sport issues not only associated with welfare-related objectives, but also associated with international relations, economic development and nation-building. It is not suggested that sport is unique in this regard: indeed, very similar debates have taken place in relation to education and the arts. However, what is being argued is that sport seems especially vulnerable to inadvertent spillover from other more powerful policy areas and to deliberate incorporation into the policy response constructed by interests far removed from sport. Examples of the former phenomenon can be found in relation to the education and health policy subsectors while an example of the latter phenomenon can be identified in relation to the government's concern to tackle the issue of social exclusion.

MODERNISATION, JOINED-UP POLICYMAKING AND SOCIAL WELFARE REFORM

The discussion of developments in education and health cannot be divorced from the policy context that foregrounds the pre-eminence of social inclusion as the dominant policy paradigm of the period between 1997 and 2005. The discussion also highlights the potential overlaps between these policy sectors, especially in light of Labour's ambitions for joined-up policymaking. And, as will be shown, from 1997, the salience of sport (and physical activity) policy and programmes assumed increasing significance as one of the ways in which policy problems in these areas of social welfare policy might be addressed. There is, in other words, gathering evidence of 'spillover effects' between sport policy interventions and social welfare programmes (Houlihan and Green 2006).

It should also be noted that it is now almost an orthodoxy that social exclusion and inclusion are contested concepts (cf. Dean 2004), but, according to Dean, they are concepts colonised by New Labour (through its recourse to the Third Way) 'in a manner that subordinates concerns with structural inequality to a concern for social cohesion, albeit a notion of cohesion premised on a predominantly liberal-individualist conception of citizenship' (2004, p. 182). For example, the promotion of equal employment opportunities, not guaranteed jobs, and promoting an obligation to engage with the labour market through, for example, welfare-to-work employment or training programmes, rather than job creation, as the first resort of policy action. This assessment accords well with the concepts of governmentality and NPM for, as Dean suggests, New Labour had adopted a ' "managerial" . . . human capital approach [that] accords recognition to the productive potential of every citizen and to the ideals of self-development and individual empowerment' (2004, p. 192). In short, 'Opportunity and responsibility as the means of achieving social inclusion and revitalised communities are perhaps the most central principles of New Labour's approach' (Lewis 2004, p. 213). In this context, the valorisation of 'active citizenship' became emblematic of New Labour's social inclusion agenda, as will be illustrated in exploring the education and health sectors which emerged as crucial sites for the party's modernising reform of the country's public services. Furthermore, for New Labour, sport policy was identified as playing an increasingly important role in the promotion of active citizenship, interweaved as it was with policy reform in the education and health sectors.

The toleration or active acceptance by key policy actors such as Sport England, local authorities and, to a lesser extent, NGBs and clubs of spill-over into the sport subsector was, in part, the result of the government embrace of the vision of social capital creation promoted by Robert Putnam. Putnam defined social capital as 'connections among individuals—social networks and the norms of reciprocity and trust-worthiness that arise from them' (2000, p. 19). In essence, social capital was considered by the Labour government to be a neutral resource which helped to establish communities that had strong social norms which permeated and maintained strong social networks that led to the generation and maintenance of mutual trust and reciprocity. According to Putnam, communities that have a higher density of civic associations, such as voluntary sports clubs, possess strong networks, and a greater depth of mutual trust will consequently have lower transaction costs, that is, there is less need for systems of audit, inspection, monitoring and supervision as communities are self-regulating. For Putnam, 'A society characterised by general reciprocity is more efficient than a distrustful one' (2000, p. 21) and 'life is easier in a community blessed with a substantial stock of social capital' (1995, p. 67) (see Houlihan and Groeneveld 2011 for a fuller discussion of the relationship between social capital and sport).

Education

During the 1997 election campaign Tony Blair made it clear that education was a clear priority. That electoral commitment was reflected in the substantial investment that followed in the early years of the new government. The Audit Commission (2008) reported that net current expenditure on education increased in real terms by some 40 per cent between 1998–1999 and 2003–2004 and that capital expenditure more than doubled over the same period. Labour's prioritisation of education was based on the argument that 'The success of our children at school is crucial to the economic health and social cohesion of the country as well as to their own life chances and personal fulfilment' (Department for Education and Skills 2001, p. 5).

Although, according to Bache (2003, p. 305), 'partnership became a key theme for the government's approach to education' as exemplified by the establishment of School Sport Partnerships in England; service provision under New Labour still relied heavily on the role of the state as regulator. As Power and Whitty (1999, p. 537) argued, despite expressions of confidence in the new world of quasi-markets 'the New Labour government has, in some respects, sought to control education more directly'. This conclusion was reinforced in Bache's (2003) analysis of education policy under New Labour in which he argues that, despite encouraging greater private sector involvement, 'the desire of the centre to retain control over its highest priority highlights a paradox at the heart of contemporary politics: how the centre governs in the context of governance' (p. 300).

Such an analysis leads Hodgson (2004), for example, to conclude that New Labour—through its strong policy narrative of enabling self-governing communities, generating local solutions to social problems and partnership working—is attempting to produce a 'manufactured civil society'. Hodgson argues that while New Labour's rhetoric 'is one of collaboration, the government has in fact continued its "command and control" . . . style of governing through "criteria-setting", auditing and centrally-imposed initiatives' (p. 156). Therefore, what appears to be emerging in education and elsewhere is that, rather than a redistribution of (central) power and influence suggested by Labour's policy narrative, we appear to be witnessing the extension of state power via a range of social actors involved in a mixture of 'networked partnerships' (Bache 2003; Hodgson 2004; Penney and Evans 1999).

The government's concern to improve the overall quality of the school system had significant implications for sport. Acknowledging the ambiguities surrounding the various interpretations of quality, Le Grand (2007, p. 65) interpreted the concept as referring to 'the contribution of school education to the training of the workforce, to labour productivity, to citizens' understanding of social and cultural values and to enhancing their creative potential'. It is clear that from 1997 Labour government policies for sport and physical activity programmes emerged as increasingly significant policy mechanisms in this respect. Bearing in mind the importance placed by the secretary of state for culture, media and sport (in *Game Plan*) on the contribution of sport and physical activity to improving all-round educational performance, confidence building, leadership skills and teamwork in children and young people, of particular relevance to the current discussions is that this discourse of 'sport benefits' was articulated against a broader political programme for combating social exclusion, reducing crime and building stronger communities. It is also important to recall the secretary of state's ambitions for 'lifelong gains' as an outcome of such an approach: 'A 10% increase in adult activity would prevent around 6,000 premature deaths not to mention bringing economic benefits worth at least £2 billion a year' (quoted in DCMS/Strategy Unit 2002, p. 7). As one senior government adviser on education and sport policy commented: 'Government haven't suddenly decided that PE is a jolly good thing, they have decided that PE and school sport can help them deliver their agenda, improve standards, a change in school ethos, tackling behaviour, reducing truancy, creating kids with a strong sense of citizenship and increasing creativity and curiosity in kids' (quoted in Houlihan and Green 2006, p. 15).

This strongly instrumental view of education and of the place of school sport was reinforced in the 2003 Green Paper *Every Child Matters*, which identified five aspirational outcomes for children and young people, two of which were 'being healthy: enjoying good physical and mental health and living a healthy lifestyle. . . . [and] enjoying and achieving: getting the most out of life and developing the skills for adulthood' (p. 6). Improved health benefits and educational attainment, and thus greater preparedness for life after childhood, are clearly signalled in these aspirational outcomes. It is therefore perhaps unsurprising that New Labour embraced sport and physical activity initiatives as mechanisms for helping to realise these policy ambitions. For one senior civil servant at the DfES, that school sport and PE were overseen by the prime minister's Delivery Unit 'has certainly given it another emphasis. That shows how government regards it' (quoted in Houlihan and Green 2006, p. 86). Equally important, however, was this observer's comments regarding the investment of over £1 billion into school sport, PE and the landmark PESSCL strategy: 'It's not simply about PE and school sport. If what we end up with at the end of this is lots of kids having lots of fun [but] making no difference perhaps to behaviour, attitude, motivation and achievement, then actually we will have failed' (quoted in Houlihan and Green 2006, p. 86).

Health

The relationship between the sport and health policy subsectors became more intense and also more complex in recent years. While the sport policy interests, such as the various sports councils, have drawn attention to the health benefits of sport participation primarily as a way of generalising the relatively narrow interests of the sport community, there was little reciprocation on the part of health interests, especially the medical profession. However, as will be argued below, the gradual rise in concern over public health issues, such as coronary heart problems and rising levels of obesity, did push these two subsectors closer together. As Robson and McKenna

(2008, p. 172) observed at the time, the 'political attention to physical activity is in sharp contrast to the situation only two to three decades ago when the position was one of relative indifference'. In the late 1980s and early 1990s, growing concerns about rising obesity levels and general physical inactivity across the country, especially amongst lower income groups, and the emergence of a number of influential reports that chronicled the (health) risk factors associated with such inactivity had two immediate consequences. First, this 'policy problem' had, by the mid to late 1990s, become highly visible and very public, and was thus a very real 'political problem'. Second, the positive benefits to be gained from political investment in and around sport and physical activity programmes were hard to ignore as the evidence mounted promoting—if not providing conclusive evidence of—such benefits (for summaries of the accumulated evidence, see Department of Health 2004; Hardman and Stensel 2009).

The health benefits of 'active living' were set out in a systematic fashion under the Conservatives in the early 1990s following the publication of the Allied Dunbar National Fitness Survey (Health Education Authority/Sports Council 1992). At this time, the broader connotations of the term 'active living' to emerge under New Labour's modernisation project, associated with social inclusion, civic renewal, active citizenship and neighbourhood regeneration, were largely subordinated to concerns with inactivity and ill health. The Conservatives' major heath policy statement, *The Health of the Nation* (DoH 1992), set out a pathology of risks associated with coronary heart disease and stroke, cancer, mental illness, HIV/AIDS and sexual health, and accidents. Although the salience of sport and physical activity programmes for engendering benefits across at least some of these areas was not as prominent as may have been desired, physical inactivity, individual lifestyle and preventative health were now on the political agenda (Robson and McKenna 2008). Crucially, however, each of the five key areas of risk set out in *Health of the Nation* had a statement of objectives attached to it, together with 27 targets across each of the areas.

The seeds of New Labour policy continuity in this area had been sown. For example, an assessment of the *Health of the Nation* policy found that there needed to be 'further development of evidence based targets' and that 'Without the requirement for substantial performance management, particularly at local level, a new public health programme's chances of success will be reduced significantly' (Universities of Leeds and Glamorgan and the London School of Hygiene and Tropical Medicine 1998, p. 4). New Labour's own public health priorities did not take long to emerge. Just two years after taking office, these were presented in *Saving Lives: Our Healthier Nation* (DoH 1999), which, for Robson and McKenna (2008, p. 173), signalled a shift away from New Right priorities, and 'offered a social reformist commitment to tackle health problems associated with social, economic, and environmental inequalities'.

Robson and McKenna also suggest that the priorities set out in *Saving Lives* heralded a political era concerned with 'the eradication of social exclusion or conversely the promotion of social inclusion' (2008, p. 173). Although these authors claimed that New Labour distanced itself from the previous government's use of performance indicators, targets were set, and set out with some prominence: 'We reject the previous Government's scattergun targets. Instead we are setting tougher but *attainable targets* in priority areas' (DoH 1999, p. 2). Perhaps of equal importance for this discussion, greater individual responsibility for one's own health was now promoted: 'People can improve their own health, through physical activity, better diet and quitting smoking. Individuals and their families need to be properly informed about risk to make decisions' (p. 3). In line with the earlier discussion of governmentality analyses, and following Dean (2007, p. 77; see also Miller and Rose 2008), it is argued that during this period political rationalities emerged intended to act upon and 'authorise certain kinds of practices which seek to produce certain kinds of responsible, orderly, self-managing subjects' in order to move them toward prevailing socio-political objectives.

The publication of *Game Plan* in 2002 was significant for the role it played in setting out New Labour's socio-political objectives for elite sport, mass participation programmes, staging major sports events and also for a major shake-up in sport's organisational infrastructure. For the first time, clear performance targets were set for increases across the public at large of 1 per cent per year in sport and physical activity rates. For almost 40 years since the creation of the Sports Councils, the benign approach associated with national government interest in sport was now well and truly consigned to the past. Setting strategic policy ambitions is relatively straightforward: implementation, delivery and achievement of targeted outcomes are rather more difficult to realise. The organisation charged with the responsibility for delivery of *Game Plan*'s strategy and objectives in England was Sport England, an organisation which New Labour had in its sights for modernising reform. Of interest here is the ways in which the articulation of the government's welfare reform agenda for health, and social inclusion more generally, came to 'embrace' sport and physical activity as increasingly important components of its preventative programme for lifestyle change.

In response to *Game Plan*, Sport England's remit was refocused to the extent that it became the de facto national agency for sport *and* physical activity (Robson and McKenna 2008). A national framework for sport in England was published in 2004 (Sport England 2004a), with a clear mandate for 'Making England active' (p. 5) including: the creation of Active England; a commitment to partnership working and joined-up policymaking through an Activity Co-ordinating Team (across nine government departments and key national agencies); setting out clear priorities and targets; and a determination to produce evidence that shows 'what worked' through a commitment to gather data on 'the impact of sport on educational results, economic benefits, health, social inclusion and social capital, national pride and achievement, crime and community safety' (p. 20). A series of documents under the rubric of *Sport Playing Its Part* was published from 2005, which reflected these ambitions and especially those associated with health and social inclusion. For example, *The Contribution of Sport to Healthier Communities* drew on a range of recent health reports (e.g. DoH 2004, 2005; HDA 2004) to demonstrate 'the positive impact that sport has on the health of individuals and communities and how it can contribute to tackling health inequalities' (Sport England 2005a, p. 4).

Local authorities were Sport England's key delivery partners in helping to achieve these ambitious plans. Through Labour's Local Government Modernisation Agenda (considered further in Chapter 6), local authorities were also subject to an increasingly centralised regime of performance management and targets. By 2007, a national set of 198 performance indicators for local authorities had been developed within six categories of which children and young people; adult health and well-being; and tackling exclusion were three. Besides an indicator on children and young people's participation in high-quality PE and sport, the other specifically sport-related indicator that related to adult participation was included in the safer communities category. Nevertheless, given the broader policy context above, Sport England (2008) sought to emphasise the contribution sport could make to a variety of other health indicators related to well-being, obesity and mortality.

This account of the 'new' and significant role for, and priority of, sport under New Labour in relation to education and health outcomes across the wider community may at first sight appear to offer a relatively clear picture of the current policy landscape. However, the Labour government had other policy priorities for sport that presented significant challenges to its broader social welfare reform agenda, and to achieving its goals not only for raising sport and physical activity levels but also those related to engendering social inclusion and improving community cohesion.

BALANCING POLICY PRIORITIES FOR SPORT

The balancing of the two major government priorities for sport—elite development and mass participation programmes—has bedevilled sports administrators for at least four decades and is discussed in more detail in Chapter 5. Seen in this light at least, Collins's (2008, pp. 81–82) signalling of the 'uncertain see-saw of policy priorities in British sport . . . which has taken another unpredictable and apparently crazy swing' was hardly surprising. Collins was referring to the resignation of Sport England's chair, Derek Mapp, in late 2007. Mapp had spent his first year in office administering the government's challenging ambitions to get the country physically active through the '5×30 minutes' per week objective outlined in *Game Plan*. The background to Mapp's resignation was the diversion of some £56 million of Sport England's share of lottery income between 2009 and 2012 to fund the 2012 Olympic/Paralympic Games. This was 'a cut too far' for Mapp, who argued that this 'seriously endangers the creation of a sporting legacy from the 2012 Games' (BBC 2007). The secretary of state for culture, media and sport (at the time, James Purnell) 'seemed to take exception to Mapp's criticisms' (Collins 2008, p. 82) and asked him to concentrate on traditional sports in order that greater resources could be channelled towards the goal of creating a sporting legacy from the 2012 Games. At the same time, Purnell indicated that the DoH would be taking over the primary responsibility for tackling obesity and other health problems related to physical inactivity (see DCMS 2007). According to Collins (2008, p. 82; see also Revill 2007), one consequence of this abrupt change in policy was that:

> The Secretary of State's action will almost certainly slow down the already uncertain progress of increasing mass participation. This clearly shows politicians' continuing wedding to elite over community sport. Politicians' rhetoric reinforces the mythopoeic (myth-making) qualities of sport as character building and foundational to society.

At least one of the problems this policy shift raised for sport and recreation managers was highlighted by Revill's (2007) report in the *Observer*. Revill cited an unnamed sports administrator as blaming 'the "blazerati" and lobbyists working for sporting governing bodies for the shift in strategy . . . Basically it [funding] will only be going to sports where you wear a strip or are in a team'. This disgruntled administrator went on to add that 'We've all been working since 2005 on the basis that under a Labour government sports was about widening participation, not closing it down'. The implication here is that those working (e.g. in local authority departments and County Sports Partnerships) towards meeting New Labour's own participation targets for sport *and* physical activity now had an added obstacle to overcome. Moreover, for some observers (cf. Collins 2008; Green and Houlihan 2005, 2006), it is not altogether clear how NGBs could respond to any additional responsibilities on top of those already laid at their door. Collins (2008, p. 82), for example, argued that:

> The governing bodies in English sport command only some 6m members, not all playing. Without exception they argue they need more volunteers to cope with the growing roles the government expects them to play; they struggle with working out the expressed aims of equality, of increasing involvement of more women, ethnic minorities, disabled people and other hard-to-reach groups.

Closely linked to elite development, another New Labour sport policy priority to emerge was the emphasis placed by government on supporting bids for hosting major (or mega) sports events such as the summer Olympic Games, FIFA World Cup, UEFA European Championships, IAAF World Athletics Championships and the Commonwealth Games (DCMS/Strategy Unit 2002). In recent years, while the UK failed with bids to host the 2001 IAAF World Athletics Championships and the 2006 and 2018 FIFA World Cup, amidst much acrimony and associated hand-wringing over stadium development and overrunning costs there were some successes, most notably the Manchester 2002 Commonwealth Games, which was generally viewed as an accomplished and well-run event and, of course, the award in 2005 of the summer Olympic Games, in 2012. Forthcoming major sports events include hosting the Commonwealth Games in 2014 in Glasgow, the rugby union World Cup in 2015 and the IAAF World Athletics Championships in 2017.

Undoubtedly the staging of the Olympic and Paralympic Games is very likely to have a transformational effect on the infrastructure in and around the site in the Lower Lea Valley in East London (cf. Raco 2004). Once again, however, caution is the watchword as myth is often the default position when attempting to extrapolate benefits from sport policy interventions. In short, the long-term impact of an Olympic Games is a matter of some debate and much controversy. As the Institute for Public Policy Research (IPPR) noted, 'the Olympics can make and remake legends. They are also quite good at myth-making and when thinking about the potential legacy of a Games, it is wise to be wary of this' (Vigor, Mean and Tims 2004, p. 3).

One of the questions raised by the above account is clearly: why did the government bother? It is almost a truism to say that the staging of mega sports events inevitably lead to accusations of overblown predictions about the levels of sporting, social, and especially economic impacts after an event has ended. Vastly understated cost predictions for staging an event during the bidding process also lead inevitably to broad-ranging criticisms of event organisers, and so to government in the case of an Olympic Games. London 2012 was no exception in this respect. In relation to the London Olympic and Paralympic Games, Raco's (2004) analysis is revealing, particularly in the context of the discussion on sport, welfare reforms and social inclusion. For Raco, the decision by London to bid for 2012 was 'in many ways, out of character with the broader thrust of New Labour's regeneration policies since 1997' (p. 38). Flagship policies such as hosting major sports events were thought to have been eschewed by the government as it sought to distance itself from the socially divisive programmes that characterised the urban programmes of the 1980s and early 1990s (Cochrane 2003). According to Raco, Labour preferred to focus on projects which would enable 'communities [to play] a role as both policy objects—those who are to be worked on and assisted—and policy subjects—those who actively develop and implement measures' (p. 38)—e.g. the New Deal for Communities and Neighbourhood Renewal Fund, which drew on principles of partnership and community inclusion; although, tellingly, against a backdrop of centrally defined government objectives and targets. What defined these initiatives was 'Active citizenship . . . with communities and individuals expected (and sometimes compelled) to take increased responsibility for themselves and their neighbourhoods' (p. 38). Yet as Raco and others (cf. Sinclair 2008) pointed out, poorly funded, under-trained, and potentially uninterested community representatives are often not able, or not willing, to cope with the bureaucratic and technocratic processes involved in such large-scale regeneration initiatives as the Olympic Games.

Writing on the issue of 'Tony Blair and the jargon of modernisation', Finlayson (1999, p. 24) pointed to Labour's 'frequent connection of modernisation with the nation', which invoked a particular brand of 'celebratory patriotism' (p. 13). In Blair's first speech to the party conference after becoming prime minister, he argued passionately for Britain to be 'nothing less than the model twenty-first century nation' (Blair 1994, p. 1). And, in the foreword to *Game Plan*, Blair maintained that 'Sport is a powerful and often under-used tool that can help Government to achieve a number of ambitious goals' (quoted in DCMS/Strategy Unit 2002, p. 5). As has been argued, concerns regarding low physical activity rates and rising obesity levels in the population generally, and amongst children and young people in particular, were at the heart of government's engagement with sport. Indeed, Lord Carter argued that 'we've moved from the manual to a sedentary society and there are . . . great arguments to say that sport is part of the answer to all the problems that brings' (quoted in *The Guardian* 2006, p. 9). This, then, was one persuasive argument for Labour's enthusiastic engagement with sport and physical activity policy. There is another other line of reasoning, however, which arguably provides a valuable perspective from which an additional source of the momentum for the modernising reform of the sport sector might be identified. The decision by the IOC in July 2005 to award London the right to host the 2012 Olympic Games provided significant political legitimation for policy decisions taken over the previous decade to prioritise elite sport development. Indeed, on the issue of political support for the 2012 bid, Andrew Rawnsley reported in the *Observer* (2006, p. 31) that 'Blair shrugged aside opposition once he got seized by the notion of adding a *grand projet* to his legacy'. It is the grand, symbolic, almost mythical rhetoric used by politicians about elite sport success and the hosting of an Olympics Games that is of interest here. Such rhetoric was evident in comments by Tessa Jowell, then secretary of state for culture, media and sport, 'who argued that a credible bid was crucial to the future not just of sport but of national aspiration' (quoted in *The Observer—Olympics 2012 Special Report*—2005, p. 3). Again the mythmaking rhetoric about sport, much of which is wrapped around the forging of national pride and national identity, is very much in evidence.

The winning of Olympic medals and the hosting of a successful Olympic Games thus emerged as crucial political referents for the story New Labour promoted in its discourse about the construction of a modern twenty-first-century Britain (cf. Finlayson 2003). In Labour's first 'annual report' in 1998, modernisation was part of the 'story' they had to 'tell about Britain' (HMSO 1998). The reader was reminded that, although the country is 'filled with creative, innovative compassionate people' (HMSO 1998), the country had for too long 'relied on past glories' (Finlayson 2003, p. 85), and now needed to adapt to the new world and the global economy. It is not such a great leap, then, to argue that, in prioritising the development of the country's elite athletes, and in the backing of the London 2012 bid, New Labour seized upon a golden opportunity to make political capital out of a 'successful' Olympic Games as an exemplar of its progressive project of modernising the nation—both in the number of Olympic medals won and through the process of re-branding the country as a 'model twenty-first century nation', symbolised by the successful hosting of the world's major sporting event.

MODERNISING THE SPORT INFRASTRUCTURE

In marked contrast to the Conservative government's 1995 policy document *Sport: Raising the Game* (DNH 1995), where the engine of change was to be a combination of passionate commitment and the funds from the proposed National Lottery, the Labour government policy statement, *A Sporting Future for All* (DCMS 2000), was clear that the organisational infrastructure of sport was considered to be an impediment to achieving the primary policy goals of elite success and the enhancement of opportunities for young people to participate in sport. 'There is a need for a radical rethink of the way we fund and organise sport [and to this end] we offer a modernising partnership with the governing bodies of sport' (DCMS 2000, p. 19). Cooperative governing bodies 'will gain more responsibility. But if they fail to perform against agreed targets, then funding arrangements will be reviewed' (DCMS 2000, p. 20). The (paradoxical) discourse of autonomy, freedom, responsibility, cooperation, partnerships, and sanctions was re-stated with some vigour in 2008, as our earlier examples taken from *Playing to Win* have shown.

Sport England was also to be modernised. It would no longer prioritise its delivery role and would adopt a role which was 'more strategic' and concerned with ensuring that public funds were 'properly spent' (DCMS 2000, p. 20). Similar conclusions were drawn by the review of elite sport funding conducted in 2001 (DCMS 2001a) in which the primary concern was to clarify the relationship between UK Sport and Sport England and ensure that the former was given unambiguous lead responsibility. The need for reform was further reinforced by the Quinquennial Review of

Sport England, which recommended, inter alia, that Sport England 'establish meaningful, outcome driven targets against which performance can be measured [and] develop agreed and robust reporting procedures that will enable DCMS to measure Sport England's performance against objectives' (DCMS 2001b, p. 44). The work of the Quinquennial Review panel set the agenda for, but was also overtaken by, the DCMS/Strategy Unit study (published in 2002 as *Game Plan*) of long-term sports policy.

Game Plan reinforced the imperative of modernisation and argued that both the two major sports councils, Sport England and UK Sport, needed to concentrate on four key activities: strategy; investment appraisal, contract specification and monitoring and evaluation; advice and guidance, especially in relation to capacity building; and research and evidence collection. The intended outcome of this refocusing was that 'There should be less micro-management and more freedom for partners to deliver against agreed targets' (DCMS/Strategy Unit 2002, p. 175). It was recommended that both organisations should be leaner and more focused with their councils (boards) selected for their expertise and 'non-executive skills (i.e. strategy, vision, wide business experience, planning scrutiny and leadership)' rather than their representation of some stakeholder interest (DCMS/Strategy Unit 2002, p. 175).

As in other policy sectors (e.g. countryside policy, Ward and Lowe 2007), *Game Plan* acted as a high-level strategy for setting out New Labour's modernising ambitions to rationalise the operations of sport non-departmental public bodies (NDPBs), and the organisations and institutions expected to deliver front-line sport and physical activity services (e.g. local authorities, community sport partnerships, schools and NGBs). In essence, this meant that, for a policy sector characterised for many years by incoherence, divisiveness and conflicting objectives (cf. Green 2006; McDonald 2000; Roche 1993), some semblance of clarity was about to be 'imposed' upon it. For New Labour modernisation of the sector reflected the markedly higher political salience of sport and physical activity programmes and, as Freeden (1999, p. 46) noted in a related debate on the ideology of New Labour, the government 'adopted Etzioni's preference for guided persuasion over [outright] coercion'. Modernisation of sport thus served the dual purpose of a grand project of national renewal (a fit, healthy and active population and the hosting of the 2012 Olympic Games), and as a concerted approach to improving the performance of public services through administrative rationalisation and greater coordination and targeting of clarified objectives for delivery of sport programmes at grassroots levels.

Part of the process of transforming Sport England into a modern organisation and also one capable of acting as the driver of modernisation of the governing bodies was achieved through change in personnel, with the chief executive and chair of the council both departing to be replaced by David Moffett, as CEO, and Lord Carter, as chair. Carter's initial impression of Sport England was 'that it was bureaucratic, relatively passive . . . ', adding

that 'they [NGB administrators] used to remind me of little baby birds sit-
ting with their beaks open expecting someone like the Chancellor to fly over
and drop a worm of money into their mouths because they were deserving'
(quoted in *The Guardian* 2006, p. 9). Moffett's succession by Jennie Price
in 2007 and Lord Carter's in 2006 by Derek Mapp were indicative of New
Labour's valorisation of business and performance management principles.
Significantly, the then secretary of state for the DCMS emphasised 'Mapp's
extensive business and regional development experience . . . and strong
entrepreneurial background' (quoted in DCMS 2006, p. 1). As regards the
appointment of Jennie Price, Mapp himself stated that 'She will bring to the
organisation both her experience of working in a tough industry and in setting up a government programme from scratch and exceeding the challenging targets she was set' (quoted in Sport England 2006a, p. 1). As we have
seen, Derek Mapp's tenure lasted less than one year. Mapp's 'removal' by
government following his acrimonious resignation speech, which criticised
the government's reform of Sport England's remit, was arguably indicative
of the tight control by the centre of its NDPBs; a scenario that belies the supposed arm's-length relationship that Sport England is meant to enjoy (see
fuller discussion in Chapter 5). Change in senior personnel was only part
of the story, however, as the process of modernisation was also achieved
through a series of reviews of Sport England designed to change radically
its culture and management practice.

In 2003 Sport England established a Modernisation Project Board
chaired by the head of the sport division in the DCMS with a brief to implement the recommendations of *Game Plan* and the Quinquennial Review. In
the 2004 report, *The Framework for Sport in England*, it was argued that
2003 had been a transformative year for Sport England, producing 'A new,
modernised Sport England ready to provide strategic leadership for sport
in England—a new board, a new clarity of purpose, and a commitment
to bust bureaucracy' (Sport England 2004a, p. 5; see also DCMS 2004).
Perhaps the transformation is best indicated by the structure of the funding
agreements signed between Sport England and UK Sport with DCMS, both
of which have much clearer statements of targets, baseline data, milestones
and performance measures than previous equivalent documents such as
corporate plans (Sport England 2004b; UK Sport 2003).

As previously mentioned, in the mid-2000s, the Treasury/DCMS and the
National Audit Office (NAO) commissioned two reports which reviewed
the extent of change and the work still to be done. The Treasury/DCMS
report (Carter 2005a) observed that Sport England had 'radically restruc-
tured, devolving decision-making through nine Regional Sports Boards'
and that 'UK Sport [had] reviewed its functions and streamlined the organisation' (p. 13) but complained that 'measurement of baseline data and evidence through research is limited: managing performance is difficult and
allocating resources at local level is not well informed' (p. 17). The tone of
the Carter report was echoed by that from the NAO, which examined the

support provided to elite athletes by UK Sport. On the one hand UK Sport was congratulated for meeting its performance target for the Athens Olympic Games while on the other hand the report identified 'a number of . . . concerns with the way in which the performance framework is operating in practice' (NAO 2005, p. 4). UK Sport was recommended to 'secur[e] a better return on investment', use 'independent experts to undertake periodic evaluations of programmes', and cooperate with the home country sports councils to simplify the funding system (p. 4). The NAO report was reinforced by a report from the House of Commons Committee of Public Accounts (2006), which criticised UK Sport for requiring NGBs to set clear performance targets while not setting any for itself or else setting over-simplified targets. UK Sport was also criticised for misreporting previous medal performance over a three-year period.

The accumulation of momentum for reform derived from these various reports was augmented by the Gershon review, which examined the use of resources across government. The Gershon review set targets for cost savings and staff reductions and not only stressed the importance of moving resources to service delivery functions, but also emphasised the importance of 'auditable and transparent measures of performance' (HM Treasury 2004, p. 32). The changes manifest at Sport England and UK Sport since 2005 clearly reinforced the view that Gershon's recommendations had major consequences for both organisations and, as we shall see in Chapters 7 and 8, for organisations much closer to service delivery such as local authorities, CSPs and schools.

While not pre-empting the discussion in later chapters, it is useful at this stage to note the nature of reforms experienced by other organisations in the sport policy sector. First, the new sports indicators that were developed by Sport England and the Audit Commission for inclusion within the Comprehensive Performance Assessment regime for local authorities resulted in the implementation of a raft of target-driven sport and physical activity objectives under three key indicators: i) raising levels of participation; ii) increasing volunteering opportunities; and iii) providing greater opportunities for easy access to a range of quality sports facilities. Central to these objectives, as Finlayson (2003, p. 94) noted, 'is the gathering and interpreting of anxiety-inducing statistics'. In order to establish a robust evidence base against which progress in the delivery of policy objectives could be measured, Labour introduced two major new surveys—Active People and Taking Part—which were significant developments in the sport policy sector. The surveys were not only clear indications of Labour's desire to gather 'hard evidence' with which to measure the performance of its delivery agents, but were also intended to enable the application of sanctions if required.

Second, initially through the PE, School Sport and Club Links (PESSCL) strategy, and the more recent PE and Sport Strategy for Young People (PESSYP), schools were subject to annual auditing of their progress towards the government's target to be achieved by 2008 for 85 per cent of children (5 to 16 years) to experience at least two hours of high-quality sport and PE provision within and beyond the curriculum each week. Third, NGBs, key delivery agents for government's Olympic ambitions (UK Sport 2006b), as well as for social policy-related objectives in areas such as health, crime, community cohesion and social inclusion (Sport England 2005d), were grappling with the consequences of the modernising reform of Sport England and UK Sport. For example, UK Sport's *No Compromise* funding strategy for elite athlete development required NGBs to meet stringent performance-related targets aligned to winning (Olympic) medals on the international stage (UK Sport 2006a).

FROM MODERNISATION TO BIG SOCIETY

As mentioned earlier, attributing policy change solely to the reforming zeal of a new government is problematic not simply due to the difficulty of undoing established policies and processes, but also due to the fact that new governments rapidly get overtaken by events and consequently are forced to shift the perspective of their discussions from the proactive to the reactive. It would be difficult to find a better example of this highly pressurised context of government than that which faced the incoming coalition government following the electoral defeat of the Labour party in May 2010. Three factors make an analysis of the impact of the new government difficult. The first is that the Conservative party, the majority partner in the coalition government, learning lessons from Labour's three successive election victories kept its manifesto long on vision and aspiration and short on precise policy commitments. However, a recurring theme within the manifesto was the shift from 'big government to Big Society' (the use of capital letters giving the notion instant gravitas). Unlike Margaret Thatcher, who once remarked that there was no such thing as society only individuals and families, David Cameron was at pains to emphasise his party's commitment to the idea of society:

> We believe there is such a thing as society, it's just not the same thing as the state. Our fundamental tenet is that power should be devolved from politicians to people, from the central to the local. Personal ambition should be set as high as is humanly possible, with no barriers put in its way by the state. Perhaps most importantly, we believe that we are all in this together (Conservative Party 2010a, p. vii).

The second factor which complicates an easy analysis of current government policy is that it is the product of a coalition. While the Liberal Democrats shared sufficient common ground with the Conservative party to provide a foundation for a coalition agreement, many aspects of policy are mediated by an additional layer of discussion as the two partners work towards a set of policies which both feel they can sell to their respective backbench members of parliament. The final factor, which continues to have a significant and most probably long-term impact on policy, is the European and North American financial crisis that developed in 2008.

As a result, caution is needed in attributing current policy to the ideological preferences of either coalition partner. However, one theme which originated with the Conservative party and which appears to be firmly endorsed by the Liberal Democrats is that of the Big Society. Perhaps more importantly the concept of the Big Society chimes with the severe financial pressure facing the government to reduce rapidly the level of public expenditure. For this analysis the key question is what are the practical implications of the operationalisation of the concept for sport policy.

In the run-up to the 2010 election, both the Conservatives and the Liberal Democrats published policy statements on sport. The Conservative Sports Manifesto (Conservative Party 2010b) echoes many of the 'one-nation' sentiments evident in the previous Conservative government sport policy document, *Sport: Raising the Game*, in 1995. Just as John Major saw sport as important in giving the nation a sense of identity and creating stronger social bonds, so the 2010 document noted that:

> Sport brings many social benefits to people and communities. It helps people perform better at work or school, and lead happier, healthier lives. And supporting sports teams and athletes bridges social divides, bringing people and communities together, both locally and nationally.

The Conservatives promised to boost school sport (for example, through the establishment of 'an Olympic-style' sports event and the encouragement of competitive sport); reforming the National Lottery to ensure that additional funding goes to sport, especially at the community level; and continued support for the hosting of major sports events. The Liberal Democrats' (no date) policy briefing, *Sport and the Olympics*, echoed many of these sentiments and objectives particularly those associated with school sport and the Olympic legacy, but with a particular emphasis on the beneficial consequences for health of increased sport participation.

Any attempt by the coalition government to translate these themes and aspirations into policies was heavily mediated, but to an extent reinforced, by the Comprehensive Spending Review of October 2010, which announced cuts in public expenditure of £83 billion over the following five years. Both Sport England and UK Sport suffered significant cuts (33 per cent for Sport England and 25 per cent for UK Sport by 2014/15) which were to be partly offset by an increase in the share of National Lottery income from 16 per cent to 20 per cent (worth around £50m per year) and were required to cut their administration costs by 50 per cent. However, there was protection of the funding for elite athletes up to the 2012 Olympic and Paralympic Games.

The two organisations were also required to merge, a process which, at the time of writing, had stalled due to uncertainty about the likely cost savings and opposition from Scottish politicians who saw the merger as a potential erosion of the gains made in policy autonomy through devolution.

Of equal significance was the cut made to the education budget. Particularly important was the removal of the protection (ring-fencing) of the money schools received to fund their involvement in School Sport Partnerships (SSPs), which had been very successful in raising levels of participation across a range of sporting and physical activities (Institute of Youth Sport 2008), and also the removal of funding from the 400 specialist sports colleges. While the government backtracked to some extent due to the scale of opposition that the proposals stimulated, the cuts remained substantial. The Youth Sport Trust, which managed the development of the SSP network and provided continuing support for schools, had its funding removed, although it was given some responsibility for organising the new School Games.

In late 2010 the DCMS published an update on its proposals for securing a legacy from the Olympic and Paralympic Games and stated that:

> The government is committed to delivering a sporting legacy for young people, and to bringing back a culture of competitive sport in schools. School sport is in a good position in this country—and we give thanks to the thousands of people in schools, and in communities, who make sport happen every day. (DCMS 2010, p. 2)

The gratitude expressed to volunteers resonates with the concept of the Big Society and is particularly important as the most severe reductions in public expenditure are likely to be at the community level in those services provided by local authorities. The government announced a cut of 26 per cent over four years in the funding for local authorities and, given the non-statutory status of sport services, it is highly likely that the cuts to sport will be disproportionately severe.

Although, at the time of writing, the new government is barely 18 months old, it is possible to provide an initial assessment of the importance of the Big Society concept for sport and to consider whether it will turn out to have the same defining significance as 'modernisation' did for New Labour. At the level of rhetoric, the Big Society project is the antithesis of the model of centrally controlled modernisation and a response to the governmentality critique of Rose and Dean. David Cameron criticised government for being 'top-down, top-heavy, controlling' with the consequences that it has

> turned many motivated public-sector workers into disillusioned, weary puppets of government targets. It has turned able, capable individuals into passive recipients of state help . . . [and] turned lively communities into dull, soulless clones . . . The Big Society is about a huge cultural

change, where people . . . don't always turn to officials . . . for answers to the problems they face but instead feel both free and powerful enough to help themselves and their own communities. (Cameron 2010)

The notion of the Big Society is anti-state, but whereas for Margaret Thatcher the alternative to the intrusiveness and inadequacies of the state was the market, for David Cameron the alternative is the community and the network of voluntary associations with which it is populated. For Jesse Norman, one of the theoreticians of the Big Society, of central importance is nurturing affective associations which are a

> place between the individual and the state for all those intermediate 'sideways' institutions which link us all together and give fulfilment to our lives; a counterbalancing moral presumption in favour of the individual; and a recognition that what motivates human beings needs not merely be a matter of the stick and the carrot, complying with rules or achieving some collective goal, but of culture, identity and belonging. It is this new category of philic association that lays the philosophical groundwork for modern ideas of social capital, networking and connectivity—and for the Big Society. (Norman 2010, pp. 103–104).

Norman argued that the Big Society idea builds on humanity's natural predilection for association and that the formal associations that are produced can 'stand between the individual and the state, acting among other things as buffers, conduits, outlets, and guarantors of stability' (2010, p. 105).

In many respects the concept of the Big Society is not radically different from the previous government's concern to stimulate the generation of a Putnamian version of social capital through the promotion of voluntary activity. As Kisby notes, 'It does not represent a significant break with New Labour . . . so much as a continuation, albeit with a greater intensity' (2010, p. 486). With sport the third most common form of voluntary activity and with around 150,000 sports clubs in the UK, sport must be considered as both an exemplar of the Big Society in action and also a sector which should be able to take rapid advantage of the policies being introduced to foster further growth in associational life. However, the problem that the coalition government faces in promoting its Big Society project is an obvious one and relates to the challenge of attracting support for the project at a time of significant public expenditure cuts. Anecdotal evidence suggests that the loss of staff in local authority sport development units and in School Sport Partnerships will be substantial, thus offering the prospect of redundant sport development officers being encouraged to do voluntarily what they had previously been paid for. However, it remains to be seen whether the Big Society becomes a defining narrative of the present government and leaves a lasting imprint on sport services or whether it suffers the fate of so many previous grand ideas of being pushed to the margin by the demands for pragmatism in day-to-day politics. In particular, if the promotion of the Big Society is to be successful, then it will also have to negotiate the tension between the government's support for market-based solutions and its commitment to boost employment through the expansion of the commercial sector on the one hand and the promotion of voluntary effort on the other. In the sport subsector of the economy, voluntary provision is often in competition with commercial provision rather than simply intervening in cases of market failure.

CONCLUSION

Two clear themes emerge from the review of sport policy under New Labour. The first is the complex nature of Labour's instrumentalist view of sport. On the one hand, the Blair governments saw sport as a valuable tool for achieving a wide range of non-sport policy objectives, for example, related to health, education and social inclusion: On the other hand, there was a genuinely held view of sport as an important element in the quality of individual and community life. The second theme is the marked shift in the nature of the relationship between government and voluntary sport organisations (NGBs and their affiliated clubs) from one characterised by a reasonable degree of trust (that is, that NGBs and clubs could be trusted to generate social benefit with their allocation of public or lottery funding) to one based on contract and audit.

As Le Grand (2007) notes, there are essentially four models for the delivery of public services: trust—professionals and organisations are trusted to deliver a high quality service with little direct government oversight; targets—a modified Weberian model of bureaucracy in which government departments or their agencies operate through managerial hierarchies and provide direction for service deliverers; voice—service levels are determined by service users; and choice and competition—where competition between a variety of service providers allows for user choice between deliverers and between levels of service. In relation to the delivery of sport services, there was a clear move from the 'trust' model to one based on 'targets', audit and, one might add, 'distrust'. The rhetoric of empowerment and autonomy for the government's partners disguises the significant increase in the capacity of the government to control and manage the nature and distribution of sports services. Liddle's (2007, p. 412) observation that NPM 'was adopted as an attempt to shift from funding organisations and institutions to funding performance' is consistent with the shift from trust to targets and relates not only to the role of NGBs and clubs, but also to local authorities and County Sport Partnerships.

The extent to which the coalition government elected in 2010 marks a radical break with the policies and objectives of the previous government is debatable. On the one hand, the coalition government's commitment to reducing the size and scope of the state is, at the rhetorical level at least, in sharp contrast to Labour's confidence in state institutions and particularly state expenditure. On the other hand, much of the justification given for the Big Society and many of the associated policies are not too distant from those expressed by New Labour in relation to the development of social capital, reinvigorating community life and strengthening personal responsibility. While Labour tended to see individuals and old-fashioned organisational structures and practices as the source of impediments to social inclusion and modernisation, the Conservative party within the coalition see the source as located within the fabric of the state. However, the net result is much the same, namely a greater emphasis on personal responsibility and the reform of institutions of civil society.

4 The Impact of Devolution on Sport Policy

In the previous chapter it was suggested that most governments fail to leave a significant policy legacy but that Labour was an exception, with the introduction of devolution providing the clearest evidence. While sport had been a devolved responsibility in Northern Ireland for some time, the Devolution Acts of 1998 transferred responsibility for sport from Westminster to Edinburgh and Cardiff, thus enabling both countries, potentially at least, to shape the development of policy much more effectively than in the past. The emphasis on potentiality for, rather than inevitability of, divergence is important as recent research on devolved government draws attention to the dominance of incremental patterns of policy change in mature political and welfare systems (Greer 2004; Pierson 2001; Wincott 2005). Thus significant divergence may take a considerable time to become evident and poses the policy analyst the daunting challenge of calibrating divergence and determining the point at which modest differentiation becomes distinctiveness. However, a number of analyses of policy development since 1998 have concluded that devolution has resulted in divergence in some policy sectors where there was previously a high degree of uniformity with England, for example, in health (Greer 2006) or greater divergence in policy subsectors where there was already a degree of difference, for example, in higher education (Keating 2006).

In relation to sport there is perhaps an additional complexity due to the greater openness of the policy subsector to global influences especially in relation to elite sport, but also in relation to physical activity and health. Consequently, the significance of the devolution legislation notwithstanding, it must be borne in mind that in an increasingly globalised (sporting) world the potential of devolution to produce divergence has to be analysed in the context of a series of powerful and potentially homogenising factors such as changes in the global economy, fashions in public sector management, requirements of global organisation such as UNESCO and the World Anti-Doping Agency in relation to doping, changes to the sports included in the summer Olympic Games, the pace of sport commercialisation etc. With this important caveat in mind this chapter will examine the impact of devolution not only on Scotland, Wales and Northern Ireland, but also, though to a lesser extent, on England.

Table 4.1   Landmarks in Progress towards Devolution: Scotland, Northern Ireland and Wales

Scotland	Northern Ireland	Wales
Act of Union 1707	Anglo-Norman invasion 1169	Acts of Union 1536–42
Many powers remained, with services such as education and the legal system maintaining a distinctive Scottish character	Irish Football Association formed 1880	
	Gaelic Athletic Association formed 1884	
	Easter Rising 1916	
Formation of the Scottish Football Association 1873	Government of Ireland Act 1920 (partitioned Ireland thus establishing Northern Ireland)	Football Association of Wales 1876
Scottish Office established in 1885 with a secretary of state for Scotland appointed in the British government and responsible for elements of social policy in Scotland	The devolved parliament at Stormont lasted from 1921 to imposition of direct rule from Westminster in 1972	Plaid Cymru (The Party of Wales) formed in 1925
Scottish Grand Committee established at Westminster 1907	Systematic discrimination against the Catholic minority prompts the formation of the NI Civil Rights Association in 1967	
Secretary of state for Scotland given a seat in the Cabinet, 1926	Civil order breaks down in the early 1970s as sectarian para-military organisations re-emerge	Welsh Grand Committee established at Westminster 1960
Formation of the Scottish National Party 1934	The 'troubles' claimed over 3,500 lives up to the onset of peace negotiations in the 1990s	Welsh Office established 1964 with a secretary of state for Wales in the British government

(continued)

Table 4.1 (continued)

Scotland	Northern Ireland	Wales
First Scottish National Party MP elected in 1967		First Plaid Cymru MP elected in 1966
Establishment of the Scottish Sports Council 1972	Establishment of the Northern Ireland Sports Council 1972	Establishment of the Sports Council for Wales 1972
Labour government publishes a White Paper 'Democracy and devolution: Proposals for Scotland and Wales' in 1974		Labour government publishes a white paper 'Democracy and devolution: Proposals for Scotland and Wales' in 1974
Failed referendum on devolution 1979		Failed referendum on devolution 1979
Successful referendum on devolution 1997	Good Friday Agreement signed April 1998	Successful referendum on devolution 1997. Also in 1997 the Labour government publishes the white paper 'A voice for Wales', which outlined the role of the proposed Welsh Assembly
	Northern Ireland Act 1998 restored devolution to Northern Ireland	
Scotland Act 1998		Wales Act 1998
	Devolved government suspended on a number of occasions (usually over the issue of decommissioning of weapons)	
First elections to the Scottish parliament 1999	Devolved institutions suspended in October 2002 until May 2007	First elections to the Welsh Assembly 1999

BACKGROUND TO DEVOLUTION

Although the nineteenth-century campaign for 'Home Rule' in Ireland stimulated similar, but more muted, demands in both Scotland and Wales, it was in the 1970s that devolution became a realistic prospect. While the Conservative party were strongly opposed to any devolution of power, the Labour party were much more sympathetic. Attempts to achieve a majority in favour of devolution in the Scottish and Welsh referendums of the mid-1970s failed,[1] but Labour, especially under the leadership of John Smith and Tony Blair, remained committed to the policy. The second round of referendums held in 1997 resulted in a solid pro-devolution majority in Scotland and a marginal positive majority in Wales. Legislation followed in 1998 which devolved a range of responsibilities to Scotland, Wales and Northern Ireland. However, when considering the impact of the 1998 legislation it is important to bear in mind two factors: first, especially in relation to Scotland, there had been a gradual process of extending home country powers and responsibilities that stretched well over one hundred years (see Table 4.1); and second, that all three countries had a distinctive cultural identity within which sport was a prominent element that predated the legislation of the 1990s.

SCOTLAND

In 1992 Jim Sillars, the then deputy leader of the Scottish National Party, remarked that too many Scots were 'ninety minute patriots'. He was not only providing a powerful metaphor for his party's disappointing performance in the 1992 election, but was also drawing attention to, even if not consciously, the intimate relationship between sport and national identity. While Sillars was lamenting the lack of support for the SNP's programme for greater autonomy for Scotland, few would deny that Scotland had long possessed the attributes of nationhood if not those of statehood (Paterson 1994; Kellas 1991; Harvie 1977). The complex relationship between sport and identity can be traced back at least to the origins of organised sport in the mid to late nineteenth century and, at different times and through different analytic interpretations, has been variously characterised as one of mutual reinforcement (Kellas 1990), a reflection of the sub-national socio-cultural divisions (Jarvie and Reid 1999; Finn 1994; Bradley 1998) and a perversion of nationalism (Nairn 1981). For Kellas (1991) the long established institutions of Scottish sport both reflected and reinforced a sense of Scottish national distinctiveness. This view is in marked contrast to that of Nairn, who views Scottish sporting nationalism more as a shallow rejection of Britishness than an expression of a coherent Scottish identity and also to the view that elements of 'Scottish' sporting identity, such as the Highland

Games, were a British Victorian construction of a nostalgic romantic, but culturally unassertive, sporting tradition (Jarvie 1991; Giulianotti 2005).

Jarvie and Reid provide the most persuasive assessment in ascribing to sport the status of a more authentic reflection of the complexities of national identity and comment that 'Scotland has always been an uneasy partnership of very different communities. Sport, therefore, should not be used as a fallacious guide to undifferentiated Scottishness but rather a subtle reflection of social, cultural and political diversity' (1999, p. 97). The central point for the present analysis is that, despite the contested nature of Scottish sporting nationalism, the phenomenon was well established long before the late-twentieth-century debates on devolution. As is the case in all four home countries, Scotland has a firmly established organisational infrastructure of national governing bodies and has for many years competed in both major international sports such as football and rugby and major multi-sport events such as the Commonwealth Games as an independent country.

Sport Policy in Scotland since Devolution

According to one senior sport administrator, prior to devolution sport lived on the fringes and 'since devolution the political parties have increasingly latched on to sport'. However, much of the 'latching on' has been on the level of sport symbolism rather than substantive interventions in sport policy, although, as Table 4.2 shows, growth in funding has kept ahead of overall government funding albeit from a low base. Leaving aside the symbolic and rhetorical level of engagement with sport policy, the salience of sport to the Scottish government has been variable, but generally low. Increases in salience resulting in action and the commitment of resources have tended to be prompted by crisis (for example, sectarian violence at football matches between the Glasgow teams Celtic and Rangers) or have been narrowly focused (hosting the 2014 Commonwealth Games or preparing for the London 2012 Olympic and Paralympic Games). Moreover, sustained periods of government interest in sport have generally been due to policy concerns external to sport such as childhood obesity and the health of the adult population as well as due to the ebb and flow of debates on

Table 4.2   Change in Public Expenditure on Sport in Scotland 2002–03 to 2010–11

Budget heading	Percentage change
sportscotland	300%
sportscotland (excluding costs for the 2014 Commonwealth Games)	216%
Scottish Executive	36%

nation-building and Scottish independence. The marginal status of sport and the uncertainty within successive governments as to its contribution to wider government objectives are illustrated by the regular transfer of responsibility for sport between different parent departments—education, environment, tourism and most recently health and well-being—and the short 'life-expectancy' of sport ministers (Thomson 2010).

Writing just after devolution, Jarvie and Thomson lamented the lack of priority given to sport and concluded that 'perhaps sport is just not politically important enough' (1999, p. 97). However, writing more recently, Reid argued that 'sport has climbed the political agenda since devolution' (see Table 4.2), but stressed that this rise in salience was not due to a recognition of some intrinsic qualities of sport but due to 'its apparent contribution to the Executive's social policies, in particular Scotland's obesity problem' (2007, p. 73). Indeed, since devolution the continuity of government concern with the health of the Scottish nation has been a, if not the, defining characteristic of successive administrations. However, while the policy objectives for local communities were broadly similar to those evident in England and Wales, the manner in which they were funded was beginning to show a degree of distinctiveness. While most of the funding for the delivery of the *Sport 21* (**sport**scotland's strategy published in 1998 and discussed more fully below) objectives came either from the government or from the lottery, there was a significant contribution from Scottish Executive's Health Improvement Fund to support physical activity programmes (such as community walking, GP referral schemes and safer routes to schools). However, as is clear from these examples, the Ministry for Health is concerned primarily with physical activity not sport. On the one hand sport has generally benefited (if only through the provision of modest financial support) from spillover from the health agenda, but on the other, sports interests have found it difficult to establish a coherent policy for sport which integrates health-related physical activity, competitive sport and high performance ambitions.

If health concerns were the primary factors in explaining any increased salience of sport since devolution, an important secondary factor was the concern with nation-building, which is a regular reference in government policy documents (see, for example, Scottish Parliament 2002) and in the speeches of politicians, especially those of the Scottish National Party. In the wake of the poor British performance at the 1996 Olympic Games and again following the strong performance by Scottish athletes at the 2008 Beijing Games there were calls for Scotland to compete separately at the Olympic Games, but there was considerable scepticism among elite athletes regarding the willingness of the government to provide the level of financial support that would be required. It is much more likely that the calls for an independent Scottish team at the Olympics were rhetorical flourishes designed to generate newspaper headlines rather than reflecting any firm commitment to change public policy.

In terms of policy priorities, the document *Sport 21* was published just prior to the election of the first Scottish Parliament. Published by the Scottish Sports Council (now **sport**scotland), the policy, which was endorsed by the incoming government, was ambitious and sought to 'ensure that the opportunity to participate in sport is available to everyone . . . [and] to establish Scotland as a world class sporting nation' (1998, p. 3). The strategy placed a strong emphasis on the development of a comprehensive approach to the delivery of sport opportunities which sought to involve local authorities, the Scottish Executive, schools, further and higher education institutions and the health boards. One of the initial proposals was the establishment of a Physical Activity Task Force, an explicit acknowledgement of the potential of an alliance with the health sector to generalise the narrower interests of the sport strategy (for example, those associated with competitive sport). The Task Force reported in 2002 and, not surprisingly, concluded that there was a 'crisis of inactivity' which 'starts before young people have left school. Tackling this is now crucial' (Scottish Executive 2002, pp. 6 and 7). Young people and health have remained central themes in Scottish sport policy since devolution.

In the early post-devolution period sport policy exhibited a broad similarity to policy found in England and to a large extent also in Wales. The commitment to modernise Hampden Park as the national football stadium, the appointment of 245 school sport coordinators through the Active Schools programme, the establishment of area institutes to support elite athletes and the ambition to bring major sports events to Scotland (Scottish Executive 2001, section 2.14) all had close parallels in English sport policy (the rebuilding of Wembley stadium, the investment in School Sport Partnerships, the establishment of the English Institute of Sport network and the preparation of the bid to host the 2012 Olympic and Paralympic Games). Part of the explanation for this correspondence in policy objectives is that both countries were facing broadly similar problems (especially in relation to the health of schoolchildren, poor elite level performance and the need to refurbish/replace historic stadiums).

Even the major review of *Sport 21*, *Reaching Higher* (Scottish Executive 2007), gave little indication of the emergence of a distinctive Scottish sport policy. In most respects *Reaching Higher* endorsed the policy direction set in the earlier strategy. The review was undertaken by a group representative of the major interests in Scottish sport (the Scottish Executive, **sport**scotland, the Scottish Sports Association, local government and NGBs) and was led, on behalf of the Executive, by a representative from the Scottish Sports Association. *Reaching Higher* noted the achievements of the previous strategy (especially the introduction of the Active Schools programme and the establishment of the Scottish Institute of Sport network) but emphasised the need for: greater clarity of the respective roles of sport partners; closer cooperation between NGBs; improved PE in schools; investment in club development; and more efficient use of existing sport facilities such as those located at schools. In many respects this list of objectives is very similar to those found in England at the time and once the Commonwealth Games were awarded to Glasgow the policy similarities between the two countries intensified as the following extract from the recent government's programme for 2010–11 (Scottish Government 2010) indicates. The government would

> continu[e] to invest in new and refurbished sports facilities and increas[e] our support for high performance sport to help our medal chances in both the 2012 Olympics and the 2014 Commonwealth Games. We will use the Games as a catalyst to leave a lasting legacy throughout Scotland of which we can all be proud. In particular, Active Nation will use the spirit and excitement of the Games to motivate Scots to get more active and get more out of life. (Scottish Government 2010, p. 22)

If there is a noteworthy difference in policy between Scotland and England, it is in relation to the prominence of health concerns as the underlying rationale for much of the interest of the Scottish Executive. However, identifying health as a more prominent rationale for sport is not meant to suggest that significant contributions to the funding of sport participation projects came from the mainstream health budget. Indeed, as one academic observer commented, 'sport was resented by health which tried to control the Active Schools programme so that it focused strongly on health benefits'. The extent to which health objectives dominate community and youth sport programmes, rather than skills development, investment in coaching and increased competition opportunities, is in part a reflection of the fragile resource base of Scottish NGBs and clubs and the extent of their dependency on public funding which, in general terms, is significantly more acute than that of their counterparts in England. However, the dominant impression is of broad similarity of policy priorities between Scotland and England with politicians in both countries giving prominence to sport due to assumptions about its capacity to deliver a range of welfare benefits despite civil servants in both countries, especially in the health and education ministries, being much more sceptical about the role of sport and far less willing to underwrite sports programmes with mainstream funding.

As regards the organisation of sport, while English sport policy has demonstrated a marked lack of consistency and stability of objectives since 2000, it has at least had a stable location within the machinery of central government, thus allowing sports interest groups to build relationships with civil servants and for sport to be incorporated into the routine of government. In contrast, Scottish policy objectives have been more stable, but the policy sector has failed to find a long-term location within the Executive with the consequence that sport has been perceived by Executive staff as 'temporary lodger' rather than a 'permanent resident' and there has consequently been a lack of ownership and integration within the mainstream concerns of the various departments that have hosted the function. One implication of this history is that the stability of policy objectives is explained, at least in part, by the fact that no department was host long enough to reflect on the problems of implementation or be held accountable for progress. Had the proposal by the Scottish National Party in 2005 to incorporate sportscotland into the Scottish Executive been successful, it might have stabilised the location of sport and also raised its profile. However, the proposal was withdrawn, although in preserving their formal independence it has been suggested that the agency lost substantial autonomy: In the words of one academic observer, 'in saving themselves they constrained themselves'. In the policy document *Reaching Higher*, the government asserted the role of the Scottish Executive, naming it as the 'lead on policy and direction for the national strategy' while limiting the role of sportscotland to the provision of 'advice to [the] Scottish Executive, Parliament and other stakeholders' (Scottish Executive 2007, pp. 41 and 43). Consequently, since the mid-2000s the Scottish Executive has exercised close supervision of sportscotland even if it has rarely provided strategic leadership on policy.

If the lack of a stable home location within the Scottish Executive is one distinctive feature of the organisation of sport, a second is the central role identified by sportscotland (and reinforced by the Scottish Executive) for local authorities, which have a statutory duty to provide sports facilities for their population. However, the nature of the statutory responsibility is limited and vaguely refers simply to the duty to make 'adequate provision' for sport and recreation. Moreover, the implication was that the concept of 'adequacy' was something to be determined locally, resulting in Audit Scotland reporting in 2008 that 'Scotland has a national strategy for sport, but there are no clear links between local and national strategies' (Audit Scotland 2008, p. 5; see also Thomson 2010). The report noted that, while sportscotland set requirements for local authorities, the latter were not obliged to adopt them and indeed only half had strategies in place by 2007; sportscotland faces the same problem as Sport England insofar as local authorities are the main providers of sport opportunities (especially facilities) in local communities yet do not feel obliged to subordinate locally developed sport policy objectives to the objectives of the national sports council. Whereas Sport England attempted to bypass local authorities by partnering with NGBs and establishing County Sport Partnerships, sportscotland had not had that option due, in large part, to the organisational and financial weakness of most Scottish Governing Bodies (SGBs). However, in 2009, sportscotland attempted to reinvigorate its network of regional sport partnerships first introduced in 2003. It remains to be seen whether the new Regional Sporting Partnerships will have a significant impact on the policy decisions of local authorities (sportscotland, no date). As regards NGBs, there is the suggestion that the current relationship between sportscotland and the NGBs is too cosy, with the latter exhibiting an 'entitlement culture' where financial support from the 'bank of **sport**scotland' is expected with little corresponding obligation.

Although sport is a devolved function, there are a number of issues on which a UK-wide policy is either required (for example, in relation to anti-doping) or desirable (for example, in relation to the preparation of elite athletes for the Olympic and Paralympic Games). Coordination is achieved primarily through the work of UK Sport and the regular meetings of the British Cabinet for Sport established in 1998 by the Labour government. With regard to both these organisations, the home country sports councils have been keen to resist what they see as Labour/Westminster centralisation by emphasising the autonomy they enjoy due to their royal charters. However, there was little evidence of tension with regard to cooperation in the development of high-performance athletes, and the relationship between **sport**scotland and UK Sport was described by more than one administrator as being very positive.

Conclusion

Dramatic changes in policy salience or direction since 1998 which are causally related to devolution would be surprising given a) the history of a degree of separate administration of sport prior to devolution, b) the lengthy history of sporting nationalism in Scotland, c) the broadly common socioeconomic context across the England, Wales and Scotland, d) the dominance for much of the post-devolution period of social democratic parties in Westminster and Edinburgh, e) the extent to which management practices associated with new public management affected all levels of government in the UK, and f) the strong common interest in elite sport success across the four home countries. Thomson concluded that 'there is much continuity of policy and purpose, and remarkably little change. It is only in PE and school sport that England has diverged significantly from Scotland. There is no equivalent of the PESSCL programme, which has benefited from massive government investment' (2010, p. 134). Reid reinforced this general assessment, commenting that 'While McConnell felt devolution aided focus and leadership towards sport, the reality has been self-congratulatory parliamentary motions, a committee addressing sport only in a crisis, a cross party sport group focusing on presentations, and a minister with an overly extensive portfolio' (2007, p. 75).

Differences in organisation and funding are generally slight and difficult to trace to devolution rather than other possible causes. For example, there has arguably been a more consistent concern to accept the promotion of physical activity as an element of sport development within schools. In addition, there has been greater consistency in the relationship between **sport**scotland and the Scottish Executive on the one hand and local authorities on the other. Neither of these examples are necessarily the product of devolution, as the former might just as easily be explained by the location of sport for a time within the health ministry and the latter by the absence of alternative partners due to the relative weakness of Scottish NGBs.

Since the election of 2011, which Hassan described as being 'of watershed proportions' (2011, p. 365) in which the SNP became the majority party, there is significantly greater potential for divergence. Not only does the SNP no longer have to negotiate policy from a position of weakness as part of a minority government, but its broadly social democratic policies are now in marked contrast to the budget-cutting neoliberalism of the Westminster coalition government. Moreover, it is arguable that a majority government in Edinburgh will be less constrained by other policy actors than would the Westminster government. The Scottish Sports Association, which represents Scottish NGBs, is an active lobbying group, but lacks leverage; the local authorities association, Convention of Scottish Local Authorities (COSLA) is hampered by the variable emphasis given to sport by member authorities; and the Scottish universities are, according to one administrator, 'catching up with the sports agenda, not setting it'. There is consequently considerable potential for policy change led by the Scottish Executive and divergence from the English pattern due to the relative lack of restraining interests. However, the impact of devolution to date has been to produce a more intimate network of relationships between policy actors and possibly a more open policy sub-sector with the potential to diverge from the other home countries in policy process and policy, although at present it would be fair to conclude that devolution has not altered in any fundamental way the policymaking process, has not changed how actors view their roles within the process and has not led to substantive shifts in policy when compared to pre-devolution policy or to the policy trajectories of England and Wales.

WALES

Although the Wales Act 1998 transferred from Westminster to the new Welsh Assembly a wide range of powers both directly and indirectly related to sport, Wales already had a separate sports council, but more importantly had a well-established sporting culture. A number of writers have commented on the symbolic significance of sport in the development and manifestation of a sense of national identity and also on the extent to which the symbolism is often more the result of manufacture than a simple reflection of an organic phenomenon (Jarvie 1993; Holt 1989; Polley 1998). In this respect sport makes more tangible the 'imagined community' of the nation. The cultural significance of sport in Wales is summarised by Holden (2011, p. 272) as follows:

> Sport has been a central tenet in inventing, maintaining and projecting the idea of a single Welsh identity in and outside its blurred borders.

It has helped to gloss over the different meanings that the people of Wales attach to their nationality, enabling them to assert their Welshness in the face of internal division and the all encompassing shadow of England.

In Wales sporting nationalism has over the years fulfilled a number of functions, including: the incorporation of English migrants; the integration of a northern agricultural Wales with an urban industrial southern Wales; and the definition of its relationship with England—its significant other. Although Wales has produced national sporting heroes in a number of sports including boxing (Tommy Farr in the 1930s) and football (John Charles and Ryan Giggs), it is rugby union that has the strongest claim to be the sport which has not only produced a series of national heroes over the years but which has also given the country its most potent defining sporting moments. The victory over New Zealand in 1905 was followed in the 1950s to 1970s by a series of victories in the Five Nations competitions, which reinforced the sense of collective identity far more effectively than other cultural products such as the Welsh language and religious nonconformity. Rugby's place in the national consciousness was further emphasised by the naming of the rebuilt Cardiff Arms Park as the Welsh National Stadium in 1970. According to Johnes, 'Sport has not only helped the Welsh to see themselves as a nation, it has also helped others to accept Welsh nationhood' (2005, p. 111; see also Evans et al. 1999). However, while the symbolic status of rugby union provides Wales with a cultural profile distinct from England in many other respects, the cultural integration with England through sport is equally notable. Although Wales has a national football league, its three most prominent teams are not members, preferring to play in the more demanding and more lucrative English leagues. Similarly, in cricket Glamorgan plays against English counties and its star players such as Robert Croft were happy to play for England. As Johnes concluded, there is an ambiguity at the heart of Welsh sporting nationalism, which, on the one hand, proclaims and celebrates a distinctive national identity, while on the other 'in sport [Wales] seems to be reaffirming its place in the United Kingdom' (2000, p. 108). This ambiguity of sporting identity mirrors the ambiguity of national identity illustrated in the responses to a questionnaire at the time of the 1997 referendum on devolution in which 43 per cent defined themselves as either 'Welsh, not British' (17 per cent) or More Welsh than British (26 per cent), but the majority defined themselves as Equally Welsh and British (34 per cent), More British than Welsh (10 per cent) or British, not Welsh (12 per cent) (quoted in Johnes 2005, p. 120). Fourteen years later, while Scottish nationalism seemed to be gathering pace, Welsh nationalism was in retreat as Plaid Cymru lost four seats in the 2011 assembly elections, falling to third place behind the Conservatives and the largest party, Labour.

Sport Policy in Wales Since Devolution

Assessing the salience of a policy area to a government is far from straight-forward. Individual indicators such as volume and trends in public expenditure, administrative location, seniority of the minister and output of strategic documents and associated initiatives are all potentially useful but not particularly valid indicators. For example, reductions in public expenditure and in specific policy initiatives might reflect a high salience to a government that is concerned to see more sports services provided by the private and not-for-profit sectors. However, collectively the abovementioned indicators should provide a basis for a cautious assessment of salience since devolution. In terms of public expenditure, sport would appear to have benefited disproportionately from the general rise in public expenditure by the Welsh Government. Although it must be borne in mind that the range of services covered by the sport budget has changed over the period, a broad calculation indicates that expenditure has increased by around 250 per cent between 2000–01 and 2011–12, whereas total Welsh Government expenditure has increased by a more modest 112 per cent.[2] The current location of sport within the Department for Housing, Regeneration and Heritage places sport on the margin of a very large and complex department and indicates a more peripheral position in the administrative hierarchy than under the previous administration. Prior to the 2011 assembly elections, ministers with responsibility for sport tended to be drawn from the middle ranks of the governing coalitions. Finally, the steady output of strategic documents confirms the government's interest in sport, although the impact of the various documents on policy is variable.

In general, prior to devolution, sport in Wales was an area of benign neglect by the Welsh Office. There was little contact between the Sports Council of Wales (SCW) and either civil servants or ministers in Westminster. The 'upside of this', according to one sports administrator, 'was that SCW was left alone, but the downside was that it was difficult to get funding increases above the rate of inflation'. However, just prior to devolution, John Redwood and William Hague, as successive Welsh ministers, requested the preparation of a sport policy for Wales (Welsh Office/Sports Council for Wales 1995, 1996). Both documents (the second was a review of progress) echoed many aspects of the British government document *Sport: Raising the Game* (Department of National Heritage 1995), insofar as there was a heavy focus on youth sport and a neglect of the role of local authorities. Where they differed was in the lack of emphasis given to elite sport success, although this omission was partially redressed in the 1996 document *Young People and Sport in Wales: Moving On*. Following devolution, there has been 'much greater ministerial interest and much more immediate contact [with the ministry]' (interview, senior sport administrator). In large part the increase in the salience of sport to the Welsh Government has been due to the concern to provide a manifestation of Welshness, which has had the impact of raising the profile of issues associated with elite athlete development. However, the concern to improve elite achievement has not been at the expense of a concern to exploit the potential benefits of sport participation for young people and for general health. Overall the salience of sport has certainly risen since, and also due to, devolution.

The creation of the National Assembly for Wales, where sport was initially the responsibility of the minister for education (then, following reorganisation, the for culture, Welsh language and sport) and where oversight was the responsibility of the assembly's Culture Committee, offered the opportunity for clearer political direction of policy. However, in the years since devolution the relationship between SCW and the Welsh Government (WAG) has often lacked integration with any complementarity in policy often being the result of similar policy priorities within SCW and the WAG rather than unified policy leadership. In evidence to the Richard Commission, which was examining the powers of the Welsh Assembly, the SCW CEO argued that as a body established by Royal Charter the council had the responsibility 'to develop sport for the benefit of the people of Wales not the benefit of the Government of the day' (Richard Commission 2003). However, Gareth Davies, chair of the SCW, admitted that 'we [SCW] are an arm's length body, although those arms are getting shorter' (Richard Commission 2004, p. 134). The source of concern was less the broad direction of WAG policy, on which there was basic agreement, and more the involvement of the government in the micromanagement of specific programmes.

As regards the policy priorities of the Welsh government, such attention as has been paid to sport has been prompted by concerns related on the one hand to young people and health and on the other to a concern with forging a collective Welsh identity. The key government document, *Climbing Higher*, published in 2003, stated as its vision for sport a desire to construct 'An active, healthy and inclusive Wales . . . where the outstanding environment of Wales is used sustainably to enhance confidence in ourselves and our place in the world' (National Assembly for Wales 2003, p. 3). The document set a 20-year time frame for the achievement of a set of targets related to participation levels, employment in the sports industries, the holding of regular Welsh Community Games, social inclusion, use of the natural environment and elite success. Underpinning the ambitions of the strategy were assumptions about the willingness of key partners, in education and health and also among the national governing bodies of sport and their clubs, to cooperate. As was acknowledged, 'This first Welsh Assembly Government strategy for sport and active recreation will only succeed if it is able to harness partners into a collective force to address the realities and challenges identified' (2003, p. 29). However, developing and sustaining partnerships which might lead to a strong policy network or even community has proved difficult. Unfortunately, there appears to have been little partnership or even consultation between the WAG and, arguably, its most important partner, the SCW, regarding the content of *Climbing Higher*. Indeed, there is only one passing reference to the SCW in the document. This assessment is endorsed by the Wharton report on aspects of Welsh sport policy which stated that 'Interviewees have suggested to us that the consultation behind *Climbing Higher* was not thorough, nor did it seek the buy-in of either SCW or the NGBs of Welsh sport. Thus, on publication, there was little or no ownership of the policy or its targets' (Wharton Consulting 2009, p. 19). Consequently, NGB performance plans were 'not routinely structured so as to fulfil the targets of *Climbing Higher*' (Wharton Consulting 2009, p. 19). Perhaps more significantly it has proved very difficult to secure effective 'buy-in' from the two key ministries, education and health. While the former did provide some funding for PE teacher professional development, this funding has declined in recent years and the current minister has requested an exit strategy by 2014. Establishing a sustained commitment from the health ministry (and health boards) to the sport and physical activity strategy of the government and SCW has proved equally difficult. For both departments there is a perception that unless their department is formally allocated responsibility for sport and the SCW, the issues associated with delivery of sport and physical activity strategy are not their concern and have little if any call on their resources.

The lack of integration of sport and physical activity into the mainstream activities of the education and health departments notwithstanding, there has been considerable continuity of policy emphasis which dates from the pre-devolution policy documents of the mid-1990s. Since 1995 there has been a consistent primary focus by SCW on young people with a secondary focus on physical activity and health, a focus which was shared by WAG on its establishment. The early post-devolution concern with the relationship between physical activity/sport and health was reinforced by the publication of the Wanless report (Department of Health 2002) and the report by the Wales Audit Office on physical activity (Wales Audit Office 2007) and is clearly evident in the 2007 WAG policy statement, *One Wales* (National Assembly for Wales 2007), which reinforced many of the sentiments and objectives of *Climbing Higher*. In relation to elite sport, the picture is more complex, although there is no doubt that elite sporting achievement has become more important since, and because of, devolution. However, the increased salience is less easy to track in Welsh policy decisions due first to the fact that the bulk of elite sport funding is controlled by UK Sport rather than being a devolved resource, and second, because the increased prominence of elite sport in Wales has been paralleled by a similar or perhaps even greater increase in prominence at Westminster.

The lack of direct control over all aspects of lottery funding poses a potential challenge to the capacity of WAG and SCW to determine the detail of sport investment. Although SCW, like **sport**scotland, is a nominated distribution board for lottery funding, the percentage allocations are set by the minister for culture, media and sport in Westminster with accountability for the use of the funding to the DCMS rather than to the WAG. For example, 20 per cent of the original lottery allocation to SCW was removed to fund UK Sport and the Great Britain elite athlete development programme. Although Welsh athletes benefit from UK Sport support, the view of the SCW was that Wales did not recoup the 20 per cent loss of lottery funding. A second example concerned the desire within the SCW to direct more lottery funding to areas of low participation which are also areas of deprivation: a change in distribution of lottery resources which is limited by the UK-wide objectives set for the use of lottery funds. However, the lack of local control over funding should not be exaggerated as there was little evidence that the minister for culture, media and sport was setting policy objectives for the use of lottery funds which seriously undermined the objectives set by the Welsh administration. Nevertheless, the lack of full local autonomy regarding lottery funds introduced a degree of uncertainty into the Welsh sport planning process and also reduced the extent to which policy could be fine-tuned to suit local requirements.

Further policy complexity was created due to the blurred remits between Cardiff and Westminster in sport-related services such as education. While Wales has considerable discretion in relation to education policy, there are elements of Westminster education legislation[3] that affect the capacity of the SCW and WAG to implement policies. Such policies would include the dual use of school facilities which, given the rural character of much of Wales, is a much more important element in sport policy than in England, where the more urbanised population are likely to have easier access to municipal facilities.

An overview of the policy process suggests that prior to devolution many key sports policy actors were oriented to Westminster rather than to Cardiff. Since 1998 SCW has become a much clearer hub for policy discussion and initiatives and has been central to the emergence of a more sharply defined Welsh network of interest for sport. However, though SCW may no longer be bypassed for Westminster and Whitehall, there is still some way to go before one could refer to a Welsh sport policy community. Among the key relationships which underpin the policy process are those between SCW and WAG, SCW and local authorities, SCW and the Welsh NGBs, and SCW and UK Sport.

As regards the relationship between SCW and the WAG department responsible for sport, there has generally been a close correspondence of policy objectives for sport with a common focus on young people and community health. However, there has been only limited support, for example, in the form of finance, expertise or organisational resources, from the education and health departments (see Wharton Consulting 2009, p. 12, para. 1.49). By the mid-2000s there were only token contributions to the sport and physical activity objectives established in *Climbing Higher* with much of the health-related funding coming not from the Exchequer health budget but from health-related lottery projects (Welsh Assembly Government

2006). The lack of 'buy-in' from these two key departments was prompted in part by the attempt to integrate the physical activity agenda with wider health and education agendas. According to the Wharton report, this attempt 'created some tension between SCW and WAG and . . . this has coloured relations between the two since that time' (2009, p. 19). However, it should be borne in mind that the reluctance of civil servants and ministers to look beyond the remit of their own department is a common phenomenon and one that is certainly not restricted to Wales.

The relationship between SCW and local authorities and NGBs shares a number of similar features as both sets of organisations are varied in terms of capacity and priorities and share few common interests except at the most general level. Consequently, it is only on a few occasions that SCW receives a collective view which can be factored in to policy discussions with the result that both sets of organisations tend to be on the periphery of the sport policy network.

Relations between SCW and UK Sport in relation to elite sport are complex and are affected by the small number of elite athletes in Wales (excluding football and rugby union) and the fact that, for many athletes, Great Britain is their reference point for elite competition.[4] Consequently, in most sports Welsh organisations (NGBs and clubs in particular) fulfil a talent identification and initial nurturing role before athletes move to GB level development squads. The capacity of SCW to shape a national elite athlete development programme is further complicated by the distribution of UK Sport lottery funding through NGBs rather than through home country sports councils. While the capacity of SCW to influence how NGBs use their funds in relation to Welsh athletes is a concern, the general view is that Welsh athletes benefit from the economies of scale that a UK-wide focus on high-performance sport allows. This conclusion reinforces the observation in the Wharton report that 'the understanding and relationships between Welsh and British NGBs is mature both strategically and operationally' (Wharton Consulting 2009, p. 34).

Conclusion

The main impact of devolution for Welsh sport has been in relation to process rather than policy. Lines of communication between key policy actors, especially SCW and WAG, are shorter, with the consequence that interaction between officials and with ministers is more regular and frequent and reinforces the more general observation that 'partnership is at the heart of the Assembly Government's policy style' (Entwistle 2006). Since devolution there has been a steady process of refocusing by local authorities and NGBs away from Westminster and towards Cardiff and a recognition that sport policy, especially in relation to community participation, is not a consequence of English decisions but is a shared domestic responsibility. Although the emphasis given to youth and general health benefits of participation are distinctive features of Welsh sport policy and pre-date devolution, the advent of devolution has made it easier for that distinctiveness to be preserved. The one major area where devolution has introduced greater complexity to sport policymaking is in relation to elite sport. The preference of two of the country's main commercial sports, football and cricket, to participate in English leagues and the orientation of Olympic sports to 'team GB' weaken the development of a distinctive Welsh high-performance sport policy and the development of a Welsh sport policy community. However, as was the case in relation to Scotland, part of the explanation for the lack of policy divergence between Wales and England is that both Cardiff and Westminster have housed governments with broadly similar social democratic values for much of the period since devolution.

DEVOLUTION AND SPORT IN NORTHERN IRELAND

Unlike Scotland and Wales, devolution is not a recent development in Northern Ireland. From the partition of Ireland in 1921 following the civil war and until 1972, Northern Ireland had a devolved parliament at Stormont with responsibility for most services apart from economic policy, defence and foreign affairs. However, in 1972 direct rule from Westminster was imposed due in part to the renewal of civil conflict by the Provisional Irish Republican Army and in part to the deeply embedded abuse of governmental power, by the Unionist-dominated Stormont government, especially in relation to the allocation of public housing and the drawing of constituency boundaries for elections. Direct rule, which lasted until 1999 and which was designed to eliminate corruption and to bring the country more closely into line with policies and administrative practices found in the rest of the UK, remained a highly distinctive form of administration insofar as it was highly centralised and lacked any significant accountability to the local population.

The suspension of Stormont was followed by a long series of unsuccessful attempts to restore a degree of devolution until an agreement was reached between the Unionist and Nationalist political leaders and, more importantly, between the governments of the UK and Ireland (Shirlow 2001) in 1998. The 'Good Friday Agreement', as it became known (at least to the Nationalist community), was less concerned with facilitating the development of 'local policy solutions for local problems' and far more concerned to find a political formula which would prevent the abuse of power by either section of the NI population, which would encourage consensus decision making and which would lead to a 'normalisation' of policy (to a UK pattern) in key areas such as housing, public sector employment and education (Paris et al. 2003). The post-1998 system contained an elaborate system of checks and balances which tended to constrain innovation, with functional responsibility (for example, for land use planning) often divided between departments and with NI Assembly committees having a strong policy development and scrutiny role (Berry et al. 2001; Carmichael and Osborne 2003).

Although the Good Friday Agreement was a major political achievement and has been followed by a period of prolonged peace, deep sectarian divisions remain and are, to a great extent, built in to the fabric of the agreement. Since 1999 the devolved arrangements have been suspended four times, usually due to disputes over the decommissioning of weapons by the various paramilitary groups. Unlike Scotland and Wales, there is no real or 'imagined' community to rationalise devolution. In contrast, Northern Ireland comprises two distinct communities neither of which has much concern with Northern Ireland as a geographical or political entity. On the one hand the Unionist community is defined by its commitment to Britain and the Nationalist community is defined by its commitment to a united Ireland ruled from Dublin. There is consequently no nationalist political party similar to Plaid Cymru and the Scottish National Party and no overlap with the main parties at Westminster. Indeed, the Labour party does not organise or campaign in Northern Ireland.

Alan Bairner, in an analysis of the projection of the image of the new, post-Good Friday Agreement Belfast, noted 'The absence of sporting venues from representation of the "new" Belfast' in recent guide books, which is a consequence of the generally held belief 'that sport has not only reflected inter-communal division . . . but has also contributed to and, in some instances, exacerbated that division' (2008, p. 217). The symbolism of sport is intimately interwoven into the history of ethno-sectarianism in Northern Ireland. For well over one hundred years sport and membership of sport organisations have been organised on strict segregationist lines with members of the Catholic nationalist community playing traditional Irish sports such as Gaelic football and hurling under aegis of the Gaelic Athletic Association, while the Protestant unionist community played traditional British sports of rugby, football and athletics also in culturally exclusive clubs. Sport was an integral part of the opposition to British rule prior to the partition of the country in 1921 and has retained its highly charged political symbolism to the present day. However, the symbolism is not as straightforward as it might at first appear because while some sports, such as football, are organised at the home country level, many others are organised on an island of Ireland level, including sports that have a strong association with Protestant unionism such as rugby and hockey as well as sports that are strongly associated with the nationalist community such as Gaelic football. One consequence of this organisational pattern is that, as Bairner observes, 'northern unionists often end up representing an entity (a thirty-two county Ireland) which they would not wish to see being given constitutional legitimacy' (2008, p. 224).

Sport Policy in Northern Ireland since Devolution

As should already be clear, sport, along with other elements of cultural policy, has historically had high salience across the political spectrum in Northern Ireland and also within the Westminster government during the period of direct rule, which interrupted the periods of devolved government. During the period of direct rule only those services considered less divisive were left in the hands of NI local authorities. The fact that the Westminster government decided to leave sport as a devolved responsibility reflected a staggering ignorance of Irish history and a disconcerting level of naiveté regarding the capacity of sport to build bridges between hostile communities. According to Coalter et al., mainland political parties considered sport and leisure to be 'an area of personal opinion, freedom and choice, and as such a "depoliticised" arena, properly outside the realm of adversarial politics' (1986, p. 127).

One consequence of the UK government's confidence in the capacity of sport to build bridges between the two communities was substantial investment in sport and leisure facilities. From the mid-1970s, Northern Ireland enjoyed 20 years of investment in high-quality facilities (Knox 1986, 1987). Decisions about the location of facilities were ostensibly based on a rational analysis of need and the aim to establish a hierarchy of provision across the country. However, it soon became apparent that sport facility location was no more immune from sectarian politics than education and housing and that location was determined less by rational planning than by the need on the part of the NI Office to be seen to be even-handed in investment in Protestant and Catholic areas. The substantial investment in sport and leisure had little discernible impact on the sectarian divisions in Derry and Belfast, but did provide these two cities with an enviable stock of good quality facilities.

In the years since the Good Friday Agreement, the hoped-for 'normal' politics have been slow to emerge. Since 1998 the NI Assembly has been suspended on four occasions, the longest being between October 2002 and May 2007, during which the province was administered directly from Westminster. Between the date of the agreement and May 2007, the Assembly had sat for only nineteen months. Although there has been no return to civil conflict in the first ten years since the agreement, there has been a polarisation of political opinion as reflected in election results. Both of the more moderate political parties associated with the nationalists (the Social Democratic and Labour party) and the unionists (the Ulster Unionist party) have been squeezed by the more uncompromising parties—Sinn Féin and the Democratic Unionist party. Suspensions were a reflection of the continuing suspicion between the two communities and although the Assembly has functioned reasonably effectively for the last few years, the depth of mutual suspicion and the complex decision-making process has resulted in stagnation in many policy sectors, including sport, and an acute sensitivity to policy initiatives that might be interpreted as favouring one community over another. A more charitable view would be to argue that the peace has held for over ten years and that the Assembly is dealing with issues, such as the reform of the police service, in order of importance to the maintenance of the peace agreement. Overall it is hard to avoid the conclusion that, far from the agreement leading to a normalisation of politics, it has institutionalised sectarianism (see Tonge 2006; Paris et al. 2003) and constructed a policy process which is dominated by inertia borne of a poverty of imagination that characterises contemporary nationalism and unionism.

In reading any policy document, either from the Department of Culture, Arts and Leisure (DCAL) or from Sport Northern Ireland (SNI, the NI sport council), one is acutely aware of the policy priority of maintaining the stability of the power-sharing agreement. The Sport Northern Ireland 2009–11 corporate plan refers to the maintenance of 'community cohesion' and notes that 'Sport and physical recreation provides a positive platform for communities to come together—not only helping to address community relations, but strengthening community infrastructure' (2009, p. 4). Similarly, the DCAL strategy, *Sport Matters*, notes that 'Sport can also assist in bridging community divisions' (DCAL 2009, p. 2) while sport features prominently in the Programme for Government 2008–11 in relation to the objective to 'Promote tolerance, inclusion and health and well-being' (NI Executive 2008, pp. 11–13).

If it is possible to put to one side the overarching concern with community cohesion and the maintenance of the power-sharing agreement, then the sport policy priorities in NI are broadly consistent with those in the other three home countries, especially Wales and Scotland. The three priorities for the period 2008–11 are: 'increased participation in sport and physical recreation; improved sporting performance; and improved efficiency in the administration of sport' (Sport NI 2009, p. 5) and are the product of similar concerns and pressures such as those related to the health of young people and adults, the potential contribution of sport to the economy and the capacity of sport, especially high-performance sport, to improve the image of a country. The objectives and associated targets are specified in detail and are supported by an impressive body of research. However, the extent to which progress towards targets is mediated and at times thwarted by the sectarian context is easily illustrated through an examination of two contrasting issues—the building of a national stadium and the improvement of coaching in schools.

In October 2000, the then minister for culture, arts and leisure established an advisory panel to recommend steps 'to be taken to develop and secure soccer as a thriving and successful sport for the longer term' (Hamilton 2001, p. 11). One of the issues concerned the lack of a national stadium that met current standards and led to the recommendation that 'this is not acceptable and that steps should be taken immediately to address this deficiency' (Hamilton 2001, p. 73). The report also noted that 'the venue should meet international standards and be acceptable to all sections of the community' (Hamilton 2001, p. 74). As Bairner (2008) noted, this recommendation led to a lengthy debate not only about the viability of the new stadium and whether it should be used for other sports such as Gaelic football and rugby union as well as soccer, but also where the stadium should be located. Partly because the government already owned the land, the suggested location was at the site of the former Maze Prison. There are few locations more strongly associated with the recent period of civil war. The prison was used as an internment camp mainly for nationalist prisoners, but also for a small number of unionist prisoners, and was the site of the republican hunger strike in 1981, which resulted in the death of ten prisoners. In the discussions over the development of the site for the national stadium, it was proposed to retain block H6 as an International Conflict Transformation Centre, and also the prison hospital building where the hunger strikers died. The proposal prompted concern that just as the existing football stadium, Windsor Park, was too strongly associated with the unionist community, the new stadium would be too strongly associated with the nationalist community because of the preservation of such evocative buildings. For this reason, and others associated with access, use and cost, the proposal was shelved in January 2009 by the Democratic Unionist party (DUP) minister for sport.

The second example concerns the decision by the Sinn Féin education minister in 2007 to appoint 24 Irish Football Association coaches and 32 Gaelic Athletic Association coaches to work in primary schools. The decision was apparently taken without consultation with the DUP minister for culture, arts and leisure and has proved controversial because it has been interpreted as a device for introducing GAA sports into schools in the unionist community. There have been reports of a school principal who apparently cancelled a planned GAA coaching session for pupils which had been arranged in discussions between the GAA and one of his staff. Although the principal later agreed to the involvement of the GAA in coaching, it would not be at the school but through the local federation of schools. More recently, when asked by a DUP member of the legislative assembly to reveal the names of the eight controlled schools (that is, schools attended mainly by protestant children) which offer GAA coaching, the minister refused on the grounds that it would place the schools in an 'invidious position' and might endanger their security (BBC 2009).

Despite the delicate context for sport, one of the few constant organisational features in Northern Irish sport policy over the last 40 years has been the Northern Ireland sports council (Sport NI). Working at times in extremely difficult circumstances, the council has negotiated its way through a turbulent period with remarkable success. Its most notable achievement has been to avoid being defined as irredeemably either a nationalist or unionist organisation. However, its relative organisational neutrality has been at the cost of rational facility planning, though this has been masked by the relative over-provision of facilities during the height of the troubles. Evenhandedness in the distribution of resources, at times irrespective of need, has enabled the organisation to survive. However, few other sports organisations could make similar claims to neutrality. The GAA and the major team sports of football and rugby are closely linked with one section of the community or the other and are deeply suspicious of one another and consequently reluctant to cooperate in service provision. The failure of the Maze Prison redevelopment was, in part, due to the depth of mutual suspicion between the three major sports organisations. The school system is similarly divided along sectarian lines and extremely wary of sports initiatives which appear to challenge the link between the school and their respective religious-political constituencies. Finally, in the brief period since the restoration of devolved power, the two most important ministers in relation to sport policy—the minister for education and the minister for culture, arts and sport—have maintained a formal evenhandedness while at the same time arousing suspicions of favouring their respective religious-political communities. One way in which the incipient sectarian tensions are kept in check is through relatively generous funding. Between 2007–08 and 2010–11, the total NI government budget was scheduled to increase by just under 18 per cent and that for the Department of Culture, Arts and Sport by just under 3 per cent, while that for the sports element of the DCAL budget was due to increase by 24 per cent.

In summary, the most notable aspect of the policy process for sport in Northern Ireland is the lack of stability over the last 20 years or so as the country moved from periods of direct rule from Westminster, during which sport policy was largely led by the NI sports council to (shorter) periods of often fractious devolved rule. During the latter periods the sports council remained a central organisation, but, as was the case with Scotland and Wales, had a much closer relationship with the home country minister and civil servants. However, what is clear, irrespective of whether sport policy was being made during periods of direct rule or during periods of devolved rule, was that there were two levels to the policy process—one public, overt and ostensibly cooperative and the other private, covert and arguably subversive. The public process revolves around a set of topics that would be familiar in the other three home countries such as sport and young people/schools, sports, physical activity and health and sport's contribution to economic growth. The private process is a calculation of sectarian advantage and the acute suspicion of motives of other policy actors.

Conclusion

Even the most cursory study of the history of Northern Ireland would demonstrate the depth of embeddedness of cultural symbolism, of which sport was a major element, in the region's history. Such is the significance of cultural politics that rather than assessing the extent to which devolution has had an impact on sport policy it would be more appropriate to assess the extent to which sport/cultural politics has had an impact on devolution. Whether the focus is on the period of direct rule or the more recent period of devolution, it is clear that the defining characteristic of the region—sectarian suspicion and animosity—has adapted itself to whatever political system was in place. However, such observations should not detract from the achievement of the Good Friday Agreement and neither should it be a surprise if the primary policy objective is the maintenance of the fragile peace rather than progress in substantive policy areas. As Knox argued, the NI power-sharing administration 'has opted for populist public policies and neglected the more difficult policy choices on which there are fundamental differences between the DUP and Sinn Féin' (2010, p. 38). Populist policies include many designed to lower the cost to the citizen of accessing public services while among the 'more difficult policy choices' is the Sinn Féin proposal to abolish selection for secondary education by means of examination at the age of 11. Knox's assessment is that the achievements of the administration have been modest and he concludes that 'Squabbling over seemingly innocuous policy issues between the DUP and Sinn Féin does not instil confidence in the minds of the public and the populist policies adopted to date are short-term sweeteners' (2010, p. 41). In the context of devolution, the sport policy subsector is a sensitive barometer for measuring progress towards normal politics as well as being a substantive policy area in its own right. Currently, sport policy is still very much the barometer rather than a normal substantive policy subsector.

DEVOLUTION AND SPORT IN ENGLAND

There are two aspects to any discussion of devolution and England. The first concerns the experiments with regionalism in England and the second concerns the extent to which devolution in the other three home countries has had an impact on English sport policy and administration. As regards the first of these aspects, the UK government's flirtation with devolution to the English regions was both short-lived and generally unhappy. The white paper *Your Region, Your Choice: Revitalising the English Regions* (ODPM 2002) extolled the benefits of regions which would draw their strength from regional assemblies. According to the prime minister in his introduction to the white paper, regionalism would give 'people living in the English regions the chance to have a greater say over key issues that affect them . . . to devise tailored regional solutions to regional problems . . . offering people more accountable, more streamlined and more joined-up government' (ODPM 2002, p. 5). However, the claimed benefits of stronger accountability, reduced bureaucracy and bespoke services failed to generate public support and regionalism for England quietly drifted off the Labour government's agenda and was further diminished by the incoming coalition government, which closed the government offices of the regions in March 2011 and returned their functions to Whitehall. The general retreat from regionalism in England was paralleled by the specific experience of sport. Sport England had for many years had an extensive regional structure, initially with a network of regional councils which comprised representatives of sport interests from within the region, and later, following the abolition of regional councils, a network of boards responsible for the distribution of lottery funding. Both the councils and the boards were supported by well-staffed regional offices of Sport England. However, from the mid-2000s the regional structure of Sport England began to contract due initially to criticism from NGBs that too much Sport England grant was spent on bureaucracy and too little was getting through to service delivery, and more recently to the government's desire to reduce public expenditure. Currently, Sport England has a set of very small regional outposts which are a pale shadow of the rich regional structure of the late 1990s.

It is possible to defend or at least rationalise the loss of a strong regional presence by Sport England by reference to three arguments. First, it could be argued that the cost of maintaining the regional infrastructure did not deliver value for money and, as argued by some NGBs, diverted money from grassroots provision. Second, it might be argued that English regionalism has generally been the product of administrative need (e.g. arising from the complexities of issues such as economic development) or the geographical imperatives of a service which has a clear regional dimension (such as land-use planning and transport). Sport has a weaker claim on both these counts. The third justification could be that with the establishment of County Sport Partnerships there is less need for regional offices. While each of these arguments has some plausibility, they all lack an evidence base. Regarding the first argument, there has been little analysis of the effectiveness of regional offices in optimising the allocation of lottery funding, leveraging additional resources and supporting local authorities in their strategic planning. The second justification has less substance in relation to sport facility planning especially when the location of specialist facilities is being considered. The final rationalisation is also weak insofar as County Sport Partnerships have yet to demonstrate their value in many areas and have only a very limited strategic service planning function.

The net effect of the diminution in Sport England's regional presence has been to greatly reduce the day-to-day contact between Sport England and the major providers of sports opportunities—the local authorities. As will be discussed in Chapter 5, there is little evidence that NGBs, armed with their Whole Sport Plans, are an adequate substitute partner in the attempt to deliver increased participation. It is hard to avoid the conclusion that the shrinking in the regional presence of Sport England was, at best, undertaken on a suspect evidence base and, at worst, has weakened significantly the links between national policy and the partners (local authorities) who had the greatest capacity, and more importantly, the greatest interest in delivering increased participation.

As regards the second aspect, the extent to which devolution in the other three home countries has had an impact on English sport policy, the answer would appear to be very little indeed. According to one sports administrator, the DCMS 'has little awareness of developments in the other home countries' and one might add little interest. Formal contact is occasional and provides the opportunity for a perfunctory exchange of information rather than a forum for discussion of common policy problems. When civil servants in London refer to the minister for sport, they invariably mean the one located in the DCMS. The proposed merger of Sport England and UK Sport will undoubtedly pose some challenges for the devolved system as Scotland, Wales and Northern Ireland might well be concerned that English interests will be more influential than they are at present in shaping the policy of UK Sport and that the merged body will reverse, if only marginally, the gains made since 1998.

CONCLUSION

Devolution needs to be seen as a long-term process of change in the British constitution in which distinctive sport policymaking processes, cultures and outputs were well established and institutionalised particularly in Northern Ireland and Scotland. With this in mind, the 1998 devolution legislation, though significant, did not represent a dramatic break with the past, but rather the continuation of a long-established trend towards greater regional autonomy, initially through administrative devolution and, in 1998, by political devolution. In assessing the impact of devolution to date it is important to acknowledge that divergence might affect a variety of aspects or dimensions of policy. Table 4.3 identifies seven dimensions along which divergence might be measured (Houlihan 2012) and indicates that devolution has had, at best, a modest impact on sport policy. Such a conclusion is hardly surprising when one takes account of the strong pressures for convergence in sport policy at both the domestic and international levels. At the domestic level the broadly common socioeconomic circumstances and cultural heritage of the four countries, the level of investment in the established infrastructure for sport, the broadly similar set of social issues, and the broadly similar ideology of the governing parties are all powerful pressures lessening the likelihood of divergence. At the international level there are also powerful homogenising forces including the monopoly positions of the international federations and the IOC, the role of UNESCO and WADA in imposing conformity in anti-doping and the role of the World Health Organisation in advising on physical activity and health.

However, as was noted earlier in this chapter, there are some policy areas, the health services, for example, where divergence has occurred

Table 4.3 Dimensions of Divergence

Dimension	Description	England	Scotland	Wales	Northern Ireland
Agenda and aspirations	Acknowledgement of an issue or the vision or ambitions for the impact of potential or actual policy outputs	Young people, national identity and increased participation in competitive sport	Health, participation and self-sufficiency in sport services	Health, young people and national identity	Community building, health and young people
Motives	Refers to the factors that prompted the aspirations and the factors which influenced the extent (amount and duration) of resource commitment	Projection of national prestige; assumption of character-building benefits of competitive sport	Symbolic value of sport to national identity; significant health problems of the Scottish population	Symbolic value of sport to national identity; health and socialisation of the young; celebration of natural environment	Sectarian advantage within the limits of the Good Friday Agreement
Contextualising discourse/ ideology/ values	Covers a range from i) the deeper structural values which shape not only policy aspirations, but also the selection of policy instruments and delivery mechanisms; to ii) the more transient policy fashions which can significantly affect policy, but which tend to be short-lived	British nationalism; belief in the value of competitive sport as a tool of social/personal development	Nationalism; assertion of cultural independence from the significant other—England; an element in the rhetoric of political independence; social democratic ideology	National identity; sport as a manifestation of Welshness; social democratic ideology	Competing nationalisms; ethnic-religious tension and limited mutual trust; cultural conservatism; populism
Policy design and implementation	The selection of specific instruments and delivery mechanisms	Centralised control over elite sport; reliance on NGBs and clubs to deliver participation	Central control by parliament; main partners for delivery are schools and local authorities	Leadership by sports council; main delivery partners are local authorities and education institutions	Fragmented policy process (between sports council, DCAL and Ministry of Education)

Inputs: tangible and intangible	Range from the tangible to the intangible: finance, administrative capacity, expertise, evidence and ideas	Heavy reliance on finance from the national lottery; importation of foreign elite-level coaches; development and support for specialist agencies such as UK Sport & English Institute of Sport	Increase in financial inputs, but fragmented control over financial and other delivery resources. Limited administrative capacity and expertise beyond **sportscotland**	Increase in financial inputs, but fragmented control over financial and other delivery resources. Limited administrative capacity and expertise beyond Welsh Sports Council	Generally well resourced, but ideology competes with evidence for influence
Momentum	The weight of support, especially political support, behind a policy aspiration	Strong in relation to elite level sport and also, but to a lesser extent, youth sport (14 to 25 year olds). Weak in relation to adult community sport participation	Strong in relation to aspects of policy that impact on identity (elite success and hosting events), but more diffuse in relation to community sport participation	Strong in relation to aspects of policy that impact on identity (elite success and hosting events), but more diffuse in relation to community participation	Frozen policy landscape. Frozen policy positions between the main two political parties
Impact	The effect of policy on the identified target issue/problem within a specific jurisdiction	Success in delivering elite-level Olympic and Paralympic objectives, but continued failure to make an appreciable impact on the level of adult participation or the 'drop-off' in youth participation	General concern within Scottish Executive to defend investment in sport, but policy community weak, therefore more vulnerable to sport being used as an instrument to achieve non-sport objectives such as increased physical activity and nation-building.	General concern within the Welsh Assembly to defend investment in sport and physical activity. Policy community weak, therefore vulnerable to change of attitude of the WAG	Sport investment generally well supported, but motivation is often derived from the pursuit of sectarian (non-sport) interests

Source: Adapted from Houlihan (2012).

since devolution. Where this has been the case it has often been as a result of an ideological gap developing between the various governments and a desire, on the part of Scotland and Wales in particular, not to follow the Labour government's neoliberal path (Mitchell 2004). Since the election of a Conservative-led coalition government at Westminster, the ideological divide is likely to widen and policy divergence might consequently become more pronounced.

5 Elite Success and/or Increased Participation

Not so long ago it was common to represent the sport policy subsector as constituting a continuum in the shape of a pyramid with four distinct levels. The base comprised the foundation level and was the stage at which young people learnt basic generic sports skills. The school, with trained physical education teachers (at least in secondary schools), was central to service delivery at this level and prepared young people to move upwards to the participation (or community sport) level where adults would be catered for by a combination of public, voluntary and commercial service providers. Those who wanted to take part in organised competitive sport would do so at the performance level mainly through the network of 100,000 or so sports clubs in England affiliated to their parent national governing body. The pinnacle of the pyramid was the excellence level occupied by athletes competing in international competition often as full-time sportsmen and -women. The pyramid, as a visual metaphor, indicated not only the notion of progression, but more importantly indicated the conceptual, organisational and practical unity of interest between the young person learning basic coordination skills and the most accomplished high-performance athlete. The latter would have acquired at least some of her foundational skills, in tennis, for example, at school from PE teachers and possibly visiting coaches in after-school sports clubs which were part of the School Sport Partnership. She might then have progressed to playing at a local club and taken part in inter-club competitions at which she might have been talent-spotted by a Lawn Tennis Association coach and asked to take part in a trial for a regional development squad. From there she would move through the hierarchy of regional and national competitions, before she turns professional and joins the Women's Tennis Association competition circuit.

While reference is still made to the sport development continuum, it is much more common to come across visual metaphors which comprise more discrete elements indicating a much greater organisational, financial and conceptual separation between levels of sport activity. School sport, community sport and high-performance or elite sport became, during the early part of the century, more self-contained and increasingly in competition for resources such as lottery and Exchequer funding, political support

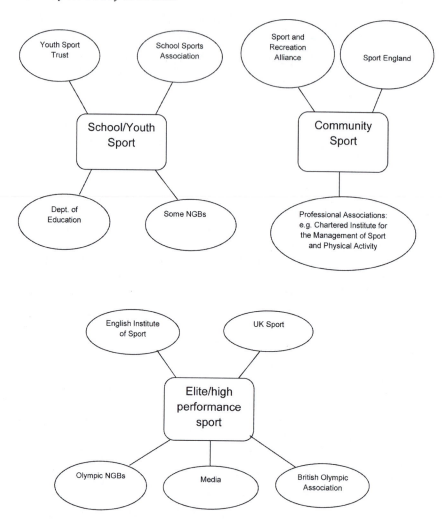

Figure 5.1   Sport policy clusters of interest, 2012.

and organisational expertise. Sport interests have progressively coalesced around elite, community and school/youth sport forming three clusters, two of which have demonstrated a determination and a modest capacity at least to protect the gains made over the previous ten to fifteen years and to limit inter-cluster cooperation (see Figure 5.1).

The fragmentation of the sport policy 'community' has become more apparent in recent years, especially since the formation of the coalition government and the substantial cuts in public-sector budgets. However, it is also the case that the unity implied by the description 'policy community' or reference to a continuum was exaggerations and that the inherent tension between different sports interests were muted either by the occasional coincidence of interests (for example, for more indoor facilities or for the inclusion of physical education within the national curriculum) or by the relative abundance of financial resources from the lottery, the Exchequer and the growing commercialisation of elite sport. Inter-cluster conflict was further diluted from the mid-1990s onwards by the high level of bipartisan political support within Parliament.

The first part of this chapter traces the development of the policy context within which the interests described above emerged and began to consolidate. An assessment of the significance of the policy document, *Sport: Raising the Game*, published by John Major's government, is followed by a discussion of the way in which, and the extent to which, the governments of Tony Blair built on the foundations laid by his predecessor. The second part of the chapter focuses more directly on assessing the impact of government policy in relation to first, community sport and then elite sport. The chapter concludes with reflections on the problems of achieving successful policy implementation in these two policy areas.

SPORT: RAISING THE GAME

The mid-1990s was a highly significant period for sport in the UK. The introduction of the National Lottery in November 1994 and the publication of *Sport: Raising the Game* in the following year were not only important in their own right, but they marked the beginning of a sustained period of government intervention in sport that continued to the time of writing in early 2012. The introduction of the lottery was important less because it established an additional source of funding for sport and more because it provided the government with leverage in a policy area dominated by powerful interests beyond the direct control of government such as local authorities, schools and NGBs.

As discussed elsewhere (Houlihan and White 2002) and in Chapter 2, *Sport: Raising the Game* was notable for its prioritisation of school sport and elite sport and its ignoring of community sport. While the document promised 'to put sport back at the heart of weekly life in every school' (DNH

1995, p. 2) and 'to help our best sports men and women make the very best of their talents' (DNH 1995, p. 3), no similar commitments were made with regard to the sports opportunities at the community participation level. The key partners identified in the strategy included schools, NGBs, clubs and further and higher education institutions: Mention of local authorities was conspicuous by its absence. However, the strategy was consistent with the announcement made the previous year by the secretary of state, Ian Sproat, that he wanted 'local authorities to concentrate on recreation and leisure and the Sports Council to concentrate on performance and excellence' (House of Commons debates 11 July 1994, Vol. 246 cc650–1). The terminology 'performance and excellence' was a clear reference to the sport development continuum, but his use of the phrase 'recreation and leisure' rather than 'participation' also indicated a rejection of (or at least a refusal to endorse) the fundamental assumption of the continuum that the four levels were interdependent. It would have been much more difficult to justify the exclusion of local authorities and the fostering of community participation from the national strategy if the secretary of state had acknowledged that there was a structural relationship between participation sport and performance sport. However, the assumption of interconnectedness and interdependence of levels within the continuum was always vulnerable to challenge and was certainly exaggerated. Even a cursory examination of the admittedly rudimentary talent identification processes of the early 1990s would have made it clear that a large participation base and the local authority facilities that support it were becoming progressively less significant. Apart from swimming, which relied very heavily (and still does) on public facilities, most other sports were rapidly moving to the use of more specialist facilities and talent development processes which involved removing potential elite sportsmen and women from the participation level and placing them in development squads.

Sport: Raising the Game was significant primarily because it set a general direction of policy which was still evident in early coalition government policy. The central priority given to elite sport success was reinforced by the Labour governments of Blair and Brown and has been endorsed by the coalition minister for sport, Hugh Robertson. Running parallel to the priority given to elite sport was the support for school sport, although here there is generally less consistency regarding the precise objectives for school sport with, at various times, the primary emphasis being given to: increasing participation in sport and physical activities; using sport to generate 'whole school' benefits such as improved attendance, behaviour and educational achievement; and fostering competitive sport and facilitating talent identification. Although funding for School Sport Partnerships was severely cut by the coalition government, it has emphasised its continuing support for the promotion of competitive sport in schools. These two central and consistent priorities were supported and reinforced by the steady development of a specialist organisational infrastructure with an associated network of stakeholders. With regard to elite sport, the development of the specialist network of facilities and support services under the aegis of the English Institute of Sport was supported by a cluster of interests including UK Sport, the British Olympic Association, the major Olympic NGBs and most of the media, forming the basis for what was to prove to be an effective advocacy coalition. The central organisational interest in relation to school sport was the Youth Sport Trust, which was supported by a slightly less coherent, but nonetheless reasonably effective, cluster of interests that included some NGBs and a number of politicians.

Apart from the acceleration given to the development of specialist clusters of interests around elite sport and school sport, the other notable feature of the period of Conservative government was the uncertainty about what the 'participation' level of the continuum meant in terms of programmes and objectives, how, if at all, it related to performance and excellence, and which organisations were responsible for delivery. In the early 1990s the Sports Council published a policy statement which endorsed the sport development continuum and argued strongly for the interconnection between levels, stating that 'whatever stage in the continuum a person may be, he or she should be able to find a structure of provision to meet their needs and aspirations. This implies the existence and nurturing of an integrated system of private, voluntary and public facilities and support services' (Sports Council 1991). The next 20 years were to witness the scope of 'participation' or community sport at times widening (to include forms of sports-related or even non-sport physical activity) and at other times narrowing (to focus on competitive sport) and the government, or its agent Sport England, alternating between seeking and rejecting partnership with local authorities. Not surprisingly, the recent history of participation/community sport is one of frustration (on the part of local authorities) and absence of direction. A key decision by the government which had a long-term impact on community sport was the removal of responsibility for sport from the Department of the Environment (which had overall responsibility for local government) and its transfer to the Department for Education and Science (which largely ignored it) and then to the Department of National Heritage, which had only weak links with local government and little leverage within local authorities. Thus, while it was evident that the mid-1990s marked the beginning of a period of consolidation and ambitious development in relation to elite and youth/school sport, it also marked the beginning of a period of steady decline and marginalisation for community sport.

In many respects the publication of *Sport: Raising the Game* was a landmark in two important senses. As mentioned previously, it marked the beginning of a period of sustained public-sector investment in elite and school sport and it also marked the undermining of the work accomplished by the GB Sports Council in building links with local authorities and encouraging them to take more interest in sport services. As Collins makes clear, the experimental Action Sport programme of the 1980s, which involved partnerships with local authorities, was largely successful not only in terms of its specific objectives, but more generally in building momentum within local authorities to support the appointment of sport development officers (SDOs). 'In policy terms, within months [the Action Sport programme] was an unqualified success . . . it had been taken up by other local authorities across the country and soon there were over 300 SDOs' (Collins 2010, p. 15). Although popular with local authorities and successful in raising the profile of sports initiatives at local level, Action Sport also drew attention to what was to become a persistent weakness in local authority-based sport development: First, as noted by the Sports Council, was the tendency for projects to 'drift . . . from initial objectives, with non-sporting objectives being allocated a higher priority' (Sports Council 1991, p. 31, quoted in Collins 2010); and second, for local authorities to assume that sports initiatives brought funding with them, thus obviating the need for sport development to have a call on mainstream authority budgets.

NEW LABOUR AND SPORT

There is significant continuity between the policies outlined in *Sport: Raising the Game* and the policy of the Labour government elected in 1997 and expressed in its strategy document, *A Sporting Future for All*, published in 2000. The Labour government adopted a number of the programmes introduced by the outgoing Conservative government, such as specialist sports colleges, and added considerable momentum to improving sports opportunities for young people at school. The strategy contained five elements related to school sport: first, using lottery and Exchequer funding to rebuild school sport facilities; second, accelerating the establishment of specialist sport colleges in order to have 110 designated by the end of 2003; third, providing funding to support the expansion of after-school sport; fourth, appointing 600 school sport co-ordinators who would facilitate after school sport and especially inter-school competitive sport; and fifth, providing coaching support for talented young athletes.

As regards high-performance or elite-level sport, there was also a high degree of continuity in relation to ends, but importantly the beginnings of a significant divergence in relation to means to achieve those ends. Adopting the Conservative government's proposal to establish a national elite performance centre, the Labour government committed lottery funding for a network of centres known collectively as the UK Sports Institute. Although the Conservative government acknowledged that achieving elite success required substantial investment of public money, it was reluctant to use Exchequer resources, preferring to rely on the newly introduced National Lottery. Labour adopted a similar funding strategy but in subsequent years, especially after the award of the Olympic and Paralympic Games to London, proved to be more willing to use taxpayers' money.

Where there was a degree of discontinuity between the Labour government and its predecessor was in relation to community sport (see Table 5.1). Not only did Labour revise the guidelines for the distribution of national lottery funding in order to channel a greater proportion of funds to areas of relative disadvantage, but in *A Sporting Future for All* it provided a fuller discussion of the government's objectives in relation to participation. The 1998 National Lottery Act resulted in two important changes to the use of lottery funding. First, the act gave the sports lottery distribution board the power to solicit applications for funding thus enabling Sport England to adopt a more strategic approach to the development of sport opportunities by approaching local authorities and sports clubs in areas of under-provision and inviting bids for funding. The second change was the production of a lottery distribution strategy by Sport England which prioritised community sport projects and ring-fenced £12.5m for revenue projects in areas of deprivation which were designed to address 'social exclusion or . . . under representation in sport participation' and to produce benefits for 'ethnic communities, disabled people, women and those on low incomes' (Sport England 1999a, p. 41). While the strategy was politically astute insofar as it echoed the social inclusion priorities of the new government, there was an inevitable dilution of sporting objectives. Thus, although reference was made to enhancing the role of sports development officers and the need to fund the improvement of local facilities, the objectives were framed by a series of welfare, rather than purely sporting, objectives. Consistent with the government's concern with social inclusion, investment in community participation was intended to 'reduce, over the next ten years, the unfairness in access to sport' (DCMS 2000, p. 11).

What was clear from an analysis of the content of *A Sporting Future for All* was that while sport had, to some degree at least, consolidated its higher position on the government agenda it was viewed in a much more instrumental fashion by Labour than by the previous Conservative government. Prior to the publication of the strategy the then minister for sport, Tony Banks, told the 1998 Central Council of Physical Recreation (CCPR) conference that the strategy would focus on five themes: improving health; access; lifelong learning through sport; higher achievement through sporting competition; and a maximisation of the wealth-creating capacity of sport. These five themes reflected the policy core beliefs of the incoming government, especially its concern to see the delivery of greater social inclusion as a priority across all government departments. This commitment was also reflected in the establishment of 18 Policy Action Teams, one of which examined sport and the arts (DCMS 1999), to support the Social Exclusion Unit's objective 'to develop integrated and sustainable approaches to the problems of the worst housing estates, including crime, drugs, unemployment, community breakdown and bad schools et cetera' (Tony Blair, quoted in Social Exclusion Unit/CMAP 2002).

Table 5.1   Continuity and Change: From the Conservative Government of John Major to the Coalition Government of David Cameron, 1995–2012

Policy area	Conservative government of John Major (November 1990 to May 1997). Sport: Raising the Game published in 1995	Labour government (May 1997 to May 2010)	Coalition government (Conservative party with the Liberal Democrat party) (May 2010–2012)
Excellence	Proposed a British Academy of Sport underpinned by the introduction of the National Lottery	Established the UK Sports Institute—a network of nineteen sites.	Funding for the English Institute of Sport guaranteed up to 2012.
	Revenue funding for athletes (World Class Performance)	Revenue funding for athletes continued and increased by Labour	Continued by the coalition government at least until 2012
	Talent identification programme planning encouraged	Continued by Labour through UK Sport. Long Term Athlete Development programme adopted by many sports with encouragement of UK Sport; in preparation for the 2012 Olympic Games, UK Sport introduced a number talent transfer initiatives	Support for talent identification/transfer initiatives from the coalition government
	Pledged to bring major sports events to UK	Similar pledge	Similar commitment to an ambitious hosting strategy
Community Sport	Concern with raising adult/community sport participation gradually dropped by Conservative government in preference for a policy of targeting, usually socially problematic groups, especially urban adolescents and the young	Central policy at 1997 election within the context of the broader concern with social inclusion. Tended to lose its central position in sport policy (and in broader government policy) as problems of making progress became more apparent	Sport England targets for increased adult participation set under the previous government dropped. New DCMS strategy 'Creating a sporting habit for life: A new youth sport strategy' targeting 14- to 25-year-olds rather than whole adult population on the basis that developing a lifetime commitment to sport participation involves complex behavioural change and may take a generation to introduce. NGBs still the preferred partners for the implementation of the new strategy
Funding	Introduced the National Lottery, but continued to squeeze local authority spending	Lottery funding still crucial to funding of school and elite sport initiatives, but little sign of an increase in local authority spending	Allocation of lottery fudning between 'good causes' to be amended to increase the proportion going to sport

The degree to which sport policy objectives were being set outside the subsector was made clear by the dismissive attitude of the government to the efforts of the English Sports Council (later Sport England) to develop a policy trajectory for sport. In its strategy document, *England, the Sporting Nation: A Strategy*, the English Sports Council (1997) identified four objectives focused on the development of skills and competence for sport, a lifestyle which included active participation in sport, personal achievement in sport and the development of excellence and success in sport at the highest level (English Sports Council 1997, p. 4). However, as Houlihan and White (2002, p. 101) noted, the minister (Kate Hoey) perceived the publication of the strategy as an attempt to pre-empt government policy decisions and 'sought to rein in the organisation'. As a result, the strategy was quietly dropped and, on its publication in May 2000, *A Sporting Future for All* became the reference document for the work of Sport England. The relationship between Sport England and the government is aptly summarised in the conclusions of the quinquennial review[1] 'the strategic planning process appears to start with DCMS objectives rather than objectives for the development of sport—this dominates Sport England's strategic planning processes . . . Efforts to join up government can sometimes leave Sport England vulnerable to short term shifts in priority, rather than setting course on long term goals, driven by the needs of sport' (2001, p. 23). As will become clear, much the same statement could be made today.

The explicit shift towards welfare instrumentalism had a significant impact not only on the work of Sport England but also on that of local authorities. The Sport England Lottery Board used its control of financial resources to ensure the greater prioritisation of areas of social deprivation which were, however, also generally areas of low sports participation. The Priority Areas Initiative (PAI) and Sports Action Zones (SAZ) were typical of the range of welfare-related sports policy programmes introduced at the time. The Priority Areas Initiative was intended to ensure that a greater proportion of capital funding for sport facilities was directed to the 100 most deprived local authorities. However, it was only a limited success as, even though grants of up to 90 per cent were available, finding the remaining 10 per cent was all too often out of the reach of the clubs in poorer areas or with a set of members with lower incomes. Moreover, local authorities were also wary of the PAI due to a concern with the likely continuing revenue obligations. The lack of enthusiasm for the PAI led to its replacement in 2000 with Sports Action Zones, which were not only more sharply concentrated on areas of low participation and social disadvantage but were also designed to provide revenue support rather than fund capital projects. This incremental, but nonetheless significant, modification to the PAI furthered Sport England's contribution to the achievement of greater social inclusion, but also heightened the emerging tension between the pursuit of welfare goals and the pursuit of increases in sport participation. As Sport England pointedly noted in a press release which accompanied the announcement of the first round of zones, it was acknowledged that they could help to 'allevi-ate some of the effects of poverty and deprivation', but the government was also reminded that 'Sport England is a sport development agency' and that its primary concern was to increase sport participation (Sport England, press release, 17 January 2000).

Evaluation of the Sports Action Zone programme was broadly posi-tive, but they were nonetheless replaced by Community Sport Partnerships (CSPs), the first of which were introduced in 2003 (Mackintosh 2011). The evaluation emphasised the importance of policy continuity in underpin-ning success in delivering increased sport participation in the twelve SAZs, all of which were in socioeconomically disadvantaged communities. More importantly, the report stressed the centrality of ensuring that any national initiatives were firmly integrated with the infrastructure of local sports clubs, schools and local authority facilities in a particular area or what was increasingly referred to as the local delivery system (Sport England 2006b). The report also noted the importance of working with 'wider partners beyond sport', of ' "bending" existing local authority and other partnership mainstream funding rather than . . . [relying on] its own funding' and of taking 'a medium to long term view about the length of time this approach will take to generate impact' (Sport England 2006b, p. 5).

The use of Sports Action Zones and their replacement with County Sport Partnerships provide evidence of a process of incremental policy change and a degree of policy learning. However, the transition from Priority Area Initiatives, via SAZs, to County Sport Partnerships also highlights the extent to which local authorities were becoming marginal to policy development on community sport. Despite repeated indications from ministers that community sport was the proper responsibility of sub-national government, most local authorities appeared content to rely on Sport England initiatives (and funding) and also content to cede policy leadership to Sport England.

However, during the 2000s the opportunity for policy leadership by Sport England was highly constrained and the extent to which the organisation had become marginal to community sport policymaking was illustrated by the process by which the government produced its policy document, *Game Plan: A Strategy for Delivering Government's Sport and Physical Activity Objectives*, and also by its content. As regards the policy process, rather than give the responsibility for strategy development to Sport England, the task was given to a group of economists within the Cabinet Office's Strat-egy Unit. As Tessa Jowell commented in her foreword to the document:

> The Strategy Unit . . . was asked to . . . challenge our thinking and help us set clear priorities. Their aim has been to refine the Govern-ment's objectives for sport and physical activity and to identify ways of improving the delivery of Government support. (DCMS/Strategy Unit 2002, p. 6)

Clearly, Sport England was not thought capable of conducting such an exercise.

GAME PLAN: A STRATEGY FOR DELIVERING THE GOVERNMENT'S SPORT AND PHYSICAL ACTIVITY OBJECTIVES

Game Plan was a curious document. First, for a strategy document produced by economists, it was an odd mix of a rigorous interrogation of evidence and uncritical flights of fancy. Expressing dismay at the weakness of evidence to support some of the claimed social benefits of sport, the document noted that it was only in relation to the health benefits of sports participation that acceptably robust data were available. However, these economists' rigour deserted them when it came to evaluating the evidence in favour of funding elite sport as the authors waxed lyrical about the 'feel-good' factor generated by elite athlete success:

> We conclude that government should set itself two overarching objectives [one of which is to achieve] a sustainable improvement in success in international competition, particularly in the sports which matter most to the public, primarily because of the 'feelgood factor' associated with winning. (DCMS/Strategy Unit 2002, p. 12)

Despite the curious lack of rigour in justifying the pursuit of medal success, the document strongly reinforced the policy path set so clearly by John Major. Where *Game Plan* differed from the policy of the previous Conservative government was in the emphasis given to the importance of increasing participation. However, the emphasis was on participation as a vehicle for achieving greater social inclusion. As the then Minister for Sport Richard Caborn observed, in his speech to the 2003 Central Council of Physical Recreation's annual conference, the government would 'not accept simplistic assertions that sport is good as sufficient reason to back sport' (CCPR 2008, p. 4). To reinforce this view the phrase 'social inclusion' was repeated on numerous occasions throughout *Game Plan*. The document was significant not only for its definition of sport as primarily a tool of social engineering, but also, and perhaps more importantly, because it diluted the emphasis on promoting participation in sport by the addition of physical activity objectives. Given the identification of health benefits as one of the few well-established, robust and measurable outcomes of participation in sport, it should not be surprising that *Game Plan* strengthened the instrumental rationale for public investment in sport by linking it with physical activity. As one would expect from a report prepared by economists and prepared for a government for whom evidence of impact was a central requirement, *Game Plan* set a number of targets in relation to participation. Most notably it set the extremely ambitious target of 70 per cent for the proportion of the population who would undertake five 30-minute sessions of sport or exercise each week by the year 2020. As Coalter (2004, p. 94) noted, 'The ambitious nature of the Game Plan target is indicated by the fact that it will require an increase of more than 100 percent on the current levels of participation—only 30 percent of the population currently meet the Government's target for health-related physical activity levels'. Not only was this target näively optimistic, but there was little indication in the document regarding the means by which this revolutionary change in people's leisure behaviour was to be achieved.

In addition to the wildly over-ambitious participation targets, there were two other aspects of *Game Plan* which were noteworthy. First the protestations made by Sport England at the launch of the Sport Action Zones in 2000 that it was a 'sport development agency' had, by 2002, been disregarded. Sport England was firmly associated with the government's health-driven physical activity targets, a shift in focus which was evident in the title of the 2004 policy document—*The Framework for Sport in England: Making England an Active and Successful Sporting Nation, a Vision for 2020*. The framework adopted the vague definition of sport produced in the 1970s by the Council of Europe and referred to the development of a marketing strategy which gave the same priority to 'countryside-based exercise and healthy lifestyles through activity which connects with everyday life' as it did to participation in sport (Sport England 2004a, p. 20). The second noteworthy aspect of *Game Plan* was the effect it had on national governing bodies of sport who realised that the modest funds available to Sport England were to be spread even more thinly due to the incorporation of physical activity objectives.

The drift in the mission of Sport England was halted abruptly in late 2007 when Derek Mapp, the chair of Sport England for the previous 13 months, was sacked by the new minister for sport, James Purnell. According to one report:

> [Purnell] had already told Mapp in a meeting on Nov 14 that the organisation, which distributes £238 million a year to grassroots sport projects, would have to re-focus on community sports, a directive backed up in a letter on Nov 23. . . . Purnell believes the job of tackling obesity should be financed by the Department of Health. That, he says, would free up more money for sports' governing bodies to develop a world-class community sports legacy [from the] . . . the 2012 Olympics in London. (Daily Telegraph 2007)

Mapp's response to his sacking highlighted both his disagreement with the new minister and why NGBs were glad to see him go.

> When I headed up Sport England, I dared to challenge the Government: if the Lawn Tennis Association has millions of pounds in the bank from

private sponsorship, why are we using government money to bankroll them? Same story with the Football Association. Around 70 per cent of our funding went to the big four—football, cricket, rugby and tennis—whose governing bodies are focused on producing the next champion rather than facilities for the community.

Surely, I said, we should be getting more kids into boxing gymnasiums and helping new sports, like basketball, yoga and street-dance aerobics that are tremendously popular with young people? I had a survey which showed that despite a £1 billion investment in sport by Sport England over 16 years, there had been no increase in sporting participation, and that 51 per cent of the population did no sport at all. (*London Evening Standard* 2008)

The reorientation in sport policy was confirmed with the publication of *Playing to Win: A New Era for Sport* (DCMS 2008). In many respects *Playing to Win* harked back to the 1990s when part of the rationale for investment in community sport was that it formed an integral part of the sport development continuum and the implicit percolation model of talent identification and development that underpinned the continuum. No mention was made of physical activity targets and there was a greatly reduced emphasis on social inclusion. The document reflected the views the minister expressed at the CCPR conference in 2007, when he stated that 'sport matters in itself and . . . competitive sport is a good thing'. He went on to acknowledge the impact that participation in sport can have on non-sport policy objectives (related to educational achievement, youth crime and community volunteering), but stressed that:

> I am categorically sure that the purpose of Sport England is to deliver sport in England. . . . There should be a clear focus on sport development and sports participation. . . . That means creating excellent national governing bodies, clubs, coaches and volunteers, supported by the investment we've already made in facilities. And the sporting bodies in our country will be critical. My offer to them is clear. We want to create whole sports plans, with a single funding pot. We will free them up from the bureaucracy and bidding that they complain about today. But, in return, they will need to commit to clear goals to improve participation, coaching and the club structure. And in particular, they will need to show how they will reach groups who do less sport today, whether women, poorer groups or some ethnic minorities. (Purnell 2007)

Playing to Win was even more explicit in stating the objectives for Sport England. '[*Playing to Win*] is a plan to get more people taking up sport simply for the love of sport; to expand the pool of talented English sportsmen and women; and to break records, win medals and win tournaments for this country' (DCMS 2008, Preface). These objectives are laudable, but arguably incompatible, especially when the primary agents of delivery are national governing bodies of sport and their clubs which have, at best, a doubtful interest in catering for the enthusiastic, but unfit and poorly skilled mass of the population. This concern notwithstanding, NGBs were placed centre stage in the delivery of *Playing to Win* with 49 preparing Whole Sport Plans in which they committed themselves to achieving often wildly ambitious increases in participation rates. Despite some references to the important role for local authorities, they were yet again marginalised in the delivery process.

By the time of the 2010 general election, which ushered in the coalition government led by the Conservative party with the Liberal-Democrats as junior partners, the outgoing Labour government had reinforced its commitment to elite success and to promoting youth/school sport. With regard to community sport, the ambition and optimism of the early years of the Labour government, that sport could contribute significantly to the alleviation of social exclusion, had long been abandoned to be replaced by a much narrower view of sport as an instrument of health improvement and as a foundation for talent identification.

COALITION GOVERNMENT SPORT POLICY

For most political parties, entering office during the worst economic recession in two generations would seriously undermine efforts at policy innovation. However, for the coalition government the recession, unwelcome though it was, provided an external rationale for the introduction of a set of sport policies which were strongly consonant with the economic neoliberalism of the Conservative party. Cutting public expenditure, culling quangos and deregulation were easier to implement within a context of economic crisis. As outlined in Chapter 3, the Comprehensive Spending Review proposed a series of budget cuts for sport which were spread across three departments (Culture, Media and Sport, Education and Communities and Local Government). In addition, the government proposed to merge UK Sport and Sport England both to save money and to reduce the number of quangos.

As regards elite sport investment, the government was much more willing to commit future resources. For example, while Sport England's budget for programmes was scheduled to reduce by 33 per cent, that for elite athlete programmes would contract by only 15 per cent over the same period. In part this cushioning of the severity of cuts in public expenditure was possible because of changes to the range of 'good causes' funded from the National Lottery which benefited sport and especially elite sport. However, it would be politically unwise to announce cuts in the support to be given to UK athletes with the Olympic and Paralympic Games less than 18 months away. Whether the current funding commitments are maintained once the Olympic caravan has moved on to Rio de Janeiro is questionable.

In summary, the current serious financial crisis notwithstanding, the coalition government has retained a strong policy commitment to elite sport, reinforced the association between school sport and competition though with substantially reduced funding and demonstrated a lack of concern (or at least policy innovation and imagination) in relation to community sport.

COMMUNITY SPORT: A FAILURE OF POLICY OR A FAILURE OF POLICY MAKING?

The introduction of policies designed to increase participation date from the 1970s with an initial emphasis on facility provision. By the 1980s, policy had moved from facility development to targeting under-participating groups through the 15 Action Sport schemes which were considered to be a success and were consequently widely adopted by local authorities. Targeting continued into the 1980s with the funding of a series of national demonstration projects 'launched to extend the proven Action Sport methods to other groups' (Collins 2010, p. 17). The decline in the relative prioritisation of community sport began in the late 1980s with the replacement of participation targets with income targets for local authority sports facilities due to the imposition of Compulsory Competitive Tendering. The movement of community sport towards the periphery of public policy for sport was confirmed by the government of John Major in the 1990s with the publication of *Sport: Raising the Game* and only partially restored by the Labour government elected in 1997. Further restoration followed the abandonment of the ill-judged attempt to subsume sport participation within a broader physical activity agenda in 2008.

The 40 years or so of community sport policy have the following characteristics:

- Specific initiatives have tended to be short-term (three- to five-year) interventions which were often successful over the period of funding, but which often failed to leave a lasting change in participation behaviour.
- In the 1980s there was extensive appointment of sport development officers by local authorities. However, many were dependent on external funding rather than being funded from the mainstream budgets of local authorities. For many local authorities SDOs were a free resource to which they had only shallow and opportunistic commitment.
- A highly variable level of central government interest in participation.
- Shifting central government motives for involvement in community sport.

- A weak evidence base to inform policy/programme design and against which progress could be measured.

Given these characteristics, it should not be surprising that progress in raising participation levels has tended to be short-lived and localised. Indeed, an examination of long-term trends in participation suggests substantial policy failure. By almost every measure community sport initiatives have failed. However, it must be acknowledged that assessing long-term trends in participation is not easy, mainly due to the changes in the questions asked and the survey tools used. The longest time series data (from the General Household Survey [GHS]) that are available cover the period from 1987 to 2002. The introduction of the Taking Part survey in 2005 and the Active People survey also in 2005 provide more robust data sets than the General Household Survey but are very recent, thus making the identification of trends more problematic. Even with these caveats in mind there is sufficient evidence to indicate clearly the dramatic lack of success in increasing community sport participation (see Tables 5.2 and 5.3 and Figure 5.2).

The longest time series is from the GHS and paints a depressing picture of steady decline in participation since 1990. More worrying was the pattern of activity that contributed to the decline. The decline was especially noticeable among the younger age groups with participation falling from 82 per cent in 1990 to 72 per cent in 2002 among the 16–19 age group and from 72 per cent to 61 per cent among the 20–24 age group. When analysed by gender, the data showed that by 2002 men's participation had declined by eight percentage points from the high point of 58 per cent in 1990 and by two percentage points from 39 per cent for women over the same period. The only positive trends were first, that there had been a slight increase in participation among the group aged 70+ and that the gap in participation between men and women had narrowed. As the commentary to the data indicated, 'It appears that we [Sport England] have a bigger challenge than

Table 5.2   Trends in Participation in Sport (Excluding Walking) 1987 to 2002. Adults in Great Britain Aged 16+ Participating on at Least One Occasion in the Previous Four Weeks

Year	Percentage
1987	45
1990	48
1993	47
1996	46
2002	43

Source: General Household Survey.

Table 5.3   Trends in Participation in Sport 2005/6 to April 2011. Participation by Adults (16+) in England in at Least 3 30-Minute Periods of Moderate-Intensity Sport per Week

Year	Number participating
2005/06	6.296m
2006/07	n/a
2007/08	6.815m
2008/09	6.930m
2009/10	6.938m
2010/11 (April)	6.924m
2012/13 (Target)	7.815m

Source: Sport England, Active People 5, June 2011.

we thought! Our target is to increase participation by an average of 1% a year to 2020—but in the 6 years between 1996 and 2002 it has declined by an average of 0.5% a year' (Sport England 2004c, p. 6).

The data presented in Table 5.3 from the Active People survey is not directly comparable to the GHS data, but it does not suggest a radically different set of conclusions. The initial increase in participation from 2005/06 to 2009/10 was modest and appears to have stalled. As a report from the

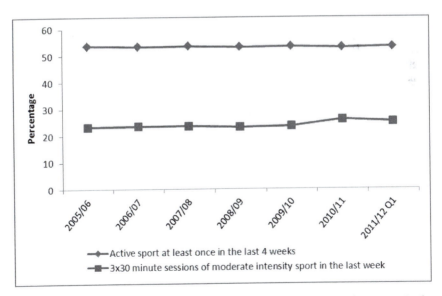

Figure 5.2   Percentage of adults who have participated in sports at least once in the last 4 weeks and at least 3 30-minute sessions of moderate intensity in the last week, 2005/06 to July 2010–June 2011.

Centre for Social Justice noted: 'In the two years since the baseline survey (Active People 2), the total number of adults in England participating in the desired level of sport has increased by just 123,000. This is just 30% of Sport England's targets, which anticipate an increase of 200,000 over each of the next five years' (Centre for Social Justice 2011, p. 44). The report also noted that between 2008 and 2010 the £75m that had been invested in the five major English sport NGBs (cricket, rugby union and league, tennis and football) had produced a decrease in participation of around 200,000. The overall lack of progress is confirmed by the data from the Taking Part survey, which recorded participation on two scales (once in the previous four weeks and three times of at least 30 minutes' duration in one week). While the Taking Part data do not show a decline, there is no evidence of an increase in participation.

In the four years between 2009 and 2013 Sport England invested £450m in the 49 NGBs which were pivotal to its strategy for increased participation. However, in the Active People report published in June 2011 only four NGBs, for athletics, netball, mountaineering and table tennis, had recorded a statistically significant increase in participation: whereas 17 sports, including swimming and football, recorded a statistically significant decrease in participation. In response to these disappointing figures Sport England reduced the grant allocation to some of the failing sports (for example, rugby league lost just under £1m and golf lost just over £100,000).

It is hard to avoid the conclusion that the participation strategies of successive governments have been a failure and that the hundreds of millions of pounds of public money invested in sport have had little discernible impact on the country's sedentary lifestyle. It is a damning indictment of sport policymaking that the cycle of setting over-ambitious participation targets— failure to reach those targets—and then setting new, equally naïve, targets seemed to continue without a pause to reflect more deeply on the nature of the policy objectives that were being pursued and the effectiveness of the means by which they might be achieved. Consequently, rather than apportion too much blame to Sport England, the real culprits are to be found within government—in the prime minister's office, the Department of National Heritage and its successor, the Department of Culture, Media and Sport and particularly among the succession of ministers who led these departments. Over the last 30 years community sport policy has suffered from periods of neglect and disdain compounded by ministerial weakness (much of the 1980s) which resulted in policy drift, periods of intense prime ministerial and ministerial enthusiasm (for elite and youth sport and less so for community sport) with consequent relative marginalisation of community sport (much of the 1990s and 2000s). Periods of attention and policy review focused mainly on the utilisation of sport for the achievement of non-sport policy objectives such as social control, health improvement or social inclusion (early 1980s and much of the late 1990s and early 2000s). The inconsistency of policy emphasis is compounded by a staggeringly naïve view of how behavioural change associated with increased sport participation might be achieved. After 30 years of policy failure, ministers still perceive sport as magic dust which has only to be sprinkled around in the form of sporting heroes, mega-sports events, six-week taster sessions for children, and Olympic and Paralympic medals, for example, and people will turn off their televisions and join their local sports club. Achieving a lasting increase in sport participation among the general population is comparable to attempts to reduce smoking, encourage healthy eating, and encourage moderate use of alcohol. While progress in each of these three areas has been slow and uneven, governments have, in general, recognised the complexity of the challenge and the need for perseverance and a long-term commitment. Public authorities have generally also acknowledged that a range of policy instruments (sanctions, information and inducements) need to be deployed in order to effect change. Furthermore, public authorities have, if only slowly, accepted that policy design will be more successful if underpinned by a theory of behavioural change (see Biddle and Foster 2011 for a review of the evidence in relation to physical activity policy). In relation to the promotion of participation in sport acknowledgement of complexity, the need for a long-term strategy, sustained application of a range of policy instruments and an underpinning theory of behavioural change are conspicuous by their absence.

ELITE SPORT: EXPLAINING POLICY SUCCESS

The contrast between the history and impact of community sport policy and elite sport policy is stark. Since the mid to late 1990s, when government intervention in relation to elite sport began in earnest, there has been a steady improvement in performance in the summer Olympic and Paralympic sports and particularly at the Olympic and Paralympic Games themselves (see Table 5.4).

Table 5.4   UK Performance at the Olympic Games 1992 to 2008

Year	Gold medals	Silver medals	Bronze medals	Total	Position in the medals table
1992	5	3	12	20	13th
1996	1	8	6	15	36th
2000	11	10	7	28	10th
2004	9	9	13	31	10th
2008	19	13	15	47	4th

The improvement in performance since 1992 or 1996 is clear and might indicate that there were lessons that community sport could learn. However, a comparison between the two policy sectors needs to take account of the contrasts not simply in outcome, but also in the nature of the problem to be solved, the resources invested and the extent, continuity and quality of political support. The complexity surrounding community sport in terms of specification of objectives (how much participation, what type of participation and for how many people) contrasts with the relative simplicity of the elite sport objectives (fourth in the Olympic medals table and second in the Paralympic medals table as a target for 2012). The lack of specialist research centres for community sport contrasts with the network of elite institutes of sport and the wider network of university sports science departments focused on aspects of elite sport performance. The erratic funding and general under-funding of community sport (not a statutory service in local authorities and the erosion of the share of lottery funding going to community sport) is contrasted with the substantial funding for elite sport (see Table 5.5). The poor quality and inconsistent ministerial leadership in relation to Sport England and community sport (regular changes in policy direction and in funding and administrative arrangements) contrasts with the strong and consistent support given to UK Sport. In short, it would be a devastating indictment of UK Sport if it had failed to deliver its objectives given the strongly positive environment in which it was operating.

Since the mid-1990s there has been continuity of political support and consistency of policy augmented by regular policy refinement. The publication of *Sport: Raising the Game* (DNH 1995) set the policy direction and, through the introduction of the National Lottery, provided the central resource for effective delivery. The publication of the policy document was followed two years later by the establishment of UK Sport, the first of a number of specialist organisations responsible for delivering success. The establishment in 1999 of the network of high-performance centres, known collectively as the UK Sports Institute, enabled the concentration of scarce coaching, medical, lifestyle and sport science resources required for

Table 5.5   Funding (Estimates) and Olympic Medal Success 1992–2008

Olympic Games	Funding for elite sport	Cost per gold medal	Cost per medal
Barcelona 1992	£62m	£12.4m	£3.1m
Atlanta 1996	£67.4m	£67.4m	£4.5m
Sydney 2000	£171.7m	£15.6m	£6.1m
Athens 2004	£166.6m	£18.5m	£5.3m
Beijing 2008	£394m	£20.7m	£8.4m

Source: Zheng 2011.

Olympic and Paralympic success. By the early 2000s and the publication of *Game Plan,* the prioritisation of elite sport success was so securely established that Bergsgard et al. were able to note that '*Game Plan* does not discuss . . . *whether* international success should be pursued, it only discusses *how* it should be pursued' (2007, p. 164, emphasis in the original).

While continuity of objectives distinguishes elite sport policy from community sport policy, the means adopted to achieve elite sport objectives also provide an instructive contrast with community sport. The Labour government in the early 2000s made a series of interventions in relation to elite sport which provided evidence of its commitment to elite sport policy objectives and also added momentum to the work of its partners in the delivery of those objectives. First, as discussed in more detail in Chapter 3, Labour emphasised the need for modernisation and tightened its control over UK Sport (and also Sport England) by insisting on the reform of the UK Sport governance model such that internal accountability was to a governing board selected more on the basis of their functional skills and less on the basis of their representation of sport interests. External accountability to the DCMS and to Parliament was tied more closely to formal performance targets.

The modernisation of UK Sport was cascaded down to NGBs, who were required to demonstrate that they too were fit partners in the delivery of elite objectives. National governing bodies were expected to professionalise, to organise themselves at board level in a similar way to that of their funder and to implement the same accountability regime which often resulted in a higher degree of internal organisational separation between elite performance and club development. Professionalisation was evident not only in the changing composition at board level but also in relation to internal functions such as coaching. The recognition not only of the central importance of high-quality coaching to elite success, but also the scarcity of world-class English coaches, resulted in considerable investment in attracting foreign coaches. According to Hubbard (2011) in the *Independent* newspaper, 'At least 21 of the 26 sports in which Team GB compete in London will have performance directors or senior coaches who have been expensively head-hunted . . . In all there are 52 foreigners working at various levels. Several are on six-figure salaries'. It is arguable that the re-engineering of the relationship between NGBs and UK Sport was the most significant indicator of the government's determination to ensure the achievement of elite sport objectives. Reinforcing the internal organisational differentiation within NGBs was a more rigid hypothecation of funding with far less scope for cross subsidy between youth, community and elite objectives.

The combined effect of these developments has been to compartmentalise policy. For example, the percolation model of talent identification and development which provided, in many sport, a strong link between the interests of elite sport and the activities of grassroots clubs has been eroded by the introduction of talent spotting and transfer schemes, such

Table 5.6   A Comparison of Elite and Community Sport Policy Implementation with Gunn's Ideal Typical Model of Top-Down Implementation

Gunn's conditions	Elite sport policy	Community sport policy
Circumstances external to the implementing agency do not impose crippling constraints.	The political, economic and cultural environment is generally supportive.	The political, economic and cultural environment is not hostile, but is inconsistent in its support.
Adequate time and sufficient resources are made available for each stage of the implementation process.	Considerable time pressure, but other resources (funding, expertise, political legitimacy etc) are generous.	Inadequate resources and no sense of urgency to address the issue of under-participation.
The policy to be implemented is based upon a valid theory of cause and effect.	Policy was underpinned by considerable research.	Much research at the level of data collection, but far less at the level of problem analysis, policy analysis and issues associated with behavioural change.
The relationship between cause and effect is direct with few intervening links.	Reasonably easy to insulate relationship from mediating/ environmental variables.	Extremely difficult to insulate relationship from mediating/ environmental variables.
There is a single (or very few) implementing agency(ies).	Direct relationship between UK Sport and NGBs. Clubs bypassed in many sports due to the role of development squad systems.	Direct link between Sport England and NGBs; weaker links between NGBs and their clubs; variable links between County Sport Partnerships and local authorities.
There is complete understanding of, and agreement upon, the objectives to be achieved throughout the implementation process.	Yes, clear public statement of objectives in relation to the Olympic and Paralympic Games since the 2000 Games.	No. While current Sport England policy is clear, there is a lack of agreement throughout the implementation chain especially among schools and local authorities. More importantly there is a lack of confidence in the stability of policy objectives.
In making progress towards the policy objectives, the tasks to be performed by each implementing agent can be specified in complete detail.	Specification of responsibilities is reasonably clear.	Considerable ambiguity of organisational responsibility.
There is perfect communication between implementing agents.	Communication is generally effective and the messages tend to be consistent.	Communication is reasonably effective.
Those in authority can demand and will receive perfect obedience.	The slogan 'no compromise' indicates UK Sport's ambitions to be authoritative, but compliance is as much the product of substantial resource dependency by NGBs on public and lottery funding as it is on respect for the authority of UK Sport.	Such compliance as exists is often the result of coincidence of objectives between organisations and resource dependence.

as Girls4Gold and Pitch2Podium, which fast-track talented athletes to elite development squads. Such schemes can only reinforce the perception of self-sufficiency at the elite level and undermine the interdependence between elite and community sport interests and replace it with a culture of self-interest and self-absorption. Over the longer term there is a risk that the increased reliance on talent identification systems that bypass the club structure and the importation of elite level coaches will weaken the capacity of sports clubs to fulfil non-elite competition and lower level participation objectives (for a fuller discussion see Houlihan et al. 2012).

CONCLUSION

It is not hard to see why elite sport policy has been so successful. If one were to compare the arrangements for elite sport policy implementation with the ideal type of top-down implementation devised by Gunn (1978), the contrast between elite and community sport policy implementation is stark (Table 5.6).

Some of the explanation for the lack of progress in addressing the issue of low levels of participation are indicated in Table 5.6. Of particular importance are the inconsistency of political support, the complexity of the problem and the ambiguity regarding responsibility for delivery. The problem of inconsistency of support is not just a consequence of the limited attention span of ministers and their preference for addressing problems which are more likely to show an improvement in the short term, but also as a consequence of the lack of an effective lobby on behalf of community sport. It is all too easy for ministers to let community sport issues drift while they focus their attention on the next Olympic and Paralympic Games or the next major sports event that the UK is bidding for. It is only when participation targets receive the same public, political and media attention as do elite level targets that community sport will move from the periphery of the government's vision.

6   The Forgotten Partner
Local Government

Given the scale of its involvement in sport, the significance of local government to sport policy should be difficult to overlook. Local government spending represents just over two-thirds of the total public funding for sport in England corresponding, in 2005, to an approximate £1.4bn annual spend on facilities and other services (Carter 2005a). A survey conducted in 1999 by Sport England (1999b, cited in Audit Commission 2002) estimated that over 80 million visits were made annually to the 1,600 indoor and outdoor sport facilities owned or operated by local authorities in England.

It was the major programme of building sport facilities in the 1970s that largely established the role of local authorities in the provision of sporting opportunities (Roberts 2004). As well as owning and operating facilities, local authorities also provide funding and other forms of support for other local sporting organisations, including voluntary clubs. Since the early 1990s, local authorities have also employed an increasing number of sports development officers whose varied roles have included the operation of sport programmes and outreach work within communities. Increasingly, local authorities have also had a role in planning for the overall provision of sport across their geographical localities (Robinson 2004).

The scope of the different sport services provided by local authorities is, therefore, very broad (Torkildsen 2005). There is significant variation as to the specific services provided and the level of expenditure across different local authorities (Audit Commission 2002). To an extent, this level of variation is the result of the status of sport as a discretionary service for local authorities in England and Wales. Even in Scotland and Northern Ireland, where local authorities have a greater duty of provision, variation remains due to the lack of clarity as to precisely what this legal duty entails. Provision in England, which is the main focus of this chapter, is further complicated by the different structures of local government, which comprises both two-tier arrangements (including county and district councils) in some areas as well as single-tier unitary and metropolitan local authorities in other areas.

The approach taken in this chapter will be to examine sport policy as it relates to local government alongside the more general changes in local government policy, practices and structures throughout the period covered in this study. While the influence of these broader changes on sport within local government will be considered and demonstrated, it should be borne in mind that sport is a somewhat unusual local government service (being one that can potentially generate income) (Robinson 2004) as well as one that occupies a very small proportion of overall local government spending (Audit Commission 2006). Nevertheless, a useful structure for considering local government sport is provided by themes identifiable within local government policy more generally. The chapter will therefore examine in turn central-local relations, service management in local government, reform of local government structures and local government's role in leading and 'joining up' service provision.

NATIONAL POLICY AND CENTRAL-LOCAL RELATIONS

Despite John Major lacking the personal antipathy that Margaret Thatcher displayed towards local government, the policies enacted by his government broadly represented a continuation of those of the preceding Conservative administrations (Young 1994b). Central to these policies was the underpinning belief that local government was inefficient (Sullivan 2004) and, as such, Loughlin (1996, p. 417, cited in Wilson 2003) commented that

> the basic thrust of the (Conservative) government's programme seems to deny that local authorities should any longer be treated as institutions of governance; they seem now to be treated merely as agencies for delivering centrally-determined policies.

While the Major government developed new policies that sought to alter the structure and management of local government, the primary tool by which control of local authorities was exercised continued to be measures that limited local authority income and expenditure (Stewart and Stoker 1995a). The introduction of Compulsory Competitive Tendering and the Council Tax were two exemplar measures aimed at controlling local authority expenditure (Young 1994b; Entwhistle and Laffin 2005). Controls on income meant that local authorities also became progressively more dependent on central funding, which was, through newly enacted bidding processes and other conditions, increasingly directed towards specified services (Wilson and Game 1994; Stewart and Stoker 1995a).

These broader policies undoubtedly impacted on local authority sport. CCT was extended to almost all leisure and recreation services in 1992 and Henry (2001) indicated that leisure budgets came under particular pressure during the period of the Major government. Moreover, despite the publication of *Sport: Raising the Game* (DNH 1995), significantly increasing the overall policy profile of sport, mention of local government in this document was conspicuous by its absence. For Houlihan and White (2002, p. 109), exclusion of local government from *Sport: Raising the Game* 'represented a triumph of prejudice over the realities of sports provision' especially in relation to opportunities for community participation. However, it could also be suggested that the lack of national policy prescription enabled individual local authorities a degree of freedom to determine their own policy priorities. King's (2009) study of sport policy in Liverpool offers a case in point. Within a Labour-dominated council characterised by resistance to central government intervention, local sport policy was driven by the lead officer for sport, who had 'relative freedom' to prioritise performance sport in a number specific sports (King 2009, p. 243).

The replacement of the Major government in 1997 saw a dramatic change in national policy towards local government (Stoker 2004), which found itself at the forefront of the New Labour government's programme of modernisation. A specific white paper on local government modernisation, *Modern Local Government: In Touch with the People* (DETR 1998a), was published early in the first term of the New Labour government. Subsequent Local Government Acts affecting England and Wales were passed in 2000 and 2001 with a second white paper published in 2001 (DLTR 2001). Similar legislation was enacted in Scotland and Northern Ireland (Martin 2002). Together these policies formed the basis of what was known as the Local Government Modernisation Agenda (LGMA), which was considered by Bovaird and Martin (2003, p. 18), among others, to be 'a particularly ambitious and potentially far reaching programme of reforms'.

This is not to say that the reforms that collectively formed the LGMA were necessarily coherent or consistent over time. In fact, Stoker (2004, p. 78) contended that 'the [modernisation] message to local government has been more muddled and mixed than in other policy sectors', a view that Cowell and Martin (2003) suggested was widely shared within local government itself. The main themes identified within the LGMA by prominent authors (Stoker 2004; Downe and Martin 2006) provide the structure of this chapter's subsequent sessions. A further recognised element of the LGMA, that of democratic renewal, had limited impact on local authority sport and, in fact, lost prominence as the Labour government focused increasingly over time on community leadership and improving local public services (Prachett 2002).

In pursuing the LGMA, the Labour government did set out to improve relationships between central and local government. Striking a particularly positive note, Midwinter (2001, p. 311) commented that 'after nearly twenty years of conflict between central and local government, Labour's election victory heralded the prospect of a return to a more consensual mode of relations'. Whereas previous Conservative governments were highly prescriptive and directive in their use of legislation and financial controls, the Labour government utilised a broader range of strategies in promoting the LGMA (Geddes 2006). In part, there was a stronger emphasis on 'persuasion and exhortation' (Martin 2000, p. 213) as central government recognised the need for a constructive relationship in order to achieve its broader policy goals through local authorities (Lowndes and Wilson 2003). Conversely, central powers of regulation, inspection and intervention were strengthened, reflecting a lack of trust in some local authorities on the part of the Labour government (Wilson 2003; Stoker 2004). The metaphor of 'carrots and semtex' was widely used to characterise this dual approach, with many authors believing the latter to be the more dominant (Lowndes and Wilson 2003; Laffin 2008).

Linked to the 'carrots and semtex' dichotomy, two further aspects of generic central-local relations are noteworthy. Firstly, in terms of finance, Stoker (2004) noted a 'cautious' improvement in overall local government spending. On the other hand, and at much the same time, Wilson (2003, p. 336) observed that 'local authority dependence on central government finance has never been greater than it is today'. A trend that was especially evident was that the funds provided by central government for specified services increased from 4.5 per cent of local government funding in 1997/98 to 11.1 per cent in 2004/05 (Downe and Martin 2006). Secondly, a particularly distinctive element of the LGMA was the differentiation in central government responses to individual local authorities (Martin 2002). Greater freedoms and autonomy were available to local authorities that demonstrated progress in the delivery of public service priorities. Conversely, those authorities that were deemed to be 'underperforming' were subject to increased central intervention that, for example, enforced the outsourcing of particular services to external contractors or other organisations that were beyond the direct control of the local authority (Prachett and Leach 2003; Stoker and Wilson 2004a). Stoker (2004) referred to the overall approach to local government as 'steering centralism', terminology which differs from the Labour government's own descriptors of 'earned autonomy' or 'constrained discretion'.

In reflecting on the impact of LGMA on local government, it could be suggested that Stoker's (2004) terminology is more apt. Cowell and Martin (2003) indicated that even supportive local authorities were unhappy with what they perceived as central government 'initiativeitis' and, more generally, Downe and Martin (2006, p. 471) found that 'many councils have struggled to keep pace with the rate of change or to make sense of the multiple, often competing demands that have been placed on them'. That policies and programmes emanated from a variety of central government departments only added to the difficulties faced by local authorities (Cowell and Martin 2003). Despite recognising these issues, Laffin (2008) identified that local authorities were 'largely passive' in their overall response to the LGMA, perhaps because they lacked resources for more active resistance (Llewlyn 2001). Moreover, in contrast to previous Conservative governments, relations between central and local government were not necessarily dependent on matching party political allegiances, as the positive relations between Conservative Kent and the Labour government demonstrate (Stoker and Wilson 2004b).

Similar to the boarder LGMA, there were changes over time in the prominence and position of local authorities in national sport policy. It was certainly the case that, in contrast to *Sport: Raising the Game*, the status of local authorities as being a major financial contributor to sport was subsequently recognised in national sport policies (e.g. DCMS/Strategy Unit 2002; DCMS 2008). Especially in the first two terms of the Labour government, local authorities were identified as a central component of attempts to use sport to deliver broader policy objectives. For example, *A Sporting Future for All* (DCMS 2000, p. 39) encouraged local authorities to 'place sport, along with the other cultural services, at the heart of councils' corporate objectives and as a central part of the lives of their communities'. Subsequently, the emphasis on the place of sport in local authorities' community planning was reiterated by both the government (DCMS/Strategy Unit 2002) and Sport England (2004a) in *Game Plan* and the *Framework for Sport in England*, respectively.

It was in relation to local authorities' role in delivering sporting, rather than broader social, objectives that changes in national sport policy were more apparent and influential. Again, early policy documents supported a significant role for local government and Houlihan and White (2002, p. 109) noted that *A Sporting Future for All* 'acknowledged that local authorities had a role to play across all elements of the sports development continuum'. Perhaps initial indications of a less supportive stance can be identified in the *Review of National Sport Effort and Resources* undertaken by Lord Carter of Coles on the instruction of the Treasury and DCMS. Carter (2005a) was critical of the lack of alignment between central and local policy for sport, identified a lowering of the priority given to sport within local authorities and suggested that weaknesses in the local delivery system 'risk[ed] not achieving the key policy objective of increasing and widening the base of participation' (p. 6). Given the Labour government's lack of patience in its dealings with local government (Downe and Martin 2006), a change in national policy was perhaps inevitable and duly arrived in 2008 when James Purnell signified the changed focus of national sport policy through the publication of *Playing to Win* (DCMS 2008). Local authorities' role in responding to local needs was recognised in this policy document. However, a lack of policy clarity, inefficiency and bureaucracy were cited as reasons for installing NGBs as the key delivery agencies in community sport (DCMS 2008). This sidelining of local government was reinforced in Sport England's (2008) complementary strategy for 2008–2011 in which the priority accorded to local authorities was little more than that in *Sport: Raising the Game* more than two decades previously.

While national sport policy during the period of the Labour government was inconsistent with regard to the position of local authority sport, there was more uniform change in the underlying relations between national agencies and local authorities. Corresponding to the increased central control over local government expenditure more generally, Houlihan and White (2002) reported that Sport England's status as a distributing body for National Lottery funds 'resulted in [it taking] a more assertive and interventionist stance towards local authorities after a long period of relative quiescence'. That local authorities were 'hard pressed' to maintain an ageing stock of facilities (DCMS 2001c) at a time when their budgets for leisure were relatively static (Audit Commission 2006) only served to increase the power of Sport England. In utilising this power, Sport England began local implementation of a number of relatively uniform national initiatives, such as Active Sports, which did not necessarily complement existing local provision or needs (Houlihan and White 2002). This approach was in some contrast to the increasingly differentiated approach evidenced in the broader LGMA and the 'greater flexibility and more targeted intervention at local level' advocated by the DCMS (2001c). While it is not possible to generalise the response of local authorities to this increasing centralisation, Houlihan and White (2002, p. 162) noted that in three of their four case study authorities it was 'argued that the balance between a supportive and facilitative role [on behalf of Sport England] on the one hand, and an overly regulatory and interfering role, on the other, often swung too far to the later end of the spectrum'.

In contrast to the increasing central government control under the Labour government, the subsequent coalition government claimed to have a distinctive localism agenda offering a significant decentralisation of power and control. To this end, the Department for Communities and Local Government introduced a localism bill that gained royal assent in late 2011 which 'stripp[ed] away much of the regulatory infrastructure governing local authorities' (Lowndes and Prachett 2012, p. 27) and gave them a 'general power of competence' which allowed local authorities to become involved in any local matter that was not specifically prohibited by law. In addition, further decentralising policies were also introduced in other government departments, for example, Education and Health, although Stoker (2011) noted that the precise nature of decentralisation that was proposed differed and, perhaps conflicted, across these different policy sectors.

Nevertheless, the greatest potential constraints on decentralisation were the cuts imposed on local authorities by central government (Cox 2010; Raine 2011). In the Comprehensive Spending Review of October 2010, particularly severe cuts representing 26 per cent of central grants over four years were imposed on local government. Local authorities in deprived areas in the north and midlands of England and in inner London were subject to the highest cuts in percentage terms (Audit Commission 2011). Irrespective of the obvious impact of cuts on local authorities' capacity, Lowndes and Prachett (2012, p. 28) further suggested that central government's continuing control of 75 per cent of local government revenue meant that the coalition's localism agenda had a 'hollow feel to it'.

The impact of these coalition policies on local government sport will be commented on in the conclusion to this chapter, although this impact remains uncertain to an extent at the time of writing. Similarly, there is insufficient evidence on which to draw an overall conclusion regarding the impact of broader national trends on the actual priorities adopted in local sport policies over the whole period of this study. A large-scale but selective survey conducted by King (2011) found that many of the responding local authorities felt that national policies, especially those concerned with health, increasingly influenced local policies. However, the recognition by the Audit Commission (2002) that the discretionary nature of sport within local government contributed to significant variations in local provision and expenditure remains important. Case studies of local sport policy emphasise this diversity. In Coventry and Herefordshire, Houlihan and White (2002, p. 160) found that the national focus, at that time, of sport contributing to wider social objectives had been 'wholeheartedly embraced' even though this had required a 'fairly rapid reorientation' in the case of the former local authority. Conversely, Kent and Derbyshire County Councils retained a degree of independence in determining local sport policy even through this was recognised as a 'little quixotic' and probably unsustainable (Houlihan and White 2002, p. 116). In this regard, King's (2009) subsequent case study of Liverpool is instructive in demonstrating how the inevitable adoption of national objectives sat uneasily with a 'jealously protected' local commitment to elite sport-specific development.

SERVICE MANAGEMENT IN LOCAL AUTHORITIES

In terms of the management of local authority services, the Major government largely continued and, in terms of sport, extended the trends begun under Margaret Thatcher. In fact, Young (1994b, p. 93) suggested that Major provided an even stronger impetus towards 'promoting more effective, speedier and more business-like decision making' within local authorities. This trend was associated with the attempt to de-politicise service delivery with managers, rather than elected politicians, at the forefront of delivery (Ravenscroft 1998; Stoker 2004). These new approaches to the management of local public services, which had begun to emerge from the 1980s onwards, have been collectively and commonly referred to as new public management.

Much of the literature on sport and leisure management within local authorities in the 1990s focused on the impact of Compulsory Competitive Tendering (CCT). The extension of CCT to sport and leisure services was enacted by the Major government despite the 'comparatively limited' impact of the previous CCT requirement for the management of other local authority services to be offered for open tender (Wilson and Game 1994). In terms of sport and leisure services, Collins (1997) similarly suggested that changes in provision as a result of CCT were largely incremental. Nevertheless, it is important not to underestimate the impact of CCT on the management of local authority sport and leisure services, and this impact was only enhanced by the alignment between CCT and other central government policies such as the Citizen's Charter that was strongly championed by John Major.

Both CCT and the Citizen's Charter required local authorities to identify performance indicators and targets for services and, more generally, encouraged the development of overarching strategic plans for these services (Wilson and Game 1994; Henry 2001; Prior 1995). Previous research by both the Audit Commission (1989, cited in Houlihan 1991) and by the Centre for Leisure Research (1993, cited in Nichols 1996) was critical of the lack of strategic planning undertaken for sport and leisure by local authorities. In practice, the extent to which CCT prompted the development of strategic plans for sport and leisure is debatable. Ravenscroft (1998, p. 147) suggested that there was generally an 'agreement that CCT . . . led to a clearer specification of policy and greater attention to customer demands, as well as initial attempts by the public sector to derive comparative performance indicators', a view that was also supported by Coalter (1995). However, case study research by Collins (1997) and Nichols (1996) questioned the extent to which such strategic development was initiated across all local authorities.

A more consistent picture emerges regarding the inclusion of performance indicators within CCT contracts. The CCT legislation allowed local authorities to focus on broader welfare objectives through setting performance targets for the participation of disadvantaged groups in sport and leisure services. However, the specification of such targets was rare, particularly in Conservative councils (Coalter 1995). Instead, performance indicators related to overall throughput and efficiency of service management were more commonly adopted (Henry 2001; Nichols and Taylor 1995). As a result, Aitchison (1997, p. 97) recognised that the organisations awarded contracts to manage sport and leisure services were 'primarily concerned with increasing user numbers rather than widening the range of users or providing facilities for all sections of the community'. For some authors, this dilution of the prioritisation of social goals was more a reflection of local authorities' inability or inexperience in setting targets and contract management than a facet of the national legislation (Coalter 1995; Stevens and Green 2002). Moreover, a focus on income generation and efficiency may well have been a long-term legacy of CCT within local authorities, as Houlihan and White (2002) identified in the case of Kent.

As well as implications for strategy development and performance measurement, CCT and the Citizen's Charter both encouraged a greater customer orientation and focus on service quality within local authorities (Stoker 2004). Despite an unease regarding the depiction of the public as consumers rather than citizens (Stewart and Stoker 1995b), an increasing ethos of consumerism was particularly evident across local authority sport and leisure services (Robinson 1999). This trend was supported by many authorities specifying the need for CCT contractors to be accredited according to various quality management standards (Collins 1997). While the adoption of such standards was not prescribed in the CCT legislation, and in fact could have been construed as illegal in contract specification (Lentell 2001), it further contributed to the advance in new public management approaches to the management of local sport and leisure services.

Upon taking office, the Labour government quickly enacted the 1999 Local Government Act, which replaced CCT with the system of Best Value that exemplified this government's initial efforts to modernise local government services (Martin 2000; Henry 2001). Central to Best Value were the 'four Cs', which required local authorities to *challenge* existing approaches to the provision of services, to *compare* the performance of services with those provided by other authorities, to *consult* with the local community and other stakeholders and to use open *competition* in order to secure the most efficient and effective management of services (DETR 1998b). Overall, the Best Value approach represented a 'continuation of the search for better management of public services first launched under the Conservatives' (Stoker 2004, p. 87). However, compared to the simplistic market mechanisms espoused in CCT, Best Value represented a more pragmatic approach in terms of its flexibility in accommodating a range of different local management arrangements (Lowndes and Wilson 2003). Moreover, there was an increased focus within Best Value on the achievement of social objectives. This aspect was emphasised by both DCMS (2000) and Sport England (1999c, p. 1), who, in guidelines provided for local authorities, 'expect[ed] sport to feature strongly on the "Best Value" agenda and to be a significant player in social regeneration and community development'.

Moreover, it is also suggested that Best Value represented something of a change in terms of the role of the public in service management. In particular, the Best Value requirement for consultation with the community represented a development of the version of consumerism that was emphasised during the period of the Major government (Henry 2001). Stevens and Green (2002, p. 135) captured the possibilities of this change particularly well in their comparison of CCT and Best Value in sport and recreation services:

> The underpinning philosophy upon which Best Value is predicated appears to be based on the belief that local government is not simply about providing 'services' to 'consumers'. Instead, it is concerned with a broad notion of citizenship, which is a political, or social rather than a managerial or market concept.

For Robinson (2004) the increased consultation generated by Best Value translated into sport and recreation services becoming increasingly accountable to local communities.

Enhancing performance management with local authorities was also central to Best Value. While a focus on performance management represented continuity with CCT, a significant difference was the development of national sets of Best Value performance indicators which were designed to allow comparison between different authorities (DETR 1998b). The development of these comparable indicators was considered desirable by local authorities (Nichols and Robinson 2000, cited in Robinson and Taylor 2003) especially as they retained control over which indicators to adopt (Henry 2001). However, both the DCMS/ Strategy Unit (2002) and academics such as Robinson and Taylor (2003) did recognise the limitation that only a small subset of the national Best Value indicators were relevant for local sport and leisure services. Addressing this issue, Sport England commissioned work to develop a series of appropriate performance indicators specifically for sport and leisure centres (Robinson and Taylor 2003) which became part of their National Benchmarking Service available to local authorities. This service sat alongside the emergence of a variety of other national sport-specific and generic toolkits and awards, such as Towards an Excellent Service and Quest, which were all orientated towards enhancing quality and performance management systems in local authorities (Taylor 2011). Similar to the selection of specific Best Value performance indicators, local authorities could choose whether to utilise the National Benchmarking Service as well as the other performance management toolkits and awards available to them. Strong advocacy for their adoption was, however, provided by central government and other agencies such as Sport England. As such, the advance of performance management approaches within local government can certainly been viewed as being systematically directed by the centre.

The 'subtle mix of control and compliance elements' (Stoker 2004, p. 88) inherent in Best Value and other nationally developed performance management systems was complemented by the enhanced role given to the Audit Commission to oversee the process of Best Value reviews and conduct their own inspections of local authority services (Midwinter 2001). Audit Commission reports on sport and recreation services were largely critical. The Audit Commission's (2002) overall review of sport and recreation Best Value reports concluded that 'one-half of local authorities will still find it difficult to improve, and one-third are categorised as providing only a fair service with uncertain prospects for improvement' (p. 8). This judgement was compounded for the Audit Commission (2002, p. 8) by the 'inward looking' nature of Best Value reviews conducted by local authorities. More specific weaknesses were identified in the collection and use of performance management information (Audit Commission 2002). The long-standing nature of this criticism was subsequently reinforced by similar comments in the Audit Commission's report on *Public Sport and Recreation Services* published in 2006.

More generally, the Audit Commission were concerned by the significant variation in the approaches to Best Value reviews in different local authorities (Prachett 2002). These criticisms led to the Labour government increasingly taking the view that Best Value had been 'insufficient to achieve the change in service delivery desired' (Stoker 2004, p. 106). As a result, central government began to develop additional and alternative measures to ensure that the modernisation of local government continued apace with the advent of a system of Comprehensive Performance Assessment (CPA) initially proposed in the 2001 white paper entitled *Strong Local Leadership: Quality Public Services* (Department for Transport, Local Government and the Regions 2001). CPA was designed to overcome the fragmented approach to reviewing specific services under Best Value (Robinson 2004) through using a variety of centrally determined performance indicators to provide an overall evaluation of performance within a local authority as well as an indication as to the possibility of future improvement. As such, CPA was presented as improving co-ordination, integration and coherence in the regulation of local authorities (Lowndes and Wilson 2003). While CPA did not formally replace Best Value reviews, it did become the major driver of performance improvement for local authorities (Downe and Martin 2006), 'enshrining the principles of objective-led performance management' (Robinson 2004, p. 13).

Many commentators are agreed that the advent of CPA represented a new phase in central-local relations. Lowndes (2004) noted that the 'animating idea' of Best Value, that of encouraging locally appropriate approaches to improve services, was lost as CPA began to become the key focus of local authorities. Moreover, it was through CPA that central government increasingly came to differentiate between local authorities, awarding greater freedoms to those authorities perceived to be responding to the government's modernisation agenda while targeting those deemed to be 'failing' for greater central intervention (Entwhistle and Laffin 2005). Prachett and Leach (2003, p. 267) suggest that local authorities largely accepted CPA, albeit 'grudgingly', despite the recognition that it 'over-rules local democracy in favour of national priorities'.

Furthermore, with CPA focusing on a small number of national priorities, such as education, health and crime, the position of sport within local authorities was weakened. Certainly prior to 2005, even the government-sponsored review of sport conducted by Lord Carter of Coles (Carter 2005b, p. 22) identified that, for local authorities, 'sport and leisure services are seen as low priority as they have a small weighting within the CPA process'. A similar conclusion had previously been reached by Sport England (2004a) in its *Framework for Sport in England*. Therefore, the inclusion of 'culture' as an assessment category, alongside others such as Children and Young People and Housing, when the CPA framework was revised in 2005 was welcomed both by Carter (2005a) as well as by managers of sport services in individual local authorities (Lindsey 2008).

Associated with the introduction of CPA, Local Public Service Agreements (LPSAs) were introduced in 2001 after an initial pilot in 20 local authorities the previous year. LPSAs offered particular local authorities further resources in return for addressing 'stretch' targets decided upon jointly with central government. However, across the whole of England, LPSAs had minimal impact on sport provision with none of the 15 national targets linked to sport and leisure. Moreover, of the 254 targets determined by local authorities across the country, only ten were related to leisure (DCMS 2002). It was, therefore, the instigation in 2007 of a more comprehensive system of Local Area Agreements (LAAs) that had a greater impact than LPSAs, especially for local sport and recreation. Of the 198 performance indicators that could be selected for LAAs, two specifically related to sport. National Indicator 8 concerned adult participation in sport and active recreation and National Indicator 57 reflected the ongoing target of children and young people's participation in two hours of high quality PE and sport (see Chapter 7). Responding to the encouragement of Sport England (2008), there was widespread adoption of the first indicator on adult participation which was included in 80 out of 150 LAAs in 2009. Ultimately, responsibility for achieving these targets rested with Local Strategic Partnerships, which brought together local authorities and a range of other key local stakeholders. However, the implicit language of government sport policy documents (e.g. DCMS 2008) and research within specific local areas (Lindsey 2010b) suggested that it was local authorities that continued to play the dominant role in prioritising and delivering the adult sport target within LAAs.

While much of the emphasis for performance management was centrally driven, Lowndes and Prachett (2012) predicted that the longer term future of such approaches would be determined by the extent to which such approaches were embedded within local authorities. In line with their decentralising agenda, the incoming coalition government abolished the Audit Commission and all centrally imposed measures of local government performance, such as Comprehensive Area Agreements. For Lowndes and Prachett (2012, p. 36) this move was as much to do with 'realpolitik [as] any idealistic move towards localism' as, in the shadow of substantial cuts, the removal of nationally applied performance management approaches would make 'it difficult, if not impossible for localities to be benchmarked or compared'. In the sport sector, the continued potential for individual local authorities to draw statistics on participation in their own localities from the Active People survey meant that some national impetus for benchmarking and performance assessment remained in place. While the funding of the Active People survey by Sport England looked set to continue, it was less likely that local authorities would continue to pay for the use of other performance management toolkits, such as Towards an Excellent Service, Quest and the National Benchmarking Service, in a time of significant cutbacks to mainstream budgets.

STRUCTURAL REFORM

The place of sport within the structure of local authority services was, at best, characterised by ambiguity at the start of John Major's premiership. While there had been a 'clear move towards the creation of comprehensive leisure departments' (Houlihan 1991, p. 55), in the majority of cases responsibility for sport resided in local authority departments whose responsibilities went beyond leisure (Coalter 1995). Moreover, fragmentation of responsibility for sport amongst local government departments was also common, particularly in two-tier authorities. Central government intervention in the structures of local authority sport was limited before 1990, however, partially due to its status as a discretionary service (Houlihan 1991).

The advent of John Major's government saw a continuation, if not extension, of the desire in central government to restructure local government (Wilson and Game 1994; Stewart and Stoker 1995a). Attempts to redraw the overall map of local authorities to extend the proportion of unitary authorities were 'shambolic' in their implementation (Leach 1995). Although unitary authorities were created across Scotland and Wales, in England many county councils were successful in resisting pressure to change to a single-tier system (Stoker 2004). As such, this broader reorganisation did not significantly affect the position of sport within local authorities.

As with service management, it was CCT that had the greatest implications for the organisation of local authority sport services. CCT allowed for three alternatives for the management of local authority sport and leisure services: the continuation of in-house provision through a Direct Service Organisation (DSO); the instigation of a new external organisation often through a buyout by existing management; and management by an alternative external contractor (Henry 2001). In both rounds of tendering within local authorities, the majority of contracts went to in-house DSOs and by 1998 only about a quarter of contracts had been won by private-sector companies (Henry 2001). The lack of market competition for the management of sport and leisure services was partly due to the particularly complex nature of the service (Coalter 1995) as well as, in some cases, 'strong political and professional resistances to simply adopting any prescribed form of reorganisation' (Collins 1997, p. 215). In fact, the awarding of contracts was influenced by the political orientation of local authorities with those that were Conservative controlled, awarding more contracts to private companies (Henry 2001). Conversely, private companies won no contracts in Scotland, Wales and areas of the north of England where the Conservative party were less well represented in local government (Aitchison 1997).

Despite CCT not leading to large-scale externalisation of management responsibilities, the process led to significant change in organisational structures even within those local authorities where an in-house DSO was awarded the contract (Coalter 1995; Aitchison 1997). The management of CCT contracts was undertaken by sections or newly created departments within local authorities separated from the day-to-day operation of services, even where this was undertaken by a DSO (Henry 2001). This fragmentation of responsibilities was enhanced by the emergence of different organisational cultures with DSOs and other contracted organisations that tended to develop a financially driven ethos whilst the 'client' local authority departments struggled to retain a more socially orientated focus (Nichols 1996).

If CCT represented a policy explicitly designed to initiate organisational change within local authorities, a more varied and nuanced approach to structural reform was enacted during the period of the Labour government from 1997. In accordance with the overall relationship sought between central and local government in its first term, 'Labour believed that the effective redesign of local government institutions required the commitment of local authorities themselves' (Lowndes and Wilson 2003, p. 285). Initially, both the flagship policy of Best Value and national sport policy (DCMS/Strategy Unit 2002) encouraged local authorities to choose from a range of institutional approaches to the management of local authority sport services (Martin 2000; Prachett 2002). While the range of approaches were not dissimilar from those possible under CCT, a fundamental difference with Best Value was that decisions on organisational reform were to a greater extent made locally on pragmatic grounds rather than being influenced by central government ideology (Stevens and Green 2002). That this pragmatism was perhaps accompanied by a degree of local conservatism with respect to structural reform was consistent with the Audit Commission (2002, p. 12) report on sport and recreation services, which concluded that a 'more robust challenge to the traditional approaches to service delivery is necessary in many of the authorities inspected'. It was, therefore, somewhat contradictory that the generic CPA regime that superseded Best Value represented 'the de facto abandonment' of central government's pursuit of external management of local authority services (Downe and Martin 2006, p. 468).

Despite these inconsistencies in Labour government policies, local authorities increasingly turned to 'leisure trusts' as an alternative institutional approach to the management of their sport services. Trusts were formally created as either Industrial and Provident Societies or Companies Limited by Guarantee, meaning that they operated on a not-for-profit basis (Reid 2003). The scale of responsibilities transferred from local authorities to trusts varied, with some instigated to manage individual facilities and others taking control of sport and leisure provision across whole local authority areas. In a few notable cases, trusts expanded to manage services across different local authorities (Robinson 2004; Simmons 2008). Simmons (2004) suggests that there was no overall pattern as to where trusts were established although they were more common in London and Scotland and less so in district authorities in England (Simmons 2003).

Nevertheless, as the pace of transfers increased from a slow beginning in the 1990s, trusts became an increasingly common management arrangement (Simmons 2004). In fact, the Audit Commission (2006) reported that in the four years until 2006, the percentage of local authority sport and recreation facilities managed by trusts increased from 12 to 21 per cent, mirrored by a similar decrease in those facilities managed 'in-house' by local authorities.

A variety of factors contributed to this expansion in the number and commonality of leisure trusts. In accordance with the pragmatism underpinning Best Value, Simmons (2004, p. 160) identified that 'trusts have been a response from local government to the changing environment rather than a policy handed down from central government'. As was noted earlier in the chapter, the ongoing lack of investment had led to increasing maintenance costs for the ageing stock of local authority sport and leisure facilities (Davis Langdon Consultancy 2003). Because of their potential to gain charitable status, leisure trusts offered local authorities potential savings on non-domestic rates and VAT as well as enabling access to a range of external funding opportunities (Reid 2003). Trusts were also more attractive to local authorities than private-sector companies due to the perception that they would better preserve the social focus of sport and leisure services. (Simmons 2003). As such, Simmons (2003) identified the expansion of leisure trusts as a form of 'creative defence' on the part of local authorities, which was enhanced by the positive policy learning that emerged from some of the early leisure trusts.

Parent local authorities were also able to maintain a high level of influence over the leisure trusts that had been created. In keeping with broader governmental changes, influence was exerted in more indirect and flexible ways than either the hierarchical control of in-house provision or the contractual basis of CCT arrangements (Simmons 2008). Ultimately, the power of parent local authorities resided in their ownership of facilities managed by trusts and the significance of the revenue grants that were paid for the management services provided by trusts (Reid 2003). However, although contractual arrangements, business plans and monitoring mechanisms were in place, relationships between local authorities and trusts largely tended to be co-operative and trusting (Simmons 2003) as evidenced by Houlihan and White (2002) in the case of Coventry. Local authorities' influence was also significantly enhanced by their representation on the board of trusts and, therefore, their involvement in strategic decision making (Simmons 2004). However, legislation in England and Wales limited local authority membership of trust boards to 20 per cent and the remainder of board members were drawn from users and other community representatives (Reid 2003). While in line with the Labour government's desire for greater stakeholder involvement, authors have questioned the extent to which trust boards represented a democratically accountable form of governance (Reid 2003; Simmons 2003; Nelson and Henderson 2005). Nevertheless, in five case studies conducted by Simmons (2004, p. 171), the broad representation on trust boards had 'in almost all cases, brought a positive payoff . . . to raise the level and quality of debate over service provision'.

Evidence from trusts themselves suggests that it was in respect of their management of services that significant changes occurred. While not in the same dramatic fashion as CCT, the expansion of leisure trusts continued the trend towards new public management and performance management approaches in leisure services (Simmons 2004). Trust managers appear to have viewed these changes positively, with Simmons (2008, p. 295) stating that

> the benefits of autonomy identified by trust managers include clearer goal setting, more proactive management to these goals, increased use of performance-related incentives, greater attention to organisational communication strategies, and improvements in the quality and usage of information management systems.

Evidence regarding the overall impact of trusts is mixed. Commenting on a major contributing factor to the expansion of trusts, the Audit Commission (2006, p. 36) reported that 'trusts have not yet unlocked significant external funding sources. Neither trusts nor private sector contractors are simple answers to an historic lack of investment in sports and recreation facilities'. Moreover, while Simmons (2008) reported indications of efficiency improvements generated by trusts, in many cases their financial stability remained uncertain and dependent on their parent authority (Simmons 2003, 2004). This evidence gives weight to Benson and Henderson's (2005) suggestion that the perceived financial benefits made trusts 'unrealistically attractive'. There is also insufficient evidence as yet to determine the extent to which trusts have retained or achieved the social goals that they were, in part, created to protect. From case studies of trusts in Coventry and Herefordshire, Houlihan and White (2002, p. 161) commented that 'clearly, well managed trusts . . . are capable of providing substantial additional opportunities, and also adding to the social capital of a community, thus contributing to the achievement of broader social policy goals'. Simmons (2004) identified that a public service ethos remained amongst many staff after the instigation of trusts. However, he also warned that the trend towards the expansion of existing trusts across a number of local authority areas may result in the direct link with local communities, which is necessary for the achievement of social objectives, being lost (Simmons 2008).

In contrast to the contextual drivers behind the expansion of trusts, the Labour government was more explicit in advocating for the internal reorganisation of local authority departments. Broader attempts to 'join up' government, considered further in the next section, included frequent exhortations for local authorities to reorganise their departmental structures on the basis of cross-cutting issues such as public health and social inclusion (Martin 2002). For example, the Every Child Matters white paper (Department for Education and Skills 2003) forced local authorities to bring together all children's services under a single department. More generic systems of local government regulation, such as Best Value and subsequent target-based approaches, were also important drivers that encouraged local authorities to reorganise departmental structures (Geddes and Martin 2000; Sullivan and Gillanders 2005). All local authority services, including sport, were therefore affected by internal reorganisations. Although national sport policies (e.g. DCMS 2001c, DCMS/Strategy Unit 2002) encouraged local authority sport to link with the broader agendas upon which reorganisations were based, formal guidance on where sport and leisure services might fit in reorganised departmental structures was not provided.

This lack of central guidance, coupled with the discretionary status of the service, meant that sport was, at best, in a position of some uncertainty with regard to departmental reorganisations within local authorities. King's (2011) survey of local authorities indicated that almost three quarters of those sampled had moved administrative location in the period 1997 to 2010. In Liverpool, for example, a Best Value review in 2002 first led to a single Sport and Recreation Service being created. However, this process did not result in the desired improvement of co-ordination, and frequent relocations between different parent departments limited the extent to which the Sport and Recreation Service became embedded within the local authority (King 2009). Similarly, Lindsey (2009) found that the priority accorded to sport was perceived to have weakened due to ongoing changes in its position within the organisational structures of one case study London borough. Houlihan and White (2002) identified that even in authorities such as Kent, where the status of sport was maintained, the institutional focus on cross-cutting issues meant that retaining an emphasis on the development of sport itself was challenging.

The Labour government took an even more directive approach to a third prominent aspect of structural reform, namely the instigation of a series of new local institutions. In contrast to the previous Conservative government's creation of quangos to take on roles previously undertaken by local authorities (Stewart and Stoker 1995a), the local institutions created by the Labour government represented partnerships that were largely inclusive of local authorities as well as other organisations (Stoker 2004). Early in the period of the Labour government, these new local institutions were largely created in specific areas of deprivation, often within the boundaries of individual local authorities. Subsequently, however, a more universal approach was adopted, particularly as Local Strategic Partnerships (LSPs) expanded over time to every local authority area in England. Each LSP was tasked with developing overarching strategies for their local area and to be ultimately responsible for the achievement of local targets. Their membership was to comprise all local public-sector bodies together with private and voluntary sector representatives (Geddes 2006).

These trends in the creation of local institutions were replicated in sport. Mirroring the initial creation of geographically focused institutions, Sport England funded the creation of twelve Sport Action Zones from 1999. These zones were created in a variety of localities across England with the aim of addressing a 'range of deprivation-related issues' including under-representation in sport (Sport England 2001, p. 3). Sport England were not overly prescriptive as to the structure of each SAZ, although the need for a partnership-based approach to management was specified (Sport England 2001). As a result, a variety of different institutional arrangements were developed across the twelve SAZs. The identified success of a SAZ in one part of Liverpool, described in an evaluation report by Sport England (2006b), contributed to the later instigation of similar area-based structures across the whole of the city (King 2009). Conversely, in Derbyshire, Houlihan and White (2002, p. 24) described the instigation of a SAZ as an example of 'at best, overlapping partnerships concerned with sports development and, at worst, a series of competing partnerships'. Similar tensions between a SAZ and an urban local authority were identified by Lindsey (2009) in a case study of local collaboration in youth and community sport. Concomitant with the ethos of locally orientated design and implementation, individual SAZs were responsible for determining their own future and securing alternative forms of support after the end of Sport England funding in 2005. A further eighteen Sports Action Zones originally planned by Sport England (2001) were never created. Thus, while SAZs were an institutional response that fitted with the general thrust of national policy at the time of their instigation, they became superseded relatively quickly by the development of a standardised and universal 'delivery system for sport' (Sport England 2005b).

County Sport Partnerships (CSPs) were the primary local component of this standardised delivery system for sport created by Sport England. As such, CSPs were very much connected to the ongoing modernisation of Sport England itself in the early years of the twenty-first century as well as replicating the government's approach to developing LSPs as universal institutional partnerships. CSPs initially emerged through the development of the Active Sports programme initiated in 1999. However, the emergence of CSPs was uncertain, at least initially, with *Game Plan* identifying them, alongside LSPs, as one of 'two existing structures which could take a lead in co-ordinating delivery at the local level' (DCMS/Strategy Unit 2002, p. 188). By 2004, Sport England had committed ongoing funding for CSP staffing and revenue budgets and by 2005 the initial 45 CSPs had been expanded by four to encompass the whole of England. Subsequently, and in contrast to local authorities, the position of CSPs was largely reaffirmed both through the change of national sport policy in 2008 and after the election of the coalition government in 2010.

While there was a large degree of consistency regarding the formal position of CSPs within the Sport England's delivery system, their precise role and place in terms of central-local relations underwent more nuanced change. Emerging from the Active Sport programme, CSPs continued to have their focus on developing sporting pathways for young people (Enoch 2010), albeit with an increasing focus on strategic co-ordination and resourcing rather than any role in direct delivery (Charlton 2010). However, CSPs' focus on youth sport was subsequently tempered in 2005 by pressure from Sport England to contribute to national PSA targets for adults as well as young people (Houlihan and Lindsey 2008). Moreover, the division of national responsibility for sport and physical activity between Sport England and the Department of Health, respectively, in 2008 meant that CSPs faced pressure, and were allocated funding, from different national agencies to address two newly distinct agendas. This reliance on funding from national departments and agencies was also key to determining the extent to which CSPs could fulfil Sport England's (2004a) initial expectation that they would connect national planning and local delivery of sport. In fact, the level of national prescription of CSP objectives became increasingly strong over time (McDonald 2005) with Sport England (2008) specifying a differentiated approach to future funding for CSPs dependent on their contribution to national targets. In terms of overall central-local relations, CSPs can therefore be identified as part of a broader trend in which newly instigated partnerships represented a 'key policy instrument in the new centralism' (Skelcher 2004, p. 37).

Due to this national orientation, it is unsurprising that a number of authors identified difficulties in the relationships between CSPs and local authorities. All CSPs' boundaries were inclusive of a number of different local authorities and both unitary and district authorities were often included even where CSP boundaries were coterminous with those of a single county council. An evaluation report by KKP (2005) identified that, where a unitary authority was included, developing a shared vision for, and commitment to, CSPs was particularly challenging. For Enoch (2010), relationship difficulties were due to larger unitary authorities wishing to 'flex their political and financial muscle', while Houlihan and Lindsey (2008) alternatively suggested that these types of authorities were unsure as to whether CSPs could add value to existing provision. Moreover, in a case study of Lancashire CSP, Charlton (2010, p. 98) reported that 'some of the smaller local authorities were suspicious that their larger, more powerful neighbours were dominating decision-making [within the CSP], often without open discussion'. Tensions also emerged where the objectives of CSPs were somewhat incompatible with local authorities' focus on wider social objectives (Houlihan and Lindsey 2008) or, in the case of Liverpool, the desire of the local authority to focus on a very narrow aspect of sporting provision (King 2009). It is somewhat ironic that, given these difficulties in the different relationships between CSPs and local authorities, the

KKP evaluation reported that other local stakeholders perceived CSPs to be 'invariably local authority focused' (2005, p. 15).

Covering an area that was to encompass all or part of a single local authority area, Community Sport Networks (CSNs) were the final and most local component of Sport England's 'delivery system'. CSNs were expected to bring together a range of local providers from sport and other sectors such as health and education (Sport England 2007). With a clarity missing from CSPs, Sport England (2007, p. 11) emphasised that CSNs were not intended to be a 'substitute for local authority responsibility for the delivery of leisure services and sports development'. Moreover, given that Sport England allocated little in the way of financial or staffing resources to this aspect of the delivery system, it could be suggested that CSNs did not represent the threat to local authority power that CSPs did. Local authorities were, in fact, expected to provide 'active support' to CSNs, often through taking a leadership role (Sport England 2005b). Studies by both Lindsey (2010b) and Baker (2011) identified that professional local authority staff exercised significant control within specific CSNs which was actually to the detriment of active involvement by representatives of other agencies. Nevertheless, it was the lack of priority given nationally to CSNs by Sport England after its reorientation in 2008 that was a major factor in the subsequent dissolution of a number of CSNs across England.

LOCAL LEADERSHIP FOR 'JOINED-UP' DELIVERY

Amongst the national policies identified in previous sections were those that contributed to, and others that were a response to, the organisational fragmentation that was strongly emergent in sport and other local public services. Even towards the end of the Conservative period of government, Stewart and Stoker (1995b, p. 194) noted that

> The institutional map of local government has been transformed. It is possible to refer to a system of 'local governance' in which local authorities find themselves increasingly working alongside a range of other agencies in their localities.

Over the next decade and a half, institutional complexity at local level only became more pronounced with Wilson's (2004, p. 18) comment that 'the world of local governance is awash with authorities, agencies, partnerships, networks and the like' being equally applicable to sport as to other sectors. Many of the national policies that encouraged the fragmentation of the institutional context also contributed to altering the position and role of local authorities within the emerging system of local governance. Reflecting on policies such as CCT during the period of the Conservative government, Aitchison (1997) recognised that the role of local authorities was increasingly becoming one of facilitator and enabler rather than the direct deliverer of services such as sport and leisure. This trend was only to continue after the election of the Labour government in 1997.

Where there was a significant difference between the Labour government and its predecessors was the policy response to the emerging system of local governance. Stewart and Stoker (1995b) equivocally suggested that the Conservatives had accepted the need for greater local co-ordination in response to the 'crisis of fragmentation' that had emerged. In a somewhat stronger representation, related specifically to the context of sport, Houlihan (1991, p. 74) identified the then minister for sport's

> preference for local authorities to move away from direct provision and to concern themselves more with an enabling role which involves planning, co-ordination and facilitating the provision of leisure services by other organisations, whether commercial or voluntary.

Nevertheless, the Labour government's approach was different from previous administrations through being representative of a 'positive embracing of [local] governance rather than a reluctant accommodation with it' (Stoker 2004, p. 58). Two particular aspects promoted within the LGMA were particularly notable in this regard. Firstly, the strength of efforts towards joined-up and co-ordinated local governance represented an important break with previous Conservative governments (Cowell and Martin 2003). Secondly, there was a more proactive realignment of the role of local authorities towards providing community leadership (Laffin 2008). Generic and sport-orientated policies that encouraged both of these elements will be examined in turn.

Although the agenda of 'joining up' was promoted throughout government, it was pursued with particular vigour at the level of local government (Geddes 2006). Commonly to be achieved through specified and unspecified partnerships, 'joining up' was envisaged as involving local authorities collaborating with a variety of other local public-sector organisations as well as those from the private and voluntary sectors (Stoker 2004). 'Joining up' was also in keeping with the broader focus of the Labour government in seeking to address so-called 'wicked' issues that crossed a number of policy areas: In the common parlance, 'joined up' problems were seen to require 'joined up' solutions (Bovaird and Martin 2003). Two distinct aspects of the locally orientated 'joining-up' agenda can be identified. Particularly associated with the types of formal partnership explored in the previous section, 'joined-up' governance was orientated towards developing co-ordinated decision making and strategic planning (Skelcher 2004). The second aspect of 'joining up' was focused on making the implementation and delivery of local services more efficient, effective and responsive to the requirements of citizens (Cowell and Martin 2003).

This broader agenda of local 'joining up' through partnerships was strongly reflected in national sport policies throughout the period of the Labour government. Furthermore, the language used in national policies encompassed both the decision-making and delivery aspects of the 'joining-up' agenda, as exemplified, respectively, in the following passages:

> At a local level, there was felt to be a need for all local authorities to . . . oversee the strategic planning for structured sport, physical education and life-long learning through sport, and informal recreational activities. This should incorporate all of the educational, public sector, voluntary sector, and commercial sector interests within their geographical boundaries and be linked to the wider 'shared priorities' for their communities agreed between the Government and local government. (Sport England 2004a, p. 19)

> Our vision is for local authorities to be at the heart of flexible and innovative partnerships with the private and voluntary sector delivering sustainable sporting opportunities to the whole community. (DCMS 2000, p. 39)

A particularly distinctive aspect of the 'joining-up' agenda as it affected local sport is also evident in these two passages and others in national sport policies. At one level, these policies advocated 'joining up' between sporting agencies in order to improve the development of sport itself. More broadly, with local authorities at the centre of attempts to use sport to deliver a broad range of social objectives, 'joining up' was also required with a range of non-sporting agencies especially in health and education sectors (DCMS/Strategy Unit 2002).

Beyond exhortation from central government and other national agencies, different policy tools were used to encourage local 'joining up'. While some of these tools have been considered to differing extents in previous sections, it is necessary to examine their specific relationship to the 'joining-up' agenda. County Sport Partnerships can be seen as the prime example of institutional reforms designed to promote collaboration between local agencies, and the instigation of School Sport Partnerships considered in the next chapter represents a further example of this trend orientated towards a specific aspect of sport policy. More generally, the overarching nature of the CPA process was designed to encourage co-ordination both within local authorities and beyond with other local agencies (Lowndes and Wilson 2003; Geddes 2006). The subsequent raft of LPSA and LAA targets were also created with the intention of fostering improvements in the 'joining up' of local services, especially as responsibility for LAA targets in particular was allocated to LSPs rather than local authorities.

National funding streams were also often used as a tool to promote local 'joining up'. Given the discretionary status of sport, and resulting uncertainty regarding budgets, gaining access to funding was generally a significant priority for local authorities and was therefore an influential driver for the instigation of local partnerships especially with health agencies that had larger and more established budgets (Houlihan and White 2002; Bloyce et al. 2008). Moreover, a number of funding streams accessible to local authorities and other local agencies involved in sport were allocated on the basis of competitive bidding processes that had partnership working of some form included in the associated assessment criteria (White 1999; Lindsey 2010a). However, much as Stoker (2004, p. 163) suggested more generally that 'partnerships were launched against a backcloth of badly designed bidding competitions', Lindsey (2010a) questioned the extent to which one specific scheme funded by the Big Lottery Fund effected more than superficial change in local partnership working. His analysis of the New Opportunities for PE and Sport programme at both national and local levels suggested that the assessment and monitoring tools enacted lacked the specificity required to affect ingrained ways of working among local agencies. More generally, however, the prominence of competitive funding streams resulted in the emergence of a 'bidding culture' across the local government sector (Stoker 2004, p. 79) that within sport services often led to difficulties in addressing long-term priorities as specific shorter-term funding opportunities were pursued.

Any overarching assessment of local responses to the 'joining-up' agenda has to be made tentatively due to the diversity and complexity of local contexts. Even with a significant body of research emerging, Skelcher (2004) suggested that it is, as yet, not possible to assess the ultimate impact of partnerships on local service delivery. A similar judgement is even more applicable to the specific context of local sport that remains under-researched in comparison to other sectors. Nevertheless, it is possible to draw on research by Houlihan and White (2002) and Bloyce et al. (2008) to suggest that, particularly for sports development services, a strong ethos towards partnership-based approaches developed within local authorities. The extent to which this ethos contributed to the achievement of 'joined-up' local governance or delivery in sport was, however, questioned in reports authored on behalf of national agencies. Commenting on local aspects of delivery, Carter (2005a, p. 6) was critical of 'the lack of a "joined up" approach to community delivery' and a subsequent report by the Audit Commission (2006) was even more scathing of the extent of partnership working by local authorities, particularly with the private and voluntary sectors. Moreover, reflecting the national desire for 'joined-up' governance across different sectors, the Audit Commission (2006, p. 43) found that 'successful strategic engagement between leisure services and the health and education sectors is not common'.

Somewhat in contrast to these national assessments, it is possible to identify specific examples where the aspirations of 'joining up' have been achieved to a greater extent. In one of two case studies presented by Lindsey

(2009), the strong collaborative ethos amongst local agencies was reinforced by the achievement of valued outcomes. A national study by Baker (2011) similarly found that a large proportion of members of Community Sport Networks perceived that their involvement in these partnerships had delivered specific benefits, although some of these benefits were considered to be 'intangible'. However, other case studies also help to identify challenges facing local actors in attempting to 'join up' local provision. A number of authors comment on the difficulties of integration and co-ordination in very fragmented local contexts that encompassed both sporting and non-sporting organisations (e.g. Lindsey 2009; Charlton 2010). For example, in considering the extended period that was required to establish a local sport forum in Derbyshire, Houlihan and White (2002, p. 120) identified that 'part of the explanation lay simply in the number of organisations that needed to be co-ordinated, but partly lay in the variable levels of commitment to the objectives of the forum'. Elsewhere Houlihan and White (2002) noted the difficulties in convincing prospective partners from other sectors of the potential contribution that sport could make to broader agendas and also the challenge of developing an integrated local sport system if there was only a limited voluntary club structure in place. These issues link with a more general problem identified by Laffin (2008), who suggested that organisations from both public and voluntary sectors may lack the same incentives as local authorities to become involved in partnership working.

In the context of efforts to 'join up' local governance, local authorities were required to adapt to the designation and acquisition of an altered role. The ongoing changes in the structure and management of service provision had, over a period of time, placed local authorities increasingly in an enabling role rather than one concerned solely with direct delivery (Laffin 2008). However, the clarity with which the scope and nature of this altered role for local authorities was prescribed by central government developed over the period of Labour rule (Downe and Martin 2006). In fact, the first Local Government Act enacted by the Labour government in 2000 broadened the role of local authorities to one of promoting the overall social, environmental and economic well-being of their localities (Stoker and Wilson 2004a). Of particular relevance to sport was the recognition in *Game Plan* that the 'promotion of public health through sport was entirely consistent' with this broader role for local authorities (DCMS/Strategy Unit 2002, p. 184). Moreover, and with an increasing central government commitment as the LGMA developed, local authorities were cast in a strategic leadership role amongst the range of local organisations that could contribute to the development of their local areas (Laffin 2008; Downe and Martin 2006). This altered role went beyond the narrow confines of the new public management agenda (Martin 2002). Furthermore, the emerging identification of local authorities as providing community and strategic leadership was replicated in national sport policies. For example, the earlier quotation from *The Framework for Sport in England* (Sport England 2004a) was complemented by similar passages in documents such as *A Sporting Future for All* (DCMS 2000), *Game Plan* (DCMS 2002) and subsequently with respect to physical activity in the *Be Active, Be Healthy* plan published by the Department of Health (2009).

There is, as yet, little evidence regarding the extent to which local authorities have been able to successfully adapt to their new leadership role or the enhanced role promoted by their being granted a general power of competence by the coalition government. During the period of the Labour government, Skelcher (2004) recognised that local authorities generally 'internalised' the emergent context of local governance, although both Stewart (2000) and Stoker (2004) suggested that not all local authorities were ready and had the capacity to undertake a community leadership role. In this regard, the identification in *Game Plan* that local authority staff had to develop new skills in strategic delivery and partnership working is particularly pertinent (DCMS 2002). The contrasting case studies of two local authorities presented by Lindsey (2009) suggested that there were significant differences regarding the extent to which such capacities were present and had developed over time in different authorities. A further case study of an urban CSN in the south of England demonstrates the challenges faced by local authorities in providing leadership while at the same time addressing the requirement to devolve power to other agencies in order to build effective partnerships (Lindsey 2010b). Houlihan and White (2002, p. 137) noted a similar concern on behalf of local authority staff that, even where they proved successful in an enabling or leadership role, their own contribution to service outcomes would be less visible to both elected councillors and the general public.

CONCLUSIONS: WHITHER LOCAL AUTHORITY SPORT?

The period covered by this study has certainly been one in which ongoing and vigorous policy activity has significantly impacted on local government sport. Local sport services have been affected both by national policies towards local government in general and by policy development within the sport sector in particular. As highlighted in the chapter, it is undeniable that these factors have had differentiated impacts on individual local authorities. Nevertheless, it remains important to offer an overarching assessment of the relative influence of this array of policy changes on local government sport. It is also apt to consider the future of local government sport given the preceding analysis and challenges that it currently faces.

In terms of the place of local government within sport policy, it is possible to suggest that there has not been significant change when considering the entire period covered by this study. *Sport: Raising the Game* (DNH

1995) largely ignored local government and instead emphasised the role of other organisations, for example, schools and universities, in the delivery and development of local sport. The terminology in the largely decentralising texts presented by the Conservative Party (2009) in their Sport Policy Paper prior to the 2010 election and by DCMS (2011b) subsequently has, in a similar vein, focused on 'local communities' rather than include significant mention of local government or authorities per se. The lack of definitional clarity as to precisely what is meant by 'local communities' and, in turn, their relationship with local government have also been commented upon as a feature of the coalition government's broader Localism Bill (Jones and Stewart 2011).

Similarity between policy at the start and end of a period is, however, no indicator of continuity throughout and it could be suggested that local government was strongly represented within Labour's sport policies from *Game Plan* in 2002 to *Playing to Win* in 2008. Nonetheless, the Audit Commission (2006) identified that funding for local government sport did not significantly increase in this period. Rather, local authorities have indicated that they became increasingly dependent on National Lottery and other short-term, ring-fenced funding sources (King 2011). The lack of more consistent funding commitment can be taken as a sign of the continued weakness of local government's position within the sport policy sector as a whole. Compared to other organisations within the sport sector, policy advocacy on behalf of local government was weak. It could be suggested, for example, that the Local Government Association lacked sufficient expertise to fulfil such an advocacy role.

Moreover, there was significant pressure on local authorities to adapt to the widespread changes enacted throughout the period of the Labour government. The chapter has highlighted the variety of policy tools utilised by the Labour government to exert increasing control over implementation of the various components of its Local Government Modernisation Agenda. Examining even a single policy tool, namely the different and changing centralised targets for local authorities, allows identification of the uncertainty and lack of consistency which those responsible for sport within local government had to manage over time. In such circumstances, long-term strategic planning, a weakness within local government sport at the outset, was undoubtedly challenging. In turn, the government-commissioned Carter report (2005a) itself recognised the impact that weak local strategic planning could have on efforts to improve adult participation in sport. A lack of identifiable increases in participation proved to be a factor in the weakening position of local government in national sport policy from 2008. Ultimately, while the period of the Labour government was one of increasing centralised control over local government, there was no progress towards the one central regulation that may have helped created a more stable status for sport within local government in England, namely making sport a mandatory rather than discretionary service.

Instead, the evidence points to sport being in a weak position within local government in general. Ongoing changes of the lead department for sport and the need for the 'creative defence' of sport services through the creation of leisure trusts are just two of a number of examples which demonstrate both the weakness of sport and the instability that was one of the consequences of such weakness. During Labour's period of relative prosperity in local government, such weaknesses may be masked, particularly where there have been innovative and resourceful local managers of sport services. With the significant cuts on local government funding imposed by the coalition government, the weakness of sport is likely to become increasingly exposed. King (2011) warned that cuts in many local authorities may leave only a 'skeleton [sport] service'. Similarly, from a wider perspective, Parker (2011, p. 4) speculated that 'by 2015, council-owned leisure centres, museums and theatres could be a distant memory'.

Responses to cuts are likely to vary across local authorities, perhaps to an extent according to local political leadership (King 2011). However, it appears likely that there will be further externalisation of local government sport services to either leisure trusts or private contractors. Although the coalition government ensured that 'communities' had the right to bid to take on the management of local facilities and services, enthusiasm from voluntary sector organisations, such as clubs, to become significantly involved in contributing to governmental agendas has previously been limited and this may well remain the case (Harris et al. 2009). If so, and in line with coalition government ideology, externalisation to trusts and private contractors will only serve to strengthen the entrenched consumerist ethos in local sport services associated with new public management approaches. The speed with which externalisation may progress also increases the likelihood of large trusts and private contractors operating provision across different local authority areas. In turn, as Raine (2011) pointed out more generally, this has implications for democratic and localised control over service provision which sit in contrast to the coalition government's stated localism.

Increasingly externalisation will also only serve to increase the fragmentation that has long existed in and affected local sport. Some structural reform enacted by the Labour government, the instigation of CSPs, for example, could be viewed as enhancing central control through creating new bodies and bypassing local government. Certainly, coalition government policies for sectors linked to sport, such as education, are likely to further marginalise the role of local government and increase fragmentation (NLGN 2010). The creation of distinct marketplaces for provision of specific local services, for example, in health, is likely to increase the challenges for those in local government sport who have increasingly looked for partnerships with such sectors in order to garner funding (Bloyce et al. 2008). For the Labour government, partnership working was a major priority, designed to overcome the identified problem of fragmentation. Irrespective of the question of effectiveness, partnership working as a process became largely embedded in the practices of local government sport. It was through partnerships that it was possible for local authorities to enact their altered role in enabling local provision and potentially providing local strategic leadership. The absence of consideration of such aspects in coalition government policy is notable. In times of austerity, there is a clear need for local leadership for sport. Whether there is the impetus and capacity for local government to provide such leadership, after a long period of uncertainty and instability, is a cause for concern.

7 Youth Sport

Previous chapters have identified the prominence of youth sport as a specific component of sport policy throughout the period covered by this study. This chapter will examine in further depth the factors contributing to the increased salience of youth sport as a whole, trace the shifting priority accorded to specific youth sport agendas and consider the governance and implementation of these agendas. These trends cannot, however, be considered in isolation from broader policies relating to young people. In this respect, consideration of the education policies of successive governments is especially relevant since, as Ball (2008, p. 1) recognised:

> Education has become a major political issue, a major focus of media attention and the recipient of a constant stream of initiatives and interventions from government.

With this prioritisation matched in other countries, Ball (2008) argued that the value attached to education by governments was on account of the need to remain competitive in an increasingly globalised and marketised economy. In a similar vein, Green (2007), Dobrowolsky (2002), Lister (2003) and others understood Labour's focus on young people in terms of being a 'social investment' for supporting the development of productive adult citizens. Policies associated with social investment in young people were not limited to education alone and Ball (2008) suggested that, rather than refer to education policy specifically, it is more appropriate to consider the agendas that comprised a broader learning policy which encompassed health, fitness and citizenship amongst other issues. Such a holistic approach to young people's development was especially prominent in influential Labour policy documents such as *Every Child Matters* (DfES 2003) and *The Children's Plan* (DCSF 2007).

The focus here on Labour's policies is not to discount those of preceding and succeeding governments. In fact, there is widespread recognition that ongoing continuities have been the most significant feature of education policy at least since 1990 (Chitty 2008; Ball 2008; Green 2010). These continuities are particularly apparent in the alterations made by successive governments to the education system within England. Ball (2008, p. 126) described the Thatcher, Major and Labour governments as 'dismantling a . . . universal and uniform welfare model of comprehensive education' that had been created during the post-war period of social democratic consensus. Instead, an increasingly diverse and fragmented system of schools developed as a result of policies enacted since the late 1980s. The Major government's instigation of schools with particular academic specialisms was continued and expanded by Labour governments. Furthermore, policies continued to encourage a diversity of management arrangements for schools with state-funded schools increasingly being outside of Local Education Authority control. In addition, the school system was subject to a general 'blurring of boundaries between the private and state sectors' that was also witnessed across other areas of welfare policy (Chitty 2004, p. 55).

Alongside this diversification of schooling, competition was instigated and developed within the education system. John Major's government was the first to publish schools' educational results and, from 1992, school league tables were continued, with minor amendments to the specific data included, ever since. Policies also encouraged greater parental choice amongst schools and as a result an increasingly market-based education system emerged (Tomlinson 2001). Compared to these competitive influences, the somewhat contradictory impetus provided by the Labour government for collaboration between schools had a more limited impact (Evans et al. 2005). An additional, particularly prominent, aspect of Labour's approach to education was the setting of numerous targets which were complemented by an increasingly influential system of inspection and audit of schools by the Office for Standards in Education (OFSTED) and other national bodies. A further significant influence on practice within schools was the National Curriculum introduced in the 1988 Education Reform Act and modified at regular intervals since then. It was through such mechanisms and policy tools that government came to exert a stronger degree of central control on the education system. This centralisation is just one of the similarities between education and sport policy. How youth sport policy has been aligned with, and also differed from, education policy will be a continuing issue explored in the rest of the chapter.

THE INCREASING SALIENCE OF YOUTH SPORT

In contrast to its recent salience, issues connected to youth sport had little priority during Margaret Thatcher's premiership. Physical education was also a marginal concern within policy debates about the education system and curricula at this time (Houlihan and Green 2006). However, these authors did note an 'emerging concern with the state of the health of young people and the perceived lack of success of elite sportsmen and sportswomen' (p. 75) in the late 1980s prior to John Major becoming prime minister in 1990. John Major's personal enthusiasm for sport has been examined in depth in Chapter 2 and, combined with the broader concerns just noted, school sport became a central component of his government's sporting agenda as evidenced in the prime minister's own forward to *Sport: Raising the Game* (DNH 1995, p. 2):

> My ambition is simply stated. It is to put sport back at the heart of weekly life in every school. To re-establish sport as one of the great pillars of education, alongside the academic, the vocational and the moral. It should never have been relegated to be just one part of one subject in the curriculum.

Two broad but distinguishable beliefs regarding the benefits of school sport underpinned this increased prioritisation. Firstly, revitalising school sport was viewed as important in contributing to future elite success (DNH 1995). Secondly, representing a similarly future-orientated but more influential perspective, involvement in sport at an early age was understood to contribute to the future 'personal, social and moral development' (DNH 1995, p. 40) of young people. While these beliefs were important in underpinning the Major government's renewed prioritisation of school sport, they were by no means new when considered within the broader history of physical education as a subject (Bloyce and Smith 2009). Moreover, as shall be identified in the following paragraphs, these same beliefs and other similar views continued to influence policy agendas after the 1997 election in which Labour came to power.

Despite the increased profile of youth sport under John Major, there subsequently remained a widespread and long-standing perception that young people's levels of physical activity had declined along with sport and physical education provision in schools more generally (Bailey 2005; Bloyce and Smith 2009). Such a view was explicitly recognised in Labour's first sport policy document, *A Sporting Future for All* (DCMS 2000, p. 7), which noted that 'in too many schools physical education and sport have declined. There has been a loss of playing fields and a decline in after school sport and competition'. Perhaps more importantly, youth sport was linked by the Labour government to the broader social investment and economic rationales that pervaded their policies associated with education and young people more generally. The future-orientated social and economic value of youth sport was explicitly stated in *Game Plan* (DCMS/Strategy Unit 2002, p. 93):

> In terms of the returns government can gain from focusing on these groups, there are particular benefits to concentrating on young people and young adults to build lifetime habits of participation and establish initial good health status.

Health became an increasingly strong rationale for government investment in sport as statistics presented by the government (Healthy Schools 2006) and statements produced by Sport England (2005c) complemented a media debate that focused on the rising proportion of adults and young people who were classified as obese.

This is not to say that the developmental agendas associated with youth sport under the Major government were not also influential in underpinning Labour's policy objectives for youth sport. If anything the narrative regarding the contribution of youth sport to personal and social development and educational attainment grew more prominent in a variety of policy documents published by the Labour government (DCMS 2000; DCMS/Strategy Unit 2002). Furthermore, linking to Labour's social inclusion agenda, the potential of sport to support the re-engagement of young people disaffected with school or involved in anti-social or criminal behaviour only served to heighten the wider salience of youth sport within education and social policy. More generally, the significant extent of this policy spillover was further evidenced in the increasing references to sport in policies and documents related to young people produced by a number of different government departments (Griggs and Wheeler 2007).

Prior to the election of the coalition government in 2010, the prospect of change in the salience of youth sport to government seemed remote to many in the sector. In the opening lines of their pre-election policy document, the Conservative Party (2009, p. 4) reiterated a very similar message to the Labour government in emphasising that 'young people who play sport tend to be happier, healthier, more socially cohesive and perform better academically'. However, by October 2010, shortly after the government's Comprehensive Spending Review, there appeared to be a significant weakening of this commitment. Michael Gove, the Conservative secretary of state for education, announced a total cut of the annual £162 million funding for the system of School Sport Partnerships introduced by Labour. While Gove (2010, p. 1) stated his belief that 'competitive sport . . . should be a vibrant part of the life and ethos of all schools', the government rhetoric initially used at the time of the announcement of these cuts differed significantly from the largely uncritical support for the wider social benefits of youth sport offered by the previous government.

This is not to say that youth sport no longer remained a salient political issue as over the following two months a vigorous campaign on behalf of the School Sport Partnership programme was undertaken by pupils, teachers and elite athletes that generated significant media coverage. As a result, in a reversal that had symbolic significance, the coalition government partially backtracked on its initial position and announced, in December 2010, reinstatement of funds that would allow a scaled-back model of SSPs to continue until 2013. The naming of the subsequent coalition government sport policy document as a 'youth sport strategy' (DCMS 2012) also indicated at least an ongoing rhetorical commitment to this policy sector. The authorship of the document by DCMS rather than the Department of Education was, however, indicative of the reduced priority given to youth sport on behalf of the latter department.

While the specifics of these policy developments will be considered further in subsequent sections, analysis of the broader politics surrounding youth sport during the initial period of the coalition government highlights important trends that have continued to develop throughout the period covered by this study. The first of these trends concerns the array of institutions and individuals that have influenced, and have sought to influence, youth sport policy. Prior to the period of John Major's premiership, advocacy for PE and youth sport from relevant organisations was neither strong nor especially coherent. Houlihan and Green (2006) criticised the two leading PE associations (the British Association of Advisers and Lecturers in Physical Education and the Physical Education Association of the United Kingdom) for their failure to coherently and effectively articulate the potential contribution that PE and school sport could make to the development of pupils. Moreover, the Sports Council's (1993a) own publication, *Young People and Sport: Policy and Frameworks for Action,* indicates this organisation's uncertainty regarding its role in relation to young people through the period before and just after the publication of *Sport and Active Recreation* in 1990. The result was that, in a generally unsupportive policy environment, any policy activism amongst sporting organisations prior to 1990 was often 'prompted more by defensiveness than confident advocacy' (Houlihan and Green 2006, p. 75).

As with sport policy more generally, the alignment of interests in the sector that began to emerge to support youth sport during John Major's premiership continued to strengthen during the period of the Labour government. Major's personal support for youth sport, which was continued by Tony Blair, created an opportunity for more proactive advocacy from within the sector (Houlihan and Green 2006). It was in this context that the Youth Sport Trust (YST) was established as a charitable organisation in 1994 through funding from the entrepreneur Sir John Beckwith. Initially prominent within the sport sector for their deployment of bags of sport equipment and training cards in schools through their TOPS programme, the YST and especially its chief executive, Sue Campbell, became increasingly prominent as an 'institutional focus' for PE and school sport (Bloyce and Smith 2009). Houlihan and Green (2006) also likened Campbell's role in the sport policy process to that of a policy entrepreneur within the multiple streams framework. The success of Campbell and the YST in taking the lead in ensuring youth sport had a high profile within Labour policies was in part due to the absence of other sporting agencies and professional interest groups capable of offering policy advocacy. More proactively, Campbell was skilful in forging positive and influential relationships with senior civil servants and Labour politicians, including

Tony Blair (Houlihan and Green 2006; Smith and Leech 2010). The influence of the YST and Campbell was associated with, and enhanced by, the alignment between their central and consistent message regarding the benefits of PE and school sport and the wider policy objectives of the Labour government (Green 2008). While this advocacy no doubt helped to increase and maintain the political salience of PE and school sport, it also enabled the YST to become increasingly influential on the detail of youth sport policy, especially as the backing provided by the prime minister and other members of the government did not extend to making detailed plans regarding policy implementation (Houlihan and Green 2006).

The emergence of the YST and its representatives as key policy actors also contributed to, and was associated with, other shifts in the alignment of institutional stakeholders in youth sport policy. Houlihan and Green (2006) noted that Sport England continued to be marginalised in policy debates concerning PE and school sport and the extent of this marginalisation was only enhanced by the prominence of the YST throughout the period of the Labour government. In fact, in the final sport policy document produced by the Labour government (*Playing to Win*, DCMS 2008), the YST was confirmed as the sole national organisation with responsibility for PE and school sport, as Sport England's role was confined to the more nebulous and less salient area of 'community sport'. Within government, however, the Department for Culture, Media and Sport (DCMS) began increasingly to assert influence within policy networks associated with the PE and school sport agenda (Green 2008). The increasing influence of the DCMS was not necessarily to the detriment of the governmental department responsible for education (at various times the Department for Education and Skills and the Department for Children, Schools and Families). The inclusion of both departments, alongside the YST and Sport England, on the short-lived School Sport Alliance that was formed in 2000 and the joint publication of the largely symbolic *Learning through PE and Sport* (DCMS/DfES 2003) document demonstrated a more co-operative approach to youth sport policy making it in line with Labour's wider commitment to joined-up government. Nevertheless, in considering the relevance of the advocacy coalition framework to the youth sport policy sector, Houlihan and Green (2006, p. 81) argued that, despite 'the increased salience and status of sport and PE', there remained an absence of 'a dominant coalition of actors/organisations' in place within the sector during the period of the Labour government.

The events subsequent to Michael Gove's proclamation of funding cuts to the School Sport Partnerships programme do, however, demonstrate the emergence of a wider network of individuals and organisations with a significant commitment to maintaining PE and sport as a salient and supported area of government activity. Gove's initial decision was one that was taken within the Department of Education where civil servants previously supportive of PE and sport at least acquiesced to, and outwardly supported, their new minister. Gove did not appear to consult significantly prior to the announcement, and the association of Sue Campbell and the YST with the Labour government meant that their previous prominence within the policy sector was reversed as they were actively excluded from the decision-making process. There were also indications that Gove's approach to policymaking stood in contrast to the co-operation between government departments in PE and school sport policy that had existed previously. In the months following Gove's announcement, articles in the *Guardian* (Campbell and Vasagar 2010) and *Observer* (Helm and Asthana 2010) newspapers indicated opposition to the school sport cuts on behalf of the Conservative minister for culture, media and sport, Jeremy Hunt, and reported concerns raised in Cabinet by Nick Clegg, the Liberal Democrat deputy prime minister, and Andrew Lansley, the Conservative minister for health.

The reported concerns of these Cabinet ministers were largely a reaction to what was, perhaps, the more significant aspect of the response to Gove's initial announcement in October 2010. In the subsequent two months, campaigns against the decision created significant publicity and garnered widespread coverage in the English media, which previously had largely ignored non-elite aspects of sport. Largely independently of the national fulcrum of school sport, the YST, a petition initiated by a school pupil from Grantham generated a reported 500,000 signatures, a letter to the prime minister written by the Olympian Gail Emms was signed by a number of present and former elite athletes and sixty head teachers from across England wrote to Gove identifying their opposition to the cuts. A debate held in the House of Commons on 30 November 2010 also heard support offered for school sport from MPs of all parties. Whilst perhaps lacking the integration of a more formally identifiable advocacy coalition, the diversity of individuals and organisations offering their support to school sport demonstrated the continued existence and developing strength of an 'increasing well established network of organisations' within the policy area that Houlihan and Green (2006) identified four years previously. Moreover, the episode demonstrated the continuing and perhaps even increasing salience of school sport as a mainstream policy issue. The involvement of both the DCMS and, especially, the Department of Health in negotiations that led to the partial reinstatement of funding for school sport only serves to emphasise this point.

The arguments put forward by both sides in the debates regarding the school sport funding cut reflected another ongoing issue, namely the contribution of forms of evidence to youth sport policymaking. Gove (2010, p. 2) justified his initial decision by stating that 'only around two in every five pupils plays sport regularly within their school and only one in five plays regularly against other schools'. Reinforcing these figures in the House of Commons, the prime minister described them as a 'terrible record' (Cameron 2010). In a response to Gove, Sue Campbell (2010) instead highlighted that overall participation in two hours of PE and school had increased to 90 per cent and others also used similarly positive findings from government surveys (e.g. Houlihan 2010) to demonstrate that Gove had been politically selective in his use of evidence.

This episode was not an isolated example in which specifically selected evidence was used to advance youth sport policy agendas. The dominant narrative of decline in young people's activity in PE and sport that influenced both John Major's and Tony Blair's governments was challenged by evidence collected by the government's own inspectors of schools regarding the provision of PE (HMI 1991) and extracurricular provision in which there was 'little to support the notion of irrevocable decline' (OFSTED 1995, p. 22). Moreover, Roberts (1996, cited in Bloyce and Smith 2009) reported that activity rates amongst young people in the mid-1990s were actually higher than in the period between 1950 and 1980. In a similar regard to the youth sport participation narrative, the Labour government's commitment to youth sport was also strengthened by the effective marshalling of evidence by Sue Campbell to demonstrate to ministers and influential civil servants that PE and school sport could make a positive contribution to the government's wider policy objectives (Houlihan and Green 2006). However, Smith and Leech (2010, p. 332) described this evidence as 'largely impressionistic, anecdotal and underpinned by the heavily ideological perceptions of the supposed worth of PE and school sport to young people'. A more overarching perspective is offered by Coalter (2007, p. 108), who surmised that there is 'mixed, inconsistent and largely non-cumulative evidence about the positive educational benefits of physical education and sport'. The ongoing utilisation (or manipulation) of specific forms of evidence described in this paragraph certainly is contrary to the more rational evidence-based approaches to policymaking strongly advocated, in rhetoric at least, by the Blair government. Instead, it was more resonant of cultural institutionalism in regards to the influence of socially constructed meaning on the policy process.

SPECIFIC POLICY AGENDAS AND PROGRAMMES

The foregoing has examined the overall salience of PE and youth sport to various governments and amongst policy actors during the period covered in the study. This is not to say that particular youth sport agendas, nor the agencies within the sector identified with them, were necessarily unified and coherent. Houlihan (2000) described PE and youth sport as a 'crowded policy space' with, at least, three separate communities of interests each with slightly different agendas. To an extent, these communities were reflective of the long-standing distinction between physical education and youth sport. With regard to the later of these, Houlihan (2000) also distinguished between specific agendas concerned with elite sport and sports development. Similarly, sports development is a practice that has been ill-defined and long contested and, in this regard, there could be considered a broad but not necessarily clear-cut distinction between the engagement and progression of young people within sport as an end in itself and development through sport intended to address some of the wider agendas highlighted in the previous section. The changing priorities with regard to each of these different policy agendas throughout the period covered by this study will be explored and explained in this section.

Even before 1990, the status of PE especially relative to other school subjects was an issue of concern to its advocates. Houlihan and Green (2006, p. 75) noted that, from the 1960s, PE teachers were growing ever more concerned about their 'increasingly marginal status within the secondary curriculum'. While the subsequent rise in the salience of youth sport may have somewhat helped to counter this isolation, PE continued to lack prominence when compared to more sport-focused agendas. In the early 1990s, the Sports Council (1993a) did seek to emphasise that the development of elite athletes should not considered as a major objective of PE. Nevertheless, Alderson (1993) still raised concerns that sport policymakers at the time continued to consider PE as the initial foundation level with the then prominent sports development continuum. Any balance that existed between PE and sporting agendas, however, was significantly altered in favour of the latter by the rhetoric and actions of John Major and his government. This was made entirely clear in *Sport: Raising the Game* (DNH 1995, p. 7) in which the downplaying of PE throughout the document was made explicit in the statement that 'the focus of this policy statement is deliberately on sport rather than physical education'. Subsequent policy statements issued by the Labour government were not as one-sided in their rhetoric but perhaps reinforced the marginalised status of PE through paying little heed to what some academics and teachers continued to view as an important distinction between the desired outcomes of PE and sport (Kirk 2004).

In reflecting and reinforcing governmental rhetoric, the creation of the National Curriculum for PE in 1992 and subsequent revisions had an ongoing and significant effect on the relative prioritisation of sport and other aspects of PE within schools. Given previous concerns, it was positive that PE gained a somewhat more secure status through its inclusion alongside other subjects in the new National Curriculum (Houlihan 1997). However, as the DNH (1995) itself recognised, the NCPE initially only established a minimum requirement in terms of taught provision and the continued prioritisation of more academic subjects may actually have led to an initial decrease in the time available for PE lessons (Flintoff 2003; Hargreaves 1995). Limitations in terms of the amount of time allocated for curricular PE by schools were actually reinforced initially by the Labour government, which for a period suspended the NCPE in order to establish dedicated time for literacy and numeracy in primary schools (Houlihan 2002). It was only after 2000 when the government began to provide impetus for the improvement of PE and school sport that the curricular time for PE started to increase (Quick et al. 2010).

In respect of the content of the NCPE, Penney and Chandler (2000) suggested that its advent in England and Wales 'legitimated a view of physical education as comprising merely a collection of activities'. Moreover, the constraints of the NCPE meant that a narrower range of activities was provided in schools than previously (Green et al. 2005) and, in line with John Major's overall agenda, competitive team sports were an especially prominent component both in the documentation and in practice within schools (Green 2008). The requirements for competitive team games were only weakened in 2000 when the Labour government began its first revisions to the NCPE. These revisions included a strengthening of the commitment to health-related activity which contributed to schools beginning to deliver a greater breadth of sports and physical activities (Green et al. 2005; Green 2008). Nevertheless, there remained concerns as to the extent to which the PE curriculum was inclusive of all schoolchildren. The focus on competitive team sports in the initial NCPE led Hargreaves (1995) to strongly criticise the lack of concern with gender inequality and, even up to the point of the most recent revision, Flintoff (2008b, p. 149) characterised the NCPE as an 'implicitly gendered text'. Haycock and Smith (2010) also suggested that the types of sporting activities prescribed in the numerous versions of the NCPE have marginalised young disabled people from mainstream PE provision.

The rebalancing of PE towards sporting activities was also evident in the changing role, status and training of PE teachers over the period of this study (Flintoff 2003). John Major viewed teachers as central to the achievement of the objectives set out in *Sport: Raising the Game* and, as such, competitive games were to become a more prominent aspect of teacher training with there being 'strong encouragement' (DNH 1995, p. 15) for all trainee teachers to undertake NGB coaching qualifications in particular sports. In respect of primary schools especially, in-service training and curriculum resources provided first through the Sports Council's National Junior Sports Programme (DNH 1996) and subsequently through the Youth Sport Trust's TOPS programme also focused on enhancing the provision of sporting activities. Whilst the subsequent Labour government sought to improve the capacity of teachers through traditional teacher training agencies rather than NGBs (DCMS 2000), the strengthening input of sporting organisations, such as the YST, into schools further marginalised the traditional PE agenda pursued by many teachers (Green 2008). Moreover, wider government deregulation enabled a trend towards the delivery of curriculum activities by non-teaching staff (Ball 2008). Primary schools especially began to increasingly employ sports coaches to deliver both curricular and extracurricular sessions (O'Gorman 2009) and sports development officers were also increasingly involved in school-based provision (Green 2008). Moreover, the need to deliver national initiatives and become involved in strategic development work across different schools increasingly encroached on the traditional roles of PE teachers (Flintoff 2008b).

This ongoing weakening of physical education as a subject independent of sport can certainly be attributed in part to the personal priorities of John Major and latterly to the emergence of the YST, which was a strong advocate of sporting agendas in schools. For Gilroy (1995), the media presentation of PE teachers as 'left wing ideologues' also helped to legitimise the weakening of their subject. However, as was suggested in the previous section, a further factor was the lack of coherent advocacy from and on behalf of the PE profession. The 'self-doubt . . . about the nature and purpose of their subject' that Houlihan and Green (2006) identified amongst PE teachers in the 1970s and 1980s continued to be recognised throughout the period of this study. Hargreaves (1995) believed that PE teachers 'capitulated' to the sport-orientated and gender-biased themes advanced in *Sport: Raising the Game*. With the 'core aims of the subject [PE] remaining far less clear and a source of apparent tension' among different PE teachers and their representatives (Penney and Chandler 2000, p. 74), it is perhaps unsurprising that the profession was not significantly consulted by successive governments as policies were determined that influenced both curricular and extracurricular provision in schools.

The overall strengthening orientation of policy towards youth sport in general should not detract from the recognition that there were ongoing incremental changes, over the period of this study, in the prioritised aspects of youth sport (Houlihan 2002). The trajectories of specific youth sport agendas are examined in the remainder of this section through analysis of the initiation and funding of specific youth sport programmes. With regard to funding, as was highlighted in Chapter 2, John Major's government struggled to match their rhetorical commitment to youth sport with the sufficient financing to meet stated policy objectives on a widespread basis. National youth sport initiatives that were launched included Champion Coaching, operated by the National Coaching Foundation with £1m of government funding, and the National Junior Sport Programme, funded by £7.7m from the National Lottery. A common theme across these programmes was the long-standing desire not only to improve young people's access to sport in schools but also to provide pathways by which participation could be continued in sports clubs and other community settings (DNH 1995). It is notable, therefore, that each of these initiatives were operated by sport, rather than educational, organisations. Other than research by Collins and Buller (2000), little information on these programmes remains available and their national impact may be gauged by the fact that they were superseded by programmes which were supported by significantly greater funds from the subsequent Labour government. Somewhat ironically, it was a specifically educational programme, which enabled schools to become Specialist Sport Colleges, that had most substantial enduring influence of those programmes initiated during the period of the Major government.

After their initial freeze on all spending increases, from 2000 the Labour government provided greater impetus to the improvement of school sport through an ongoing array of strategies and programmes, matched by the commitment of significant funding. Included in *A Sporting Future for All* (DCMS 2000) was a 'five part plan' consisting of building facilities, creating Specialist Sport Colleges, extending out-of-hours activities, appointing school sport co-ordinators and providing support for the most talented young people. As a result and in line with the ongoing trend towards diversification within the school system, £24m was allocated for three years from 2000 to expand the number of Specialist Sports Colleges to 150 across England (DCMS 2001c). Larger sums, of £240m and £750m, respectively, were largely drawn from the National Lottery to fund out-of-school-hours activities and the development of school sport facilities across the UK, the later through the New Opportunities for PE and Sport programme (DCMS 2000; NOF 2001). Funding for the deployment of school sport co-ordinators in English-maintained secondary schools also commenced in 2000. By 2006, under the then renamed School Sport Partnership programme, there was a school sport co-ordinator working up to two days per week in all secondary schools and every primary school had a link teacher who was allocated 12 days per year for work towards the development of school sport.

The various PE and school sport initiatives launched from the turn of the century were linked together within the framework of the PE, School Sport and Club Links (PESSCL) strategy that was announced by Tony Blair in 2002. PESSCL 'strands' included the five parts of the plan announced in *A Sporting Future for All* as well as a QCA PE and School Sport Investigation, the Step into Sport youth volunteering programme and a package of support for school-based swimming. While the accompanying documentation was brief and consisted of little more than descriptions of the eight strands (DCMS/DfES 2003), the PESSCL strategy had more important symbolic value in representing the government's efforts in the policy sector as well as, for advocates of PE, the continuing prioritisation of 'sporting interests in PE policy' (Green 2008, p. 39). Subsequently, in 2008, a new PE and Sport Strategy for Young People (PESSYP) was launched which committed further funding of £755m over the following three years and announced a number of further initiatives and targets for school sport. It was perhaps a sign of the embedding of the initiatives and structures that had been launched since 2000 that PESSYP included a more succinct overall aim 'to create a world class system for PE and sport for all children and young people, which will stimulate and increase their participation in sport, and sustain it' (DCSF 2008, p. 2).

If the overarching PESSCL and PESSYP documentation gives little information about the pursuit of different aspects of the youth sport agenda, it is through their component programmes that these aspects can be more fully examined. An aim to increase participation in sport and physical activity amongst young people was especially prominent within the School Sport Partnership programme and was commonly articulated in social investment terms of engendering lifelong physical activity habits (e.g. DCMS 2000; DCMS/Strategy Unit 2002). As such there was a strong focus on the provision of high-quality opportunities for young people to participate in a range of competitive and non-competitive activities (DCMS 2000; Flintoff 2008a). Part of the impetus for providing a range of activities was to encourage participation for young people who were not attracted to or were not participating in existing school sport provision (DCMS/Strategy Unit 2002). Initial outcomes and guidance for the SSP programme were also orientated towards targeting particular groups of young people who were underrepresented in sport including girls and young women, ethnic minority youth, disabled young people and those from socioeconomically deprived backgrounds (Flintoff 2008a). In this regard, there was significant confluence with the government's wider prioritisation of social inclusion at the time.

Over time, however, priorities and outcomes for the SSP programme shifted away from underrepresented groups as there became more impetus for the provision of competitive sport (Flintoff 2008a). From 2004, increasing numbers of competition managers were appointed to work alongside existing staff within SSPs. NGBs were also encouraged to work alongside SSPs to build more integrated competition structures from school to national level (NCSS 2005). Furthermore, the UK School Games was initiated on an annual basis from 2006. This increasing emphasis on competition was, firstly, underpinned by the successful bid to host the Olympic Games. Secondly, it was given greater momentum by Gordon Brown, who emphasised competition in order to make his own imprint on the youth sport agenda after becoming prime minister in 2007 (Thorburn 2009). As was indicated on behalf of Michael Gove earlier in the chapter, the incoming coalition government continued to emphasise competition after their election in 2010. After withdrawing funding for competition managers, it was subsequently announced that a number of School Games co-ordinators would be employed through funding from Sport England and the Department of Health. A nationwide 'School Games' programme, 'inspired by the London 2012 Olympics', was also announced by the secretary of state for culture, media and sport (Hunt 2011). The role of NGBs was also emphasised in the coalition government's youth sport strategy as they were 'tasked with delivery of increased participation for young people under 16' (DCMS 2012, p. 9). While the coalition government sought to emphasise that these elements were different from previous Labour initiatives, their link with a longer-term shift back towards a competitive sport agenda that had previously been supported by John Major was clear.

Another agenda that was prominent from the time of John Major, but enhanced by the Labour government, was linking school and community-based provision into a continuous youth sport pathway (Houlihan 2002). Certainly, there was a long-standing concern regarding the extent and strength of links between schools and sports clubs in their communities (Alderson 1993; OFSTED 1995) and a number of Labour policy documents highlighted this issue as a priority (DCMS 2000; DCMS/Strategy Unit 2002; DCMS 2008). While building links with sport clubs was included in the remit of SSPs, greater responsibility for developing an infrastructure that connected school and community sport was entrusted to sporting organisations. NGBs were to be set 'challenging targets . . . [for] developing sport in school and the community' (DCMS 2000, p. 20). Ten NGBs, in particular, were given funding to do so from 1999 through Sport England's Active Sports programme, one objective of which was to 'improve retention in organised sport by young people' (KKP 2005). Subsequently, the local delivery structure for the Active Sports programme transformed into newly constituted County Sport Partnerships that become one part of the school sport architecture considered further in the next section.

The youth sport pathway desired by the Labour government also involved schools and sporting organisations developing a more systematic and integrated approach to identifying and progressing talented young people to elite level. In opposition to the beliefs of educationalists (e.g. Flintoff 2008a), sport policy documents, such as *Game Plan* (DCMS/Strategy Unit 2002, p. 127), became more explicit in identifying schools as 'form[ing] a key part in the talent identification and development framework'. The Specialist Sports Colleges introduced by the Major government were given an 'explicit focus on elite sport' to be enacted in part through their flexibility to allocate school places for talented young people (DCMS 2000, p. 7). The government's wider programme for the education of gifted and talented young people was also expected to enhance the identification and development of young sportspeople. However, the desired creation of a unified school and NGB talent identification and development system was undermined as sports such as football and rugby union withdrew talented young people from school sport competition and the school sport system more generally (Houlihan 2000). Over time, Specialist Sport Colleges came to play a greater role as hubs of individual SSPs rather than as centres for elite sport development.

As was outlined in the previous section, the salience of youth sport was to a great extent premised on its contribution to successive government's wider social agendas. This aspiration manifested itself in different ways in the specific policy agendas pursued and the particular programmes that were initiated, particularly as the prominence of and funding for youth sport rose under the Labour government. Smith and Waddington's (2004) comment, that there was a lack of clarity and specificity in crime-prevention-orientated policy objectives to be achieved through sport, was largely also applicable to other agendas such as educational attainment. As a result, two broad categories of underpinning philosophies can be identified amongst the large range of programmes and initiatives that were expected to address some or all of these wider agendas.

A first category included those school-based programmes that were expected to address both sporting and social agendas on a widespread, or as Kelly (2011) termed it 'universal', basis. For example, the seven revised outcomes determined in 2004 for the School Sport Partnership programme included those that referred to 'improved attitude, behaviour and attendance in PE and whole school'; 'increased attainment and achievement in and through PE, OSHL and sport' and 'improved quality of community life' (Loughborough Partnership 2006). Specialist Sport Colleges also carried similar expectations, particularly with regard to increased academic performance across all subject areas. The commissioning of a number of independent evaluations and studies (e.g. Loughborough Partnership 2008a, 2008b, 2008c) on the achievement of these outcomes reflected their importance to government departments and the Youth Sport Trust. However, national policy documentation for these programmes contained little guidance for the numerous schools involved as to how the policy aspirations were to be delivered or achieved. There remained something of an implicit assumption that positive wider social outcomes would be a natural consequence of generating increased participation in PE and school sport. Generally, evaluations found some indications of improvement in overall academic standards as well as teachers' perceptions of attendance and behaviour although reports often included qualifications regarding the difficulty asserting a causal link between any improvements and the specific sport programmes that were evaluated (Loughborough Partnership 2008a, 2008b, 2008c). There was also likely to be differences in the impact and emphasis given to these outcomes across the large number of different schools involved in the various school sport programmes.

A further national programme, delivered through schools, that was significantly aligned with the Labour government's broader social objectives was Step into Sport. Building upon existing Junior and Community Sport Leader Awards as well as the Millennium Volunteer initiative, Step into Sport expanded from its inception in 2002 to provide differentiated volunteering opportunities for pupils aged 11 to 19 years old in a number of School Sport Partnerships across England. In one respect, Step into Sport was designed to enhance the capacity of sporting and community organisations through encouraging greater numbers of young people to volunteer. Similar to other widespread youth sport programmes, however, government support for Step into Sport was predicated on its contribution to the personal and social development of the young people involved in the programme. The 'clear links [that Step into Sport had] to citizenship', a key agenda of the Labour government, were explicitly highlighted in the document *Learning through PE and Sport* (DCMS/DfES 2003, p. 11). The programme's contribution to this particular agenda, as well as increases in self-confidence and communication skills for the young people involved, were noted in evaluation reports (Bradbury 2006), although, again, there was evidence of differential impact with higher proportions of young volunteers being white and from middle-class backgrounds (Kay and Bradbury 2008).

The second category of programmes identifiable during the period of the Labour government operated largely outside of the school context, were orientated specifically towards social outcomes and tended to have more clearly defined groups of young people that were to be targeted for intervention. Playing for Success was one such programme, launched by the Department for Education and Employment in 1997, that provided study support sessions in the alternative environment of professional sports clubs in order to improve educational attainment in underachieving pupils in Key Stages 2 and 3 (Sharp et al. 2003). However, a greater number of other programmes used sport specifically to address crime, anti-social behaviour and drug use amongst young people. Such programmes were by no means new as Simmons (2004, cited by Coalter 2007), for example, identified that significant funding was allocated to sport-orientated projects that addressed crime through the Single Regeneration Budget initially launched by John Major's government. However, the policy impetus and some funding provided by the Labour government led to a significant expansion of similar programmes orientated towards crime reduction.

Perhaps most prominent among such programmes was Positive Futures, which was launched nationally in 2000. Initial funding of £6m was granted to Positive Futures and a subsequent £15m was allocated for the period between 2003 and 2006 (Home Office 2003; Nichols 2007). In line with the Labour's aspiration of joined-up government, it is notable that Positive Futures was nationally driven and funded by a partnership of Sport England, the Football Foundation, the Home Office Drugs Unit and the Youth Justice Board. Although these organisations continued to be involved, the national management of Positive Futures was outsourced in 2006 to the charitable organisation Crime Concern, a decision that was again in keeping with the thrust of Tony Blair's modernisation project. Unlike school-based programmes, however, Positive Futures encompassed a greater level of local determination in terms of delivery structures and approaches. As such there was a significant diversity amongst the 67 Positive Futures projects that were initially funded in various locations across the country. Moreover, across different localities, many other similar small-scale projects were instigated, funded through a variety of sources and delivered by a range of sporting and non-sporting organisations from the public and voluntary sectors (Smith and Waddington 2004). Given the diversity of projects, it is impossible to assess their overall impact on crime, anti-social behaviour and drug use amongst young people (Nichols 2007), although, again, relatively positive but often qualified evaluations of specific programmes were produced (e.g. Crabbe 2006). Furthermore, the plurality of such projects meant that they were less amenable to central governance than the mainstream school-based initiatives launched during the period of this study. It is to the governance of youth sport policy implementation that the chapter now turns in the following section.

GOVERNANCE AND IMPLEMENTATION
OF YOUTH SPORT POLICY

As youth policy agendas have incrementally developed over the period of this study, so have the policy instruments utilised in the implementation of these agendas. The change in the salience of youth sport marked by *Sport: Raising the Game* (DNH 1995) was accompanied by a similar expansion in the policy instruments utilised in the sector by the government (Houlihan 2002). This expansion continued under Labour with the result that central government increasingly took a directive approach to the governance of youth sport (King 2009). The increasingly wide range of policy instruments utilised, which included both inducements and constraints, will be considered in this section. Consideration will also be given to indications of a commitment to greater local determination of youth sport policy under the coalition government as well as the potential and realised local agency by youth sport organisations throughout the period.

A significant proportion of the 'Sport in Schools' chapter in *Sport: Raising the Game* (DNH 1995) was devoted to the policy instruments used to enact John Major's agenda. Most prominent among these instruments were those associated with assessment of the delivery of PE and school sport. In line with the focus on competitive team sport, OFSTED was instructed to include an assessment of the 'quality and range of games offered as part of the PE curriculum, together with provision for sport outside the curriculum' in all school inspections (DNH 1995, p. 11). An OFSTED audit of teacher training in PE and uptake of coaching qualifications were also announced (DNH 1995). In the same vein, but presented in a more incentivising light, was the introduction of Sportsmark and Sportsmark Gold awards for those schools that met specified criteria for the promotion of school sport (Houlihan 2000). The Sports Council was tasked with undertaking 'validation' visits to a sample of schools that received these awards every year (DNH 1995). The rationale underpinning all these tools was firmly associated with ongoing aspects of the market-based ideology increasingly being introduced into the school system in that they were expected to promote a 'spirit of competition [between schools] and encourage all schools to match the best' (DNH 1995, p. 12). Furthermore, the expectation that schools would publish information on school sport provision in their prospectuses was a further step designed to enhance market-orientated competition through parents being able to make increasingly informed decisions and choices between schools (DNH 1995).

In terms of regulatory mechanisms for PE and youth sport, there was a large degree of continuity from John Major's government to those of the Labour party. OFSTED's role in assessing school-based provision was continued and the Qualifications and Curriculum Authority (QCA) were tasked with undertaking a further investigation into PE and school sport with the objective of providing guidance and recommendations for all schools (DCMS/DfES 2003). The NCPE also remained in place and, through ongoing revisions, continued to ensure that national policy agendas were addressed in school teaching. Furthermore, Sportsmark and the new Activemark accreditation award continued to be an influential governance mechanism within the school sport system (Smith and Leech 2010) and similar award schemes, such as Clubmark, were expanded to voluntary sports clubs that provided activities for young people. Further regulation was also specifically applied to Specialist Sports Colleges which were required to apply for this status in the first instance and then had to undergo specified and assessed re-designation processes every three years.

However, if the information available on PE and school sport through inspection and awards was, rhetorically at least, presented as a mechanism to increase downward 'accountability' to parents by Major's government (DNH 1995), the expansion of other policy instruments under Labour was certainly aligned with increasing upward accountability to central government. In particular and in common with the broader education sector (Chitty 2008), there was a dramatic increase in centralised target setting for PE and school sport which was accompanied by burgeoning processes of national monitoring and evaluation. The most prominent target introduced by Labour was that concerned with the delivery of 'two hours of high quality PE and school sport' (DfES/DCMS 2003). The two-hour measure was not a new one, having been mentioned fleetingly in *Sport: Raising the Game* (DNH 1995), nor did it have a basis in scientific evidence regarding recommended exercise levels (Bloyce and Smith 2009). Nevertheless, the setting of quantitative targets for the proportion of pupils participating in two hours per week and the prominence of these targets, for example, through inclusion in Tony Blair's forward to *Game Plan* (DCMS/Strategy Unit 2002), certainly enhanced its influence within schools. Initially, a target of 75 per cent of pupils participating in two hours of PE and school sport per week by 2006 was set in 2002, at which time the baseline of participation was estimated at 25 per cent (DCSF 2008). The achievement of this target and an extended target of 85 per cent of pupils by 2008 led to the ultimate replacement of the two-hour measure with a more nebulous target associated with a five-hour 'offer' consisting of two hours of PE and school sport and opportunities for young people to participate in three additional hours within the school and the broader community.

The increasing levels of participation in PE and school sport point to the efficacy of these targets on implementation within schools. This is not to say that there were not criticisms of the two-hour target and associated monitoring and evaluation systems. Despite the publication of a guidance document, *High Quality PE and Sport for Young People* (DfES/DCMS 2004), there were ongoing concerns regarding the specification and measurement of the 'high quality' dimension of the target. Smith and Leech (2010), in particular, provided evidence that schools focused on the quantitative aspect of the target at the expense of quality of provision. Monitoring of the two-hour target, and other indicators of PE and school sport provision, was undertaken through an annual School Sport Survey undertaken by the consultancy company TNS on behalf of DfES. The School Sport Survey sat alongside a number of broader evaluations commissioned by government and the YST of specific school sport programmes, including SSPs (Loughborough Partnership 2008d), Specialist Sport Colleges (Institute of Youth Sport 2004) and Step into Sport (Bradbury 2006). The government explicitly recognised that the commissioning of extensive monitoring and evaluation of PE and school sport was, in itself, a governance mechanism designed to 'raise the status of sport and PE' within schools (DCMS/Strategy Unit 2002). Moreover, monitoring and evaluation were fundamental to the government's wider agenda of evidence-based policy through providing information on which future planning could be based (DCMS/Strategy Unit 2002). However, the linking of monitoring with specific national targets can bring perverse incentives and mask a diversity of practices in individual schools (Ball 2008). This may well have been the case in PE and school sport with teachers indicating that figures provided for the School Sport Survey were exaggerated in order to demonstrate achievement of the two-hour target (Smith and Leech 2010). The contribution of monitoring and evaluation to evidence-based policy in PE and school sport, therefore, remains somewhat open to question irrespective of these mechanisms' ongoing influence as directive policy instruments.

Improvements in participation and other aspects of PE and school sport, widely and consistently recognised in published evaluations throughout the period of the Labour government, were not only due to policy tools such as regulation, target setting and monitoring. As was indicated earlier, the Labour government allocated significant new funds to the achievement of their youth sport policy goals. By the government's own figures, a total of approximately £1.5bn was provided for PE and school sport from 2002 until 2008 from a mixture of mainstream government and National Lottery funding. Plans for a further allocation of £755m until 2011 were announced in 2008 (DCSF 2008). The provision of significant lottery funding for PE and school sport, for example, the £581m allocated to school sport facilities in England through the New Opportunities for PE and Sport programme, was potentially controversial given that the legislation creating the National Lottery required its funding to be additional to areas of core governmental spending (Moore 1997). Nevertheless, such arguments were by no means prominent and additional funding was never likely to garner significant resistance given that it was 'simply making good the long-term erosion of spending' on PE and school sport since the period of Thatcher's government (Houlihan and Green 2006).

In both education more broadly (Chitty 2008) and in school sport, in particular, the Labour government used the first-order policy tool of funding decisions to drive the pursuit of their specific policy agendas. Especially in the rollout of newly funded programmes in the early period of the Labour government, allocation of funding was strongly associated with the government's social inclusion agenda. Initial lottery funding for School Sport Co-ordinators and the NOPES programme was directed towards 'communities in greatest need' (DCMS 2000, p. 32) and 'areas of urban and rural deprivation' (DCMS 2001c, p. 12), respectively. Nevertheless, other mechanisms of influence associated with allocation of funding bore greater similarity to those previously enacted by the Major government. The relatively small amounts of funding available allowed the Major government to be increasingly prescriptive in the conditions associated with competitive bidding for funds. NGBs applying for grants were required to specify their contribution to school sport in their business plans, and schools and clubs were required to enhance competitive sport in order to qualify for 'challenge funds' made available through the Sports Council (DNH 1995). Such conditions continued to be applied to funding under the Labour government with Flintoff (2003) identifying that plans to target particular groups of young people and address educational outcomes were required to access particular streams of national lottery funding. However, the extent to which conditional funding impacted on local delivery and practice is less clear. Garrett (2004) and Lindsey (2008) identified case study sports clubs and schools, respectively, that did not feel compelled to target the types of young people required as a condition of funding in National Lottery programmes. These examples point to weaknesses in post-grant governance of lottery funding and it may well also have been the case that the power associated with conditional funding actually lessened as large-scale, widespread funding became established over the period of the Labour government.

A further instrument that was utilised by the Labour government was institutional reform, consisting of the creation and modification of organisational structures and individual roles within the youth sport sector. The precursors of these changes can, once more, be traced to the period of the Major government. The alignment of the PE teaching profession with sports coaching under the Major government was subsequently strengthened, for some teachers at least, by the establishment of what Armour (2010) termed as a 'youth sport pathway' for the teaching profession. As noted earlier, the SSP programme created new sport-related roles including school sport co-ordinators, competition managers and partnership development managers that were undertaken on a full- or part-time basis by existing teachers. The creation of these roles for the mainstream teaching profession was fundamental to the instigation of School Sport Partnerships and, as such, became a constitutive part of the ongoing shift towards sport-focused aspects of PE.

A more high-profile aspect of the SSP programme, which also involved Specialist Sports Colleges, was the creation of local delivery networks comprising of groups of schools and, aspirationally at least, community organisations such as sports clubs. These networks were designed to address the long recognised problem of fragmentation between the variety of organisations, including schools and clubs, involved in the youth sport provision

(Sports Council 1993a; DNH 1995; Alderson 1993). Although there are indications of some previous incremental progress (Murdoch 1993), it was only through the additional resources subsequently provided by the Labour government that more systematic development of institutional networks for youth sport was achieved.

As their name suggests, School Sport Partnerships typically consisted of families of four to eight secondary schools, each in turn linked to four to six primary schools. At the centre of each SSP was a Specialist Sports College that employed the partnership development manager who was responsible for providing the partnership with overall strategic direction. As the SSP programme rolled out across England, 450 individual partnerships, each with a similar structure, were created. The establishment of SSPs was expected to be the primary institutional mechanism through which the Labour government's aspirations and targets for the improvement of PE and school sport were to be realised (Carter 2005a). As networks, the institutional capacity of SSPs to do so was both supported and constrained by wider educational policies. The remit of specialist schools more generally, 'to develop partnerships with their "family" of local schools and to seek to become a local/regional centre of excellence', fitted well with their role as central hubs of SSPs (Houlihan 2000, p. 188). However, the fairly standardised institutional model of SSP and its universal rollout sat in contrast to the diversity being promoted in the education system more generally and the market-based competition that was inherent in this system. This competition was commonly cited as the reason for weaker co-operation between non-specialist secondary schools within SSPs (Flintoff 2003; Houlihan and Lindsey 2008; Green 2008). It was for similar reasons that secondary schools were generally more supportive of developing links with primary schools which were seen as a way of making their school attractive to prospective pupils and parents (Houlihan and Lindsey 2008).

SSPs also made progress in addressing the long-standing gap between schools and local sports clubs. An OFSTED (2006, p. 3) report commented that schools in SSPs had 'developed strong links with local sports clubs and sports coaches in the community, giving pupils many more opportunities to play sport outside school'. However, linkages between school and community provision also remained challenging in areas where few sports clubs existed, as King (2009) identified in the example of Liverpool. More broadly, Houlihan and Lindsey (2008) also noted that there remained a potential divide between the inclusive and universal ethos of schools and the desire of some clubs to enhance their success in competition by being selective in the young people allowed to become members. The subsequent emphasis of the coalition government on the major competitive sports and their development of links with schools (DCMS 2012) were only likely to heighten this concern.

Relationships between SSPs and local public-sector sport agencies were also variable. Overall, a national evaluation of the SSP programme found generally 'close and complementary relationships' between SSPs and local authorities (Loughborough Partnership 2006, p. 12). The advent of SSPs had, however, been challenging for many local authorities whose capacity, within education departments, to support co-ordination of school sport had been weakening for some time (Sports Council 1993a; OFSTED 1995). Some local authorities, therefore, saw SSPs as being in competition with their existing services (Houlihan and Lindsey 2008), whilst others responded to incoming SSP structures by undertaking 'fundamental reviews' of their own roles and responsibilities (Lindeman and Conway 2010). CSPs were a further ingredient of this institutional mix, added on behalf of Sport England and, again, while there was movement towards better integration between CSPs and SSPs, this did take time to evolve in some areas (Enoch 2010).

The evidence from SSPs does, at the very least, suggest a degree of variation in the local delivery of youth sport policies in spite of the range and strength of policy instruments that were utilised by government and national agencies. As Bloyce and Smith (2009, p. 76) commented, the complexity of the institutional context for youth sport meant that it was 'difficult for any one group—even a group as powerful as the government—to retain control over the implementation' of national policy agendas. Flintoff (2003, 2008a) also commented on the extent to which particular SSPs were influenced by local contexts and the particular characteristics of the teachers employed in the programme in individual schools. However, Flintoff (2008a) still warned that it was unreasonable to expect school-based staff involved in local delivery to significantly challenge the nationally dominant policy agendas, for example, the strengthening orientation towards sport rather than PE.

That the subsequent coalition government strongly prioritised competitive sport in their policy rhetoric and in their allocation of funding suggested that national priorities were to continue to be a strong influence on local delivery. Alongside this clear policy steer, however, initial pronouncements of the coalition government emphasised an aspiration to loosen central control and encourage local determination of youth sport delivery by schools (e.g. Gove 2010). That there was a potential tension between national exhortation to prioritise particular sporting agendas and the broader programme of decentralisation pursued by the coalition government appeared to go unrecognised, as was captured in the following pertinent extract from a Department for Education (2010) press release:

> Previously, PE and Sports strategy was driven by top-down targets, undermined by excessive bureaucracy, limiting the freedom of individual schools on how they used their funding . . . and lacked a proper emphasis on competitive team sports.

Nevertheless, the decentralisation rhetoric was supported by the coalition government's early removal of many of the policy instruments utilised by the Labour government. Within six months of taking office, Gove (2010) announced the removal of the 'five-hour-offer' target as well as the national

School Sport Survey by which this and other indicators of performance were measured. Requirements for specialist schools, including sports colleges, to submit re-designation applications at regular intervals were also removed. Furthermore, the funding for the employment of partnership development managers who oversaw each individual School Sport Partnership programme was cut. Gove (2010) suggested that schools could individually and collectively choose to continue to employ partnership development managers and retain other aspects of School Sport Partnerships. Linked with the general trend towards increasing commercial involvement in state education (Ball 2008), some School Sport Partnerships and their staff looked towards integration into or funding from the private sector as ways to secure their future. More broadly, the institutional networks for PE and school sport created by the Labour government were likely to fracture and fragment. As the Conservative chair of the Education Select Committee recognised, this was likely to have a particularly detrimental effect on the primary school sector that had especially benefited from links with secondary schools developed through SSPs (Stuart 2010).

CONCLUSION

Perhaps to an even greater extent than in other areas of sport policy, the early decisions of the coalition government make it particularly important to consider the potential legacy of a significant period for youth sport. The prioritisation of youth sport since 1990 can be attributed to a variety of factors. That there was a commonly accepted understanding that youth sport could contribute to a variety of wider agendas certainly underpinned its salience. The increasing prominence of youth sport under John Major was on account of the broader values that he personally associated with it. During the period of the Labour government, youth sport benefited from a broader alignment with notions of a social investment state and the refocusing on a broader conception of learning that encompassed, but was not limited to, education. Although some, still limited, evidence did start to emerge as to the contribution that youth sport made to these agendas, the initial policy impetus was underpinned by a more 'commonsense' appraisal, which Whitty (2010) suggested underpinned much Labour policy despite its rhetoric of evidence-based policy. The reaction against the coalition government's cuts can also be seen as representative of the widespread strength of this 'commonsense' view of the value of youth sport as well as the evidence of increased participation that was a legacy of Labour's funding. Nevertheless, with coalition government education policies being influenced by 'prejudices and misconceptions' (Chitty 2011, p. 11), it may be that it is only in the longer term that this evidence, together with well-marshalled support, may sustain the prominence that youth sport had during the period of this study.

It can also be suggested that the progressive prioritisation of youth sport over physical education also weakens the prospects of both. Incremental policies over time led Smith (2011) to speak of the prominence of 'sport in schools' rather than physical education or even school sport. Moreover, early indications of changes to the NCPE under the coalition government, to be enacted in 2014, suggested that it would include an increased emphasis on competitive sport, strengthening the re-emergence of the focus that was criticised during the period of the Major government. In addition to being representative of this trend, the instigation of a national programme of school games also bore the hallmarks of the coalition government's broader strategy of proving the 'dynamism of government' (Ball 2008, p. 2). However, programmes such as the school games and Sports Unlimited, both funded through Sport England, certainly lacked the scale of funding provided by the Labour government. Furthermore, even the publication of the coalition's youth sport strategy in 2012 did not convincingly provide evidence of a broader governmental strategy for youth sport beyond an association with the 2012 Olympic Games. Without a strong link to an ongoing school-based infrastructure, such as that provided by SSPs, there must remain concern about whether national impetus for youth sport can be fully sustained in the period immediately after 2012.

These developments also reflect the changing institutional context within which youth sport policy was made. The example of youth sport demonstrates that not only do coalitions of actors influence policy but also policy provides the context which enables different groups to advance their own interests. The priority given to youth sport by successive governments enabled the emergence of a supportive network comprising a variety of stakeholders. This network emerged from a fragmented context and its orientation towards youth sport came to sideline those that wished to advocate for the specific merits of physical education. Caution should still be exercised when ascribing too much importance to any youth sport policy network. Certainly, the emergence of a youth sport network became more evident through campaigning efforts against coalition government cuts to school sport funding in late 2010. However successful, advocacy in opposition to specific policies should not be confused with the capacity to influence proactively the development of subsequent policies. The extent to which the rise in prominence of youth sport can be explained in terms of 'policy taking' from wider agendas is reflected in the diminished capacity for independent policymaking in the sector. As it became more pre-eminent in the sector, the Youth Sport Trust increasingly became an organisation geared towards the delivery of government policy. The early and politically motivated sidelining of the Youth Sport Trust under the coalition government was also particularly notable. The subsequent increase in prominence of Sport England within the youth sport sector offered little more for those looking for strong and independent policy leadership as capacity to do so within this organisation had been subject to continual hollowing out since the late 1980s and early 1990s.

Paradoxically, it may be an aspect of provision that was supported but stayed somewhat dislocated from the mainstream of youth sport policy throughout the period of the Labour government that could be well placed to demonstrate a certain endurance. As in wider education policy (Whitty 2010; Chitty 2008), Labour's focus on social inclusion in youth sport waned as a more universal approach was adopted especially in terms of the targets to be delivered by School Sport Partnerships and other PESSCL initiatives. Nevertheless, a diverse array of programmes utilising sport to address social issues and, in particular, crime and anti-social behaviour were continued. Many of these programmes, even those such as Positive Futures that were funded nationally, were located in and adopted approaches orientated towards particular localities. That a high proportion of these programmes were managed by voluntary sector organisations only serves to strengthen their alignment with the decentralised ethos of the coalition government's Big Society agenda. Although it can certainly be anticipated that funding cuts are likely to affect some programmes, their association with a prominent national policy agenda may generate opportunities for skilled local advocates and operators.

Local determination within schools is also likely to be a significant factor in shaping the medium-term legacy of Labour's investment in youth sport. While in place, this funding undoubtedly and unsurprisingly enabled centralised control and some degree, at least, of universal implementation especially through the establishment of the institutional infrastructure of School Sport Partnerships. The significance of other policy tools implemented by Labour, such as target setting, monitoring and evaluation, cannot be separated from the provision of funding associated with them (Ball 2008). That ongoing adjustment of targets was required to maintain their influence, as identified more broadly by Chitty (2008), suggests some relative weakness of this particular policy tool, as does the suggestion of data manipulation and perverse outcomes associated with monitoring of PE and school sport targets. In turn, this suggests that locally there remained capacity to resist central influence. The coalition government's education policies are also orientated towards greater independence for individual schools. As such, it may certainly be the case that the focus on school sport competition is increasingly mediated by local circumstances and the priorities of staff in schools. However, Chitty (2011) also observed a countervailing trend in the coalition government's education policies towards increased decision-making powers held by central government. For youth sport, the initial vision for coalition government policy did not extend significantly beyond the promotion of competitive sport. The resultant danger for youth sport is that it incrementally returns to the margins of education policy at a time when central government seeks to initiate substantial change within the school system.

8 Continuity and Change in British Sport Policy

The analysis of sport policy presented in this book makes it difficult to deny that there have been significant developments in the fortunes of sport over the last 20 years or so. However, what the analysis in Chapters 2 to 7 has also highlighted is the unevenness in the extent and, more importantly, in the intensity or depth of change. The opening section of this chapter therefore examines in more detail the nature and extent of change in sport policy in general and more specifically in relation to elite, community and youth/school sport. This examination will enable a closer consideration of the questions raised in chapter one concerning the salience of sport to government, the allocation of resources, changes to the machinery of government and the distribution of power within the subsector. A number of these questions correspond closely to the analytic schema outlined by Hall (1986) in which he identified three 'orders' of change—'third-order' changes to policy objectives, 'second-order' changes to the range of policy instruments utilised and, finally, 'first-order' changes to the resources committed to existing instruments. This assessment in the nature, direction and scale of change in sport policy will be followed by a more specific review of the concepts and analytic frameworks outlined in Chapter 1 to indicate how they contributed to the overall analysis.

With regard to continuity or change in policy objectives for sport, it is argued that it is the degree of continuity that is most striking. The emphasis given to elite sporting success by John Major in *Sport: Raising the Game* has been maintained and, as will be argued below, intensified in the intervening period. Even the present government, faced with severe pressure to cut the public budget and with a preference for market solutions, has made a clear resource commitment to support elite sport development programmes as athletes and NGBs look beyond the 2012 Olympic and Paralympic Games to the 2016 Games in Rio de Janeiro. While the funding allocated for preparation for 2016 is highly unlikely to match the funding made available to support a Games on 'home soil', it is likely that the long-term upward trend in funding elite development identified in Chapter 5 will continue. However, simply to note the broad continuity between governments in policy towards elite sport under-emphasises the significant intensification of commitment to this objective relative to other aspects of sport policy, particularly community sport, but also youth sport. To a large extent intensity of commitment to particular objectives will be reflected in what Hall would refer to as changes in first-order resources such as money, regulation/legislation and administrative capacity. Suffice to say at this point that the intensification of government commitment to elite sporting success in general (and at the Olympic and Paralympic Games in particular) has been one of the most distinctive developments over the period under review and since the mid-1990s in particular.

A similar conclusion can be drawn from an analysis of the development of school sport since 1990. Again, the catalyst for policy development in this area was John Major's enthusiasm and the initial momentum given by *Sport: Raising the Game*. However, it was under the premiership of Tony Blair and his concern to put education reform and improvement at the heart of his government's agenda that intensified the momentum for the restructuring of school sport. The extent to which school sport was able to benefit from policy initiatives in the education policy subsector was a consequence of three factors. The first of these factors was the personal endorsement of the prime minister and of the education secretary, Estelle Morris, rather than being the outcome of successful lobbying by either school sport organisations (such as PE teachers associations or school sport associations) or NGBs. Indeed, what is striking about the development of specialist sports colleges and School Sport Partnerships was the extent to which they were constructed independent of any significant contribution from the teaching profession or school sport organisations. The second factor was the opportunity to link school sport policy objectives with a much more influential policy area which provided the opportunity to argue that investment in increasing opportunities for participation in sport by schoolchildren would produce a more general benefit, for example, in relation to school attendance and pupil behaviour. However, the capacity to take advantage of this kind of opportunity depends often on the availability of a capable policy entrepreneur (the third factor) who has the necessary political skills and access to be able to take advantage of the opportunity to generalise what might be construed as relatively narrow sectional interests. As has been argued, Sue Campbell was able to fulfil that role very successfully, particularly under the Labour administrations of Blair and Brown.

The environment within which change in elite sport policy and school sport policy took place since the early to mid-1990s has a number of distinctive features. Both policies benefited greatly from having senior politicians as champions (John Major and Tony Blair in relation to elite sport and Major, Blair and Estelle Morris in relation to school sport). In addition, the environment was positive, or at least neutral, insofar as there was no significant lobby opposing a greater emphasis on elite and school sport, thus allowing policy entrepreneurs such as Sue Campbell to operate without generating significant opposition. The generally positive environment for the development of elite and school sport policy since 1990 has resulted in considerable stability of investment of public and lottery resources and, as indicated in Chapters 5 and 7, strong positive outcomes in relation to Olympic and Paralympic medal success and increased levels of participation in sport among school pupils.

The level of government commitment to elite sport and school sport and the evidence of positive impact of public policy are in marked contrast to the dominant features of adult or community sport since 1990. There is indeed continuity of policy across the governments of John Major, those of Blair and Brown and that of the Conservative–Liberal Democrat coalition, but it is a continuity characterised by low priority, policy indecision and policy failure. There are a number of possible reasons for the contrast between the treatment of elite and school sport on the one hand and community sport on the other. First, in terms of salience to government, the low level of adult participation does not manifest itself as an issue that imposes itself on either the public (media) or the governmental agenda. Unlike elite sport, there is no simple medals table against which the UK's relative performance can easily be measured. As the Compass report (1999) demonstrated, finding comparators which use a similar definition of 'sport' and of 'regular participation' makes inter-country comparison difficult. The second reason relates to the first and concerns the lack of a clear, or at least a compelling, rationale for government intervention in community sport. This issue was especially acute for Conservative governments where the paternalism associated with encouraging citizens to take part in sport was often anathema. It is arguably only in the last few years that the health benefits of sport participation, emphasised in *Game Plan*, have emerged as a justification for policy intervention that might cut across all three major political parties. A third reason is undoubtedly the complexity of the problem to be addressed. Without wishing to detract from the policy achievements of UK Sport and the Olympic and Paralympic NGBs, developing policy to deliver improved elite performance is relatively straightforward by comparison to engineering an increase in adult participation. The interplay of personal, cultural and socioeconomic factors that affect participation levels is of far greater complexity than those that affect elite success or the participation of children in sport in schools. As Collins with Kay (2003) noted, social exclusion from sport is often the result of multiple factors such as poverty, disability, family obligations and geography. Moreover, as Collins (2011) has argued, governments have ignored the fact that achieving higher levels of participation involves a significant change in behaviour and the current use of free time. Governments have a tendency to address complex problems rhetorically rather than substantively, preferring to engage with more straightforward problems that offer the prospect of a 'quick win', that is, one that will produce a positive newspaper headline before the next election. Where the government has considered the issue of the stagnation in the level of adult sport participation, it has tended to adopt short-term strategies that border on the self-delusional such as the much heralded demonstration effect of the London 2012 Olympic and Paralympic Games. The final reason for the reluctance of governments to address adult participation is their lack of control over the delivery mechanism for adult participation policy. Local authorities, with their substantial stock of sport and leisure facilities and staff, were extremely variable in their willingness to cooperate in the delivery of the centrally determined policy initiatives of the DCMS and Sport England (King 2009). The recent attempt by government to use the data collected through the Active People survey to set targets for increasing adult participation for each local authority foundered, in part at least, due to the latter's variability in their willingness to abandon locally determined strategic plans for sport particularly when neither the DCMS nor Sport England had much to offer by way financial support. In this context the adoption by Sport England of NGBs as their primary delivery agents was a consequence of the general lack of cooperation from local authorities and the assumption that NGBs and their clubs would be more biddable partners. However, as was made clear in Chapter 5, the strategy has been unsuccessful, with most NGBs failing to reach the participation targets agreed in their whole sport plans.

The most recent DCMS sport strategy (DCMS 2012) is, to some extent, an acknowledgement of the complexity and intractability of the problem of raising adult participation levels. As the secretary of state, Jeremy Hunt, commented, 'A new approach for England is needed—a more rigorous, targeted and results-orientated way of thinking about grassroots sport, which focuses all our energies into reaching out to young people more effectively' (DCMS 2012, p. 1). The new strategy, which focuses on the 14- to 25-year age group, is premised on the reasonable assumption that a change in attitudes towards sport participation will be achieved only over the long term. 'We are seeking a consistent increase in the proportion of people regularly playing sport. In particular, we want to raise the proportion of 14–25 year olds who play sport and to establish a lasting network of links between schools and sports clubs in local communities so that we keep young people playing sport up to and beyond the age of 25' (DCMS 2012, p. 3). Unfortunately, the acknowledgement that engineering a change in sporting habits needs to focus on the young and may take a generation to achieve was not shared by Jeremy Hunt's colleague Michael Gove, secretary of state for education, one of whose first actions in government was to substantially reduce the funding for School Sport Partnerships, arguably the most successful youth sport initiative of the last 20 years.

The foregoing discussion indicates not only the direction of sport policy and the relative policy priorities, but also the changes in the distribution of power among sport policy subsectors and actors. The period since 1990 has witnessed a clustering of policy actors around specific subsectoral interests, particularly those of elite sport and youth sport. With regard to elite sport, it is difficult to assess the extent to which the clustering of actors (including the

British Olympic Association, the sports media, the English Institute of Sport, UK Sport and the Olympic NGBs) constitutes a powerful advocacy coalition. The cluster certainly undertakes advocacy on behalf of elite sport and especially its continued public funding post-2012. However, it is doubtful whether the generous current level of funding and the promise of continued funding up to 2016 are the result of the exercise of coalition power, as there is little if any evidence that the elite lobby forced government to do something it would otherwise have chosen not to do. Indeed, it is arguable that the policy momentum to prioritise elite sport success emanated substantially from government, albeit within a highly supportive general political environment. Such is the momentum behind elite sport success that slowing that momentum or reversing it, for example, to save public money, would pose any government with a severe political challenge. Government investment in elite sport has elevated the public's expectations and it would be a brave or foolhardy government that would adopt a funding strategy aimed at delivering a top 15 position in the medals table (the UK's normal position in the post-war period) rather than a top five position.

Policy development over the period since 1990 offers a sharper insight into the distribution of power in the school sport sector. For much of the period of the Blair and Brown Labour governments school sport, despite varying levels of enthusiasm from successive secretaries of state for education, enjoyed strong support. Unqualified governmental support ended abruptly with the election of the coalition government, which, although endorsing the objective of increased participation, differed sharply from its predecessor regarding the means by which that objective was to be achieved and the resources that its achievement warranted. However, as discussed in Chapter 7, the cluster of interests (with the Youth Sport Trust at its heart) that had developed around school sport was able to mobilise with reasonable effectiveness to force a partial retreat by the education minister.

No such positive assessment can be made in relation to adult community sport. In the list of reasons given above for the failure of successive governments to address effectively the challenge of raising adult participation, one that was omitted related to the lack of a powerful lobby on behalf of community sport. Whereas many other European countries, the Scandinavian countries most notably, have large sports confederations that advocate on behalf of club and community sport interests, such organisations are conspicuous by their absence in the UK, although the Sport and Recreation Alliance is making progress in filling that gap. Where community sport has risen, albeit marginally, on the political agenda is in the home countries due in large part to the dominance of broadly social democratic political parties in Edinburgh and Cardiff and the exigencies of sectarianism in Northern Ireland.

Turning to consider shifts in power relations between individual policy actors since 1990, three main conclusions are suggested. The first is that individual politicians, whether prime ministers or ministers in the DCMS, remain dominant within the policy sector. However, since the mid-1990s there has been a greater degree of involvement of other interests, especially NGBs, but much of this involvement takes the form of consultation rather than a significant sharing of power.[1] While the dependence of government on the delivery network of NGBs and clubs should give sports organisations some leverage, it is generally outweighed in significance by the extent of financial resource dependence of NGBs and clubs on public subsidy. That elected politicians should occupy a pre-eminent position in a public policy network should not be surprising, but the extent to which other interests are marginalised (by comparison to health, transport and agriculture, for example) is significant.

The second conclusion concerns the rise in prominence of the Youth Sport Trust. Despite its heavy reliance on public funding, the philanthropic financial base of the organisation and the political capacity of its chair, Sue Campbell, resulted in it achieving a central location in the implementation network for a series of school sport initiatives. The election of a government committed to deregulation in 2010 undermined much of the influence of the trust but there are signs that the organisation is successfully re-establishing its relationship with government. The third conclusion is more tentative and concerns devolution and its potential impact on UK and English sport policy. At the UK level, the merger of UK Sport and Sport England proposed by the Conservative–Liberal Democrat coalition government prompted opposition from the Scottish government, who were sensitive to any attempt by Westminster to reverse the gains made under the 1998 Devolution Act, particularly in the period when the Scottish National Party is preparing for a referendum on independence in 2014. Of greater potential significance are the consequences of diverging policy directions due to governments with different ideologies in Cardiff and Edinburgh on the one hand and Westminster on the other. There is already a sharp awareness in England that Welsh and Scottish university students are treated much more favourably than their English counterparts and that the health service in Wales and Scotland imposes fewer costs on the patient than in England. If Wales and Scotland continue to give greater priority to community sport than is the case in England, it is possible that a perceived divergence in provision might stimulate political debate in England and push the issue further up the policy agenda.

1990 TO 2012: A DISTINCTIVE PERIOD IN UK SPORT POLICY?

In the opening chapter there was a brief discussion of the problem of defining and delimiting significant periods in policy. It was argued that the temptation to proclaim a particular time span a distinctive period in policy history should be resisted particularly if the period under discussion is recent, as temporal distance will provide a sharper focus on continuities and breaks with the past. The present study covered a time span in which there were two prime ministers, John Major and Tony Blair, with a strong interest in sport policy and in which one political party, Labour, enjoyed a prolonged period in office. Since 1990 there were certainly developments in sport policy, though mainly ones which Hall would class as first- or second-order changes, which were distinctive and noteworthy, including: the first central government department responsible for sport; the introduction of the National Lottery; the restructuring of the sports council; devolution; School Sport Partnerships; and data collection through the Active People survey. While the cumulative effect of these developments could arguably be interpreted as adding weight to the claim that the years from 1990 to the present (or at least until the election of the coalition government) were sufficiently distinctive to deserve the description as a discrete period of policy or, in the language of Baumgartner and Jones (1993, 2002), a period of equilibrium which was punctuated by the economic crisis of 2008 and the election of a neoliberal government in 2010.

However, it is equally easy to construct a contrary argument. On a number of occasions in this study we have drawn attention to the degree of continuity not only between the governments of Major and those of Blair and Brown, but also between the Labour governments and those of Margaret Thatcher. Blair's promotion of modernisation and his emphasis on stakeholding resonate strongly with central elements of the new public management philosophy espoused by Margaret Thatcher in the 1980s. It could also be argued that the continuities stretch back even further and are part of the gradual (though admittedly unevenly paced) progression of sport from being primarily the preserve of civil society institutions to being an instrument in the government's portfolio for dealing with a range of largely social welfare issues. The transition from an Advisory Sports Council in the mid-1960s to an Executive Sports Council in the early 1970s to Action Sport from 1982, to National Demonstration Projects in the mid-1980s to *Sport: Raising the Game* in the mid-1990s followed by the plethora of more recent initiatives provide some evidence at least of a consistent policy trajectory that stretches back to the Labour government of Harold Wilson if not further back to the Wolfenden report of 1960. According to this assessment, the Thatcher years would be defined not as a break with the past, but simply a slowing in the pace at which sport was moving into a more central position in fabric of public policy.

One way of examining the nature of and balance between policy continuity and change is to utilise the metaphor of levels of beliefs discussed in Chapter 1 and used most explicitly in advocacy coalition theory. At the level of 'deep core beliefs' there has been a strongly and consistently held belief in the value of competitive sport, especially as a character-forming experience. This positive valuation of sport is complemented by a long-established concern that leisure time should be used positively and that unstructured leisure time left society 'at risk', particularly from disruptive behaviour by the young. Although manifesting itself in different ways (for example, Action Sport in the 1980s and Positive Futures in the 2000s), the concern with the problem of free time and the belief that sport can address that concern effectively are themes which dates back to the mid-nineteenth century.

There is rather less continuity at the policy core level of belief with the most explicit tensions arising over the policy instruments best suited to achieve policy objectives rather than the policy objectives themselves. Here the tension is between confidence in government intervention and leadership (which could be described as paternalism) as opposed to confidence in the market and the promotion of individual responsibility as a means of optimising provision. However, even here the tension is often reflected more in the rhetoric of political debate than in the substance of policy with all the governments covered by this study making only modest adjustments to be the balance between government intervention and market autonomy. For example, Margaret Thatcher's commitment to market solutions (reflected most sharply in the introduction of compulsory competitive tendering for local authority sports facilities) was balanced by intervention by her government to determine a national curriculum for PE. Likewise, Tony Blair's centralist control over School Sport Partnerships was balanced by a more pragmatic attitude to voluntary sector and commercial provision of public services in sport. Not surprisingly there was far less continuity at the 'secondary belief' level where differences over funding patterns, especially the extent of use of Exchequer funding, and selection of primary delivery partners (NGBs or local authorities) were more obvious.

In summary, rather than the development of sport policy since 1990, and indeed since the 1960s, being characterised by periods of equilibrium punctuated by abrupt changes in policy, the period is characterised by a steady, though uneven, expansion in the role of the state in sport and a consistent prioritisation of elite sport success and school/youth sport over community sport. Using Hall's typology of 'orders' of change it is argued that while there is evidence of considerable movement in relation to the first two orders, there is far less movement in relation to third-order change— changes in policy goals. However, in relation to third-order changes it could be argued that the narrowing of Sport England's policy goals from a concern with the promotion of physical activity to a narrower focus on competitive sport is one example although it could be argued, indeed more persuasively, that the prominence given to the promotion of physical activity was a short-lived and unsuccessful attempt to punctuate the long established equilibrium of the focus on the promotion of competitive sport.

THE DOMINANT ROLE OF GOVERNMENT

Earlier in this chapter the pre-eminent role of government was noted and explained partly by the absence of effective challenges to its policy leadership.

A fuller understanding of the capacity of government to dominate the sport policy subsector can be gained by reference to the work of Hood and Margetts (2007) and Lowi (1964, 1970), which was summarised in Table 1.3. Hood and Margetts were concerned to identify the resources—nodality, authority, treasure and organisation—available for governments to deploy in pursuit of their policy goals. In relation to sport policy the nodality of central government is clear, particularly since the creation of the Department of National Heritage and its successor the Department of Culture, Media and Sport. For Hood and Margetts (2007, p. 6) nodality 'equips government with a strategic position from which to dispense information, and likewise enables government to draw in information for no other reason than that it is a centre or clearing-house'. Nodality, like the other three resources, fulfils a dual function insofar as each is a mechanism for effecting change and for gathering information, that is, detecting. Nodality can be sought or engineered by government or it can be acquired by default through the absence of other effective nodes. With regard to sport policy it is clear that since the 1970s governments have at some times sought nodality and at others simply accepted their nodal position, although the government's enthusiasm to exploit its nodality varied considerably across different aspects of sport policy.

Almost since the establishment of the executive sports council in 1972 successive sports ministers have sought to undermine the terms of the Royal Charter and treat the agency and its successors, Sport England and UK Sport, as extensions of the DNH and DCMS. More importantly, as noted above, there is no alternative node in the UK such as the sports confederations which exist in many northern European countries and which might challenge the government's role. As a result it is the DCMS, operating through Sport England, UK Sport and to a lesser extent the Youth Sport Trust, which has established itself as the dominant node in the sport policy landscape. However, while the government's adoption of a nodal position is most apparent in relation to elite sport and, within England, in relation to youth sport, it is far less obvious in relation to community sport, where it has been much more willing to cede nodality to home country sports councils. In summary, government holds a nodal position in the landscape of UK sport, but has considerable discretion as to whether it seeks to exploit its nodal position partly due to the general weakness of the sport lobby. Much the same can be said in relation to sport policy in Wales and Scotland, where the weakness of the sport lobby leaves the governments with a nodal position by default.

The second resource, authority, can be used by governments to require information and is a resource that has been used intermittently over the years. Some information, such as evidence of success in international sports competitions, does not require authority for its collection, but other data, for example in relation to participation by children in sport at schools, the quality of PE classes, the level of adult participation in sport and the degree of satisfaction felt by the users of public sports facilities, require the authority of government for effective collection. While few data, apart from those generated through the general household survey, were collected in the 1980s and 1990s, the period since 2000 saw a substantial increase in their systematic collection. Taking Part, Active People, the School Sport survey and the Sport England/NGBs club membership surveys fulfilled a number of purposes—establishing baseline data, measuring progress and/ or confirming achievements—and at least some of the data (those from schools and from NGBs) would not have been provided had the request not been reinforced by the authority (and control of access to financial resources) of government. Deciding what data to collect, from whom and when are significant powers and ones that government is in the best position to exploit. The decision to require data from schools about participation levels of pupils signalled the importance of youth sport participation and also gave the government a powerful resource with which to pressure schools to comply with its participation objectives. However, the decision by the coalition government to stop collecting data through the School Sport survey also reflects the power of government to decide not to require data and thus, potentially, deny to its critics a valuable resource with which to monitor the impact of government policy.

The third resource, treasure, can be used to buy information, but more importantly has often been converted into incentives through which influence could be exerted and behaviour modified. As illustrated in Chapters 5, 6 and 7, treasure, in the form of subsidies, grants and tax breaks, has been applied by the government with considerable success to aid the achievement of its sport policy goals. The most obvious examples would include the increases in the volume of treasure allocated to elite sport and school sport and the likely reduction in the allocation to community sport—although this allocation was heavily mediated by the decisions of the many local authorities throughout the UK. The final resource is organisation, 'a label for a stock of land, buildings and equipment, and a collection of individuals with whatever skills and contacts they may have, in government's direct possession or otherwise available to it' (Hood and Margetts 2007, p. 102). Some recent examples of utilisation of organisational capacity related to sport are fairly obvious and would include the establishment of the network of specialist sports colleges, county sports partnerships and School Sport Partnerships in England. The clearest illustration of the significance of this resource is the impact of the establishment of a specialist agency, UK Sport, to coordinate and drive the pursuit of elite athlete improvement and medal success.

Armed with these resources, governments over the last 20 years or so have designed and utilised a wide variety of more specific policy instruments (Hall's second order changes) of distribution, redistribution, regulation and administrative redesign (see Table 1.3) for the achievement of its objectives. As regards examples of the use of government authority to distribute resources, the clearest example is the introduction of the National

Lottery and the way in which the income has been apportioned by government. Funding from the National Lottery was crucial to the establishment of the elite sport development infrastructure, especially in supporting the elite coaching and athlete support services of NGBs and in providing direct financial support to athletes. Similarly, with regard to school sport the government used its authority to identify sport as one of the specialisms that secondary schools could adopt which required distribution of resources from the education ministry budget. National Lottery funding was also used to support the introduction and steady expansion of the School Sport Partnership programme. Although the National Lottery generated a relatively modest proportion of total public sector expenditure on sport (that is, if local authority spending is included), the fact that its use could be influenced directly by government provided substantial policy leverage. In addition to the extensive use of distributional power, governments also used their power to redistribute public resources. The use by both UK Sport and Sport England of their power to reduce the budgets of NGBs deemed to be failing to meet their medal or participation targets reflects a commitment to a 'command-and-control' style of policy implementation and is a far cry from the shift from government to governance identified in other policy subsectors. Government has also used its control over financial resources to redistribute lottery funding from Sport England to help finance the cost of hosting the London Olympic and Paralympic Games.

Further evidence of the persistence of traditional government within the sport policy area comes from an examination of the use of governmental regulatory power, particularly under the Labour governments, which exercised regulatory power both overtly and covertly. Among the many examples of overt regulation are: the ring-fencing of funding for school initiatives, such as School Sport Partnerships and other elements of the PESSCL and PESSYP strategies; the control over procedures for accessing National Lottery funding by communities and sports clubs; the use of OFSTED inspections to monitor the work of specialist sports colleges and SSPs; the introduction of criminal records bureau checks for those wishing to work with children in schools and sports clubs; the regular reviews of the content of the national curriculum for physical education; and the use of comprehensive area assessments and national indicators to measure sport outcomes. At the more indirect and covert level was the modernisation agenda of the Labour governments and the impact that it had on the management culture of national agencies, NGBs and local authorities. Similarly the rhetoric of access, health, fitness and participation was in tension with the underlying assumption that the promotion of competitive sport was the primary concern of school-level interventions. However, as noted in Chapter 7, the privileging of competitive sport became increasingly explicit through the appointment of competition managers in SSPs and the coalition government's public endorsement of competitive sports in schools and the funding of the School Games.

Administrative redesign is the fourth major tool for effecting policy change and overlaps to an extent with Hood and Margett's concepts of nodality and organisation. However, while Hood and Margett emphasise the importance of organisational nodality for the collection of information and the management of the flow of information between organisations, Lowi emphasises the role of administrative design and redesign in the management of policy implementation. Administrative redesign can be used most effectively to ensure a strong focus through organisational specialisation on a particular issue or problem and has been used widely in recent years. The clearest examples of the application of this strategy include the decision by John Major to establish the Department of National Heritage, the creation of UK Sport as a specialist agency to focus on a very narrow range of objectives—particularly international sporting success and success in winning bids to host major events—and the decision to separate the anti-doping function from UK Sport and establish UK Anti-Doping. Other examples, which are arguably less effective, include the decision to establish county sport partnerships which, to an extent at least, were perceived by some local authorities as undermining their sports development activities and the more recent decisions to dismantle the School Sport Partnerships and to require the merger of UK Sport and Sport England. Both the last two decisions were driven less by evidence of organisational failure and more by ideological prejudices towards state activity.

PUTTING THE ANALYSIS OF POLICY OBJECTIVES, RESOURCES AND INSTRUMENTS INTO PERSPECTIVE

The foregoing discussion drew attention to the problems of identifying continuity of policy and determining when a policy development constituted a significant break in the pattern of continuity. In addition, the identification and cataloguing of policy instruments tells us much about how policy change is effected or how policy stability is maintained, but it is of limited value in explaining why particular policy objectives have been set and why one combination of policy instruments was deemed more appropriate than another. Reference to macro- and meso-level theory provides a context within which to address these and similar questions such as those about agenda-setting and policy choice in relation to sport.

Although macro-level theories vary in scope and focus, they share a common concern with exploring and explaining the distribution of power in society and the implications of that distribution for the role of the state. For Abend (2008, p. 179) they provide 'a Weltanschauung . . . an overall perspective from which one sees and interprets the world'. Neo-Marxism, neo-pluralism, governance and public choice/market liberalism are all examples of this type of theory. Each of these macro-level theories provides a conceptual language and usually a set of propositions about the world which informs and structures social investigation. While at times macro-level theories can become so dominant in a branch of social science (for example, the realist perspective in international relations) that they assume paradigmatic status, this is unusual outside the natural sciences: In the social sciences, theoretical pluralism is much more common. In the practice of policy analysis it is not uncommon for researchers to choose to operate within a particular macro-level theory such neo-pluralism (Lindblom 1977) or neo-Marxism (Hill 2009) or to avoid a commitment to a particular perspective, as is the case in this study, and to use them as competing worldviews which inform research design and offer a range of perspectives which inform analysis.

In the opening chapter four prominent macro-level theories were identified as being potentially valuable in generating insights into the analysis of sport policy. While it is possible to utilise macro-level theories to investigate particular policy subsectors and specific policy decisions, it is often the case that the broad assumptions about power relations at the societal level lose some of their analytic incisiveness when applied to specific issues and decisions. However, as argued in Chapter 1, the value in utilising macro-level theory is twofold: First, it sensitises the researcher to themes, interests and power relations which, while not being overt, are likely to provide the context within which policy is made; second, the meso-level frameworks designed specifically to examine the policy process in subsectors, or with respect to particular decisions, incorporate explicitly or often implicitly macro-level assumptions about power, access to the policy agenda, decision-making processes and the nature of sectional interests that affect the way in which analysis proceeds and consequently the conclusions that are drawn.

As regards neo-Marxism there is a tendency to dismiss it as a body of theory whose credibility was undermined by the collapse of European communism in the late 1980s and the apparent triumph of capitalist democracy. However, the recent European and North American banking crisis and degree of subservience of Western governments to the interests of finance capital have prompted a revival of interest in neo-Marxism as a lens through which to examine society. Despite this, resurgence in interest neo-Marxism is severely hampered by the fragmentation of the traditional working class (one of its basic units of analysis) and by a tendency to lapse into tautology when considering the role of the state. Nevertheless, neo-Marxism is important in sensitising the researcher to the ubiquitous nature of business interests and the closeness of their relationship to government. In relation to sport policy, neo-Marxism prompts questions about the ideological underpinnings of government intervention in school and youth sport where there is a clear concern to utilise sport to achieve greater social control over young people. Over the lifetime of the School Sport Partnerships there was an increasing emphasis placed on the instrumental use of sport to achieve objectives related to improved behaviour and attendance. The enthusiasm of successive governments for competitive sport might also be seen as evidence of ideological manipulation, that is, a way of inculcating values supportive of capitalist competition. From a slightly different angle the priority given to the hosting of international sports events, the enforcement of compulsory competitive tendering and the expansion of out-of-school-hours sport could all be interpreted as efforts by governments to create new markets for commercial enterprise. In addition, the strategy adopted by many local authorities of transferring sports assets to trusts as a way of trying to avoid the perceived excesses of marketisation could also be interpreted in neo-Marxist terms as an example of the state itself being a site of 'class' conflict. However, none of these examples is especially compelling as the hosting strategy, for example (particularly in relation to Wales and Scotland), could be explained more persuasively in terms of the imperatives of nationalism rather than capitalism. Nevertheless, the capacity of business interests to dominate in policy discussions should not be under-estimated.

Part of the weakness of neo-Marxist macro analysis is that it is possible to arrive at broadly similar conclusions regarding the influence of business interests in sport through neo-pluralist analysis, which avoids the tautological problems and teleological assumptions of neo-Marxism. What is particularly valuable in the application of a neo-pluralist analytic framework is not that it highlights the privileged position of business interests (the non-sport commercial sector as well as the more commercially successful NGBs) but that it demonstrates the weakness of the representation of interests in the fields of community sport and youth sport. The underpinning assumption of neo-pluralism that the social system allows and indeed facilitates the formation of interest groups and that the political system is sufficiently open (or at least porous) to enable interaction with decision makers encourages the researcher to search for evidence of interest-group formation, activity and impact.

Although over the last ten to 15 years it is possible to trace the gradual strengthening in the voice of elite sport, it is far more difficult to determine the cause. Conventional interest-group theory suggests that effective interest-group lobbying, often supported by the media, causes the change in the government's agenda. However, while the media had certainly been prominent in promoting the 'problem' of UK international (and especially Olympic) failure, it is hard to identify a central role for interests in the major Olympic NGBs such as athletics and swimming. Indeed, a much more plausible explanation for the current strength of the elite sport lobby is that it was the side effect of central government policy to prioritise elite sport and the subsequent decisions regarding the use of national lottery funding and the organisational restructuring of NGBs and the sports councils. The availability of the National Lottery helped fund the modernisation of Olympic NGBs (inadvertently strengthening their capacity to lobby in a more professional manner), the establishment of the network of elite sport institutes and, most importantly, the creation of UK Sport as a specialist agency for the delivery of elite sport success. Reinforced by media opinion, which has such a clear interest in fostering elite sport success given the reliance on sport material by much of the media, a relatively strong coalition of interest has emerged. A broadly similar pattern of coalition generation can be found in relation to school sport. While the effective campaigning of the Youth Sport Trust was a significant factor in promoting the issue of school sport, of equal importance was the fact that the YST was offering a solution (as defined within the multiple streams framework) to a problem which had been articulated by John Major and which resonated powerfully within the backbench ranks of both the main political parties in the House of Commons.

While it would be tempting to explain the rapid expansion of the budgets for youth/school sport and elite sport as providing evidence supporting the public choice critique of state and state-dependent organisations, in the case of the Youth Sport Trust, it would be more accurate to see both the UK Sport and the YST as responding to the strong governmental support for elite sporting success. Even school sport, which had to justify its financial support from the Department of Children, Schools and Families in terms of whole-school educational outcomes, nonetheless did so in large part through the promotion of competitive sport and the establishment of programmes for talent identification and development. Rather than the increased investment of lottery and Exchequer funding in elite sport and school/youth sport being primarily the result of effective lobbying, it is much more accurate, as argued above, to see the increased profile of both areas as the outcome of departmental sponsorship (in the case of school sport) and prime ministerial sponsorship (in the case of elite sport and school sport).

It is partly due to the generally positive relationship between successive governments across the four home countries and the sports subsector that governance theory is of particular interest. As summarised in Chapter 1, governance theory suggests that the role of the state has altered in recent years due to developments such as the increasing complexity of social issues, the persistence of so-called wicked issues and the steady increase in public expectations of government capacity which can result in overload. The shift from government to governance is thus an acknowledgement by government of its limited capacity to respond effectively to many issues in contemporary society. Sport is typical insofar as the capacity of the UK government and of the home country governments to achieve their objectives is dependent on partnership with a very broad range of civil society organisations, particularly NGBs and the 140,000 or so clubs spread across the UK. The development of partnerships/networks is not just the consequence of the complexity of the issues that have emerged within sport, such as the stagnation in adult participation levels, but is also a recognition of the persistence of organisational fragmentation within the sport subsector (for example, four home countries, a large number of NGBs, few multi-sport clubs and around 500 local authorities) despite attempts by successive governments to create a more coherent organisational landscape. However, the development of an extensive and often highly complex network of partnerships should not be interpreted as a loss of power by governments or a 'hollowing out' of the state. Given the high degree of resource dependence of many partners on state grant aid, the limited organisational capacity of most NGBs and the failure of most English NGBs to deliver their participation targets, it would be much more accurate to emphasise the extension of state influence into areas of sporting activity (such as coaching, club youth sport and competition calendars) where it had previously had little influence. It is difficult to argue that the state has lost power or even shared power when so many NGBs and many clubs depend on state subsidy for their survival. Consequently, it is more accurate to see the current pattern of inter-organisational relationships, particularly in the areas of adult participation and school sport, as a series of overlapping implementation networks fostered and substantially managed by government (mainly via the sports councils). The willingness of non-state organisations to cooperate with government is, as already mentioned, partly the result of heavy resource dependence, but also partly due to a broad commonality of policy objectives such as the prioritisation of sport over physical education and the general institutionalisation of competitive sport.

The fourth macro-level theory reviewed in Chapter 1 was market liberalism, in which it was argued that the dynamic for policy development was a combination of market competition and the rational pursuit, by individuals, of utility maximisation. While Anthony Downs (1967) argued that the public bureaucrats' concern to maximise their own utility (status, career prospects, salary etc.) could at times be moderated by altruism, other theorists such as Gordon Tullock (1965) were far less willing to admit the likelihood of altruism diluting the pursuit of self-interest. However, the pursuit of rational self-interest would not necessarily undermine the achievement of public policy goals as arguably the clearest route to career advancement, increased salary et cetera is by the successful achievement of the policy goals set by ministers. However, Niskanen (1971) argued that policy outputs and outcomes are distorted as public officials will prioritise organisational growth (bigger budgets and more staff) as the most effective means of securing their personal advantage. Public choice theory thus contains a vigorous critique of state intervention not only because state intervention (for example, through subsidised entry to public leisure centres, establishing elite sport training facilities and subsidising youth coaching) inevitably distorted the functioning of the market, but also because public-sector organisations such as UK Sport and the home country sports councils would, equally inevitably, become more concerned with organisational expansion and aggrandisement than with the pursuit of public policy goals.

While the public choice critique is a useful corrective to exaggerated claims of selflessness among public officials, it is difficult to make a prima facia case that public-sector sports organisations (UK Sport and the home country sports councils) have pursued organisational aggrandisement at the expense of public policy goals. The budget and staffing levels in UK Sport have indeed grown in recent years, but if this was the result of collective organisational self-interest then the government was also a very willing co-conspirator. Both UK Sport and successive governments have pursued elite sporting success as the primary public policy goals for sport with mutually reinforcing enthusiasm. The other sports councils have arguably been far too weak to pursue organisational objectives of budget and staff expansion with any realistic prospect of success without explicit support from their governments. **sport**scotland has been on the brink of closure at least on one occasion and was probably saved from abolition by Glasgow's success in winning the right to host the 2014 Commonwealth Games. Whether the Scottish National Party will let the organisation survive once the games have finished is a moot point. Similarly, Sport England (and its various predecessors) has been subject to regular reviews and questioning as to its purpose and effectiveness. From such positions of weakness it is difficult to see scope for the aggressive pursuit of individual and collective organisational self-interest—survival has for long been the central priority.

As mentioned at the beginning of this section, one reason for examining macro-level theories is that their various assumptions underpin either explicitly or implicitly the meso-level analytic frameworks which are conventionally adopted in the study of sport policy. The second reason is that they sensitise the researcher to broad themes, interests and power relations that are of particular significance in relation to sport policy. From the foregoing discussion it is argued that the insights derived from neo-pluralism and governance theory are of particular value in explorations of sport policy. One of the distinctive features of recent sport policy has been the emergence and clustering of interests around specific aspects of sport policy. However, the acknowledgement of this feature is not to exaggerate the influence of organised interests. Indeed, the value of a neo-pluralist perspective is that while it encourages the examination of the activity of organised interests in the policy process it is also capable of illuminating the relative significance of government and state institutions. In many respects governance theory complements neo-pluralism and is of particular value in the study of sport policy due to the assumptions of the theory regarding policy complexity. If the shift from government to governance is partly explained by the increase in the intractability of some problems and the complexity of the environment for policy delivery, then sport offers a potential ideal typical case.

MESO-LEVEL ANALYTIC FRAMEWORKS

The expansion of theorising at the meso level in the 1980s and 1990s was in large part a response to the limitations of attempts to use macro-level theory to explain particular policy outputs or the policy process in relation to specific issues or subsectors. Much meso-level theorising focused on the relationship between organisations (often confined to the national level) and especially the relationship between the state and its various agencies on the one hand and civil society institutions on the other. All four meso-level analytic frameworks identified in Chapter 1 are both descriptive and ideal typical insofar as the accumulation of empirical research on which they are based provides the basis for generalisation, but once formulated as a model of the policy process they become benchmarks against which particular policy processes can be compared.

The punctuated-equilibrium model, with its ambition to explain both stability and change, offers the prospect of particular insights into the factors that prompt policy change. However, in its application to sport policy it is clear that a degree of caution is needed because of the problem of distinguishing incremental from non-incremental change. The problem is similar to that discussed in relation to periodisation in that what might appear to the contemporary observer as a non-incremental (radical) change in policy might, with the perspective that time brings, appear far less radical. In relation to school sport, for example, it is not clear whether the changes in policy (including the design of a national curriculum for PE, the establishment of specialist sports colleges, the funding of School Sport Partnerships and the more recent reduction in SSP funding) constitute a pattern of incremental change or a succession of punctuations. There is also a problem in that some 'punctuations' are better described as interruptions rather than permanent shifts in policy objectives. The short-lived involvement of Sport England in the promotion of physical activity in the mid-2000s is a case in point.

Despite its weaknesses, the punctuated-equilibrium model does prompt some important questions and observations regarding the recent history of sport policy. First, the model endorses a broadly rational view of the policy process by suggesting that the accumulation of evidence is a powerful factor in stimulating policy change. However, in relation to adult sport participation, the accumulation of data from the mid-1980s showing the broadly static level of participation led, not to a radical review of policy, but rather to sustained policy inertia. In relation to school sport, the data collected through the School Sport Survey indicated the success of the SSP programme, but this did not stop the Conservative–Liberal Democrat coalition government from substantially reducing funding and weakening the structure of the partnership arrangements. This example illustrates the limitations of evidence-based policy when confronted by ideology. A second observation concerns the model's assumptions about the vulnerability of policy subsystems to a variety/plurality of interests. In relation to UK, but especially English, sport policy, a plurality of interests capable of competing effectively for influence over the policy agenda is hard to identify. Non-state interests are generally weak and heavily resource dependent on public funding and there is certainly no equivalent to the Scandinavian sports confederations which have the resources and legitimacy to challenge government. The relative vacuum in powerful organised interests has created an opportunity for an extension of influence by NGBs, but it is an opportunity that has been taken, and then only partially, by the small number responsible for the major commercial sports. In relation to elite sport development and the promotion of increased participation, NGBs have obtained and consolidated a central position with UK Sport and Sport England, respectively, thus suggesting a progressive institutionalisation of NGB interests within the public policy process, albeit more strongly in relation to policy implementation rather than policymaking.

The significance for access to the policy agenda is at the heart of institutional analysis associated with the work of Thelen and Steinmo (1992) and DiMaggio (1988). Institutional theorising was prompted by the observation that in many areas of policy and business, societies failed to adopt policies and practices that had proved successful elsewhere and persisted with apparently sub-optimal policies and practices. Historical and cultural institutionalism sought to provide answers by drawing attention to the 'weight of history' and the extent to which cultural practices (definitions of problems and preferences among politicians and the public for particular types of solutions) become embedded in the fabric of social and political systems. Institutionalism also focuses the researcher's attention on the architecture of government and administration and suggests that factors such as the distribution of functions between central government departments, the powers of sub-national units of government and the established patterns of budget setting and legislation all foster a distinctive and deeply rooted approach to policy.

The application of institutional analysis to UK sport policy prompts two observations. The first is the unevenness of awareness among ministers of the significance of organisational institutionalism—the extent to which the structuring of organisations, the distribution of functions and authority between them and the pattern of inter-organisational resource dependencies significantly affects the scope for policy innovation and change. In respect of the position to local authorities, an underlying rationale for central government policies that successively undermined local authority autonomy and capacity can be traced to the recognition of the institutional problems of working with partners who have their own electorate to satisfy, who have a tradition of independence and a large proportion of which will, at any one time, be broadly antagonistic to the party in power at Westminster. However, within the sport policy sector in particular, there was a lack of recognition as to how these broader trends presented an institutional barrier for local authorities which, combined with the lack of concern with community participation, only served to weaken local authorities' position even further. A greater awareness of the significance of organisational institutionalism and the extent to which it could be an impediment to the implementation of government policy was shown with regard to the arcane

internal governance arrangements of many NGBs. Funding was consequently provided by UK Sport and Sport England to facilitate and encourage the modernisation of NGBs. Furthermore, the commissioning by Sport
England and UK Sport of the Foster Report (Sport England/UK Sport
2004) on athletics in the UK focused particularly on the modernisation
of the NGB, UK Athletics, while the Burns Report, which also had strong
government support (Football Association 2005), was directly concerned
with the structure and governance of the Football Association.

Rather less insight was shown in relation to the consequences of devolution for the development of sport policy. While the decision in 1997 to
dissolve the GB Sports Council and create two new organisations (Sport
England and UK Sport) was an acknowledgement of the ambiguous status
of the GB Sports Council in the eyes of the three other home countries and
also anticipated the passage of the 1998 Devolution Act, the more recent
decision by the Conservative–Liberal Democrat coalition government to
reverse the 1997 decision and re-establish a combined organisation ignored
the extent to which the devolution of responsibility for sport policy became
institutionalised in Scotland, Wales and Northern Ireland. Any proposal to
alter the status of Sport England was inevitably going to be interpreted as
a move to strengthen English influence over UK Sport and elite level policy
at the expense of the other home nations.

With the exception of the recent proposals to merge Sport England and
UK Sport, the uneven sensitivity of Westminster governments to the significance of organisational institutionalism for sport policymaking and
implementation has caused few significant problems. Where successive
Westminster governments have been far less astute is in recognising the
influence of the cultural institutionalisation on policy. The impact of cultural institutionalism on sport policy is evident particularly at the level of
the values, norms and beliefs found in communities. Two examples provide
ample illustration, the first of which is the impact of sectarianism in Northern Ireland, where, as indicated in Chapter 4, sport policy continually served
to reinforce sectarianism rather than to dilute the phenomenon. The second
example relates to the continuing inability (or at least sustained reluctance)
of successive governments to recognise that increasing adult participation
in sport required engineering a substantial change in the prevailing norms,
attitudes and beliefs towards physical activity and the use of free time.
The insights generated by the application of institutional theory reinforce
many of the conclusions drawn in connection with punctuated-equilibrium
theory. In particular, institutional theory emphasises the stability of values,
norms and policy preferences and provides further justification for drawing
distinctions between levels of embeddedness of values and norms in relation to sport policy.

The acknowledgement of the importance of organisational and cultural
institutionalism in shaping sport policy would suggest that there was little
scope for the multiple streams framework which 'shares common ground

with chaos theories in being attentive to complexity, in assuming a considerable amount of residual randomness, and in viewing systems as constantly evolving and not necessarily settling into equilibrium' (Zahariadis 2007, p. 66). While institutional theory reinforces some of the assumptions of path dependency, by contrast the multiple streams framework emphasises the endogenous and exogenous sources of turbulence that can affect the policy agenda and policy outputs. The recent history of sport policy provides ample illustrations of 'policy windows' which enabled the three streams— problems, policies and politics—to join. Endogenous sources of policy windows include elections and the accumulation of evidence (for example, in relation to overweight among children) while exogenous sources would include changes to the World Anti-Doping Code, the recent economic crisis among Eurozone countries. The appointment of John Major as prime minister in 1990 provided the policy window for the promotion of sport on the agenda of government; the election of Tony Blair's New Labour government in 1997 led to an expansion of the remit of sport policy—with particular implications for NGBs and local authorities—to embrace a series of welfare-related objectives which extended well beyond a simple concern with increased participation; and the election of the Conservative–Liberal Democrat coalition government in 2010 provided the opportunity to reduce central government regulation of school sport. In addition to there being many examples of policy windows being exploited by newly elected governments, there are also examples—though far fewer—of the effective intervention of policy entrepreneurs.

Rather than confusing the analysis of the UK sport policy, the three meso-level theories reviewed so far enable a more subtle understanding of recent policy. The application of punctuated-equilibrium theory and institutional theory draws attention to the existence of continuities in sport policy and underpinning values since the mid-1960s—particularly evident in the prioritisation of elite sporting success, the concern to promote competitive sport in schools and the lack of concern with adult participation. The application of the multiple streams framework suggests that the policy windows were more effective in enabling the linking of new solutions/policies (such as the introduction of the National Lottery, specialist sports colleges and School Sport Partnerships) to recognised problems (under-funding of elite sport development and the decline of competitive sport in schools) rather than forcing new problems onto the policy agenda.

The final meso-level theory introduced in Chapter 1 was the advocacy coalition framework, which provided insights which, with one major qualification, complement rather than undermine the assessment of UK sport policy provided at the start and throughout this chapter. The ACF emphasises the hierarchical structure of belief systems with the acknowledgement of the significance of 'deep-core' beliefs which inform fundamental norms and values and which change only slowly. The belief in the value of competition (and competitive sport), the role of civil society organisations (NGBs and clubs), the emphasis on individual responsibility (for one's health and fitness) and the confidence in the instrumental value of sport have all proved to be relatively permanent features of the ideological context within which sport policy has been made. The ACF's emphasis on the importance of exogenous factors (external shocks/scandals) in prompting policy change is balanced by the framework's insistence on the necessity of adopting a medium-term view over which to assess policy change. Such an approach prevents the premature identification of particular policy developments as significant changes in policy direction when in fact they are temporary diversions or simply turn out to be far less significant than at first assumed. The lack of concern shown towards elite sport success during much of the 1980s is, arguably, one illustration of the value of adopting a longer time frame for analysis. Similarly, it might also be the case that the downgrading of emphasis on school sport by the Conservative–Liberal Democrat coalition government does not indicate a change in policy direction (that is, policy objectives) but rather a change in the means by which those policy objectives might be achieved.

However, where the ACF needs to be qualified is in relation to the process by which the competing coalitions are formed. For Sabatier and Weible (2007) the emergence of coalitions (they assume between two and five in each policy subsector) is the product, on the one hand, of policy complexity and the consequent need for organisations and other policy actors to specialise and, on the other, a plurality of opinions regarding both the relative importance of problems (agenda control) and the most appropriate solutions/policies. In the UK there is considerable evidence of the development of coalitions of interest within the sport policy subsector most clearly around elite sport and school/youth sport. However, rather than see these coalitions as the product of interest-group activity and capacity it is far more convincing to see them as the consequence of government decisions to increase the prioritisation of elite and school/youth sport and encouraged by government as a means of providing a more effective network for policy implementation. It is accepted that a coalition that starts its life as the creature of government has the potential to develop into an independent policy actor and the recent defence of School Sport Partnership funding might indicate that this process is taking place, but a final acceptance of this analysis is certainly premature. Whether the elite sport coalition (which includes the BOA, Olympic NGBs, English Institute of Sport [EIS] and the British Athletes Commission) has developed from an implementation network into an advocacy coalition is unclear mainly due to the proximity of the Olympic and Paralympic Games and the reluctance of the government to risk accusations of withdrawing funding immediately before the London event. However, the prospects for such a development of an effective advocacy coalition are not promising due to the weak financial base of the BOA and most of the Olympic NGBs and the vulnerability of the EIS to public expenditure reductions. In summary, viewing

UK sport policy through the lens of the ACF serves to reinforce the relative weakness (if not absence) of effective defensive and promotional coalitions operating in the sport policy subsector.

CONCLUDING COMMENTS

Although this analysis of sport policy has emphasised broad continuity with regard to public policy objectives since 1990, this should not downplay the scale of change in relation to the allocation of not only financial resources, but also administrative capacity and political legitimacy. The current economic recession and the election of a neoliberal Conservative–Liberal Democrat coalition notwithstanding, elite sport and school sport are far better resourced today than they were in the early 1990s. Consequently it would be reasonable to conclude that while public policy objectives and priorities have been refined, the scale of change in resources does not mark a break with the past as the direction of policy and the relative priority between community, elite and youth/school sport have remained broadly consistent.

As regards the process of sport policymaking, government—either in the form of prime ministerial interventions or operating through the Department of National Heritage/Department of Culture, Media and Sport—remains the dominant policy actor. As argued above, evidence of a transition from government to governance and of a greater role for non-state actors in the determination of policy is limited. The networks of organisations that have developed around elite sport and school sport certainly have the potential to make the transition from being largely passive agents of policy delivery to being active participants in the policymaking process, but with the exception of the Youth Sport Trust evidence of consistent influence on policy is limited. Indeed, one of the most striking features of the last 20 years or so has been the lack of capacity building among the many interests affected by the public policy decisions of government in relation to sport, especially in the case of community sport. As discussed in Chapter 5, effective advocacy on behalf of adult recreational and competitive sport participation is conspicuous by its absence despite strong evidence of 30 years of failure to make significant changes to the profile of participation. While successive governments have basked in the reflected glory of improved Olympic and Paralympic performance, none has acknowledged the stagnation in levels of community sport participation as either their responsibility or a matter for urgent attention and have remained content to tinker with the symptoms of the problem rather than address it directly. The repeated response to evidence of lack of progress has been to set new targets rather than to seek innovative ways of making progress. It would be welcome if the same energy, commitment and concentration of resources that had been devoted to improving UK Olympic performance were applied to the challenges of increasing community participation in sport. At present this is a remote prospect.

Notes

NOTES TO CHAPTER 4

1. Due in the case of Scotland to a turnout lower than the 40% threshold set in the act of parliament authorising the referendum.
2. In 2009–10, overall expenditure on sport by SCW was £41.9m (£30.8m from the Exchequer and £11.1m from the National Lottery).
3. Legislation that impinges on the dual use of school facilities includes Education No. 2 Act 1986 (role of school governors), Education Reform Act 1988 (allocation of funding between curricular and extracurricular uses) and the Education Act 1991 (arrangements for the transfer to management responsibility for school facilities, e.g. to a local authority sport development section).
4. It should be noted that Wales contributed about one quarter of GB gold medals at the 2008 Paralympic Games reflecting the priority given to disability sport.

NOTES TO CHAPTER 5

1. Quinquennial reviews were regular assessments of the work of non-departmental public bodies of which Sport England is one. The reviews are carried out by a panel consisting of civil servants and external experts and service partners/users.

NOTES TO CHAPTER 8

1. The major exception to this generalisation is in relation to the business interests of the five most commercially successful sports.

References

Abend, G., 2008. The meaning of "theory". *Sociological Theory*, 26 (2), 173–199.

Aitchison, C., 1997. 'A decade of Compulsory Competitive Tendering in UK sport and leisure services: Some feminist reflections'. *Leisure Studies*, 16 (2), 85–105.

Alcock, P., 1997. Consolidation or stagnation? Social policy under the Major governments. *In*: M. May, E. Brunsdon & G. Craig, eds., *Social Policy Review 9*. London: Social Policy Association.

Alderson, J., 1993. Physical education, sport development and leisure management. *In*: G. McFee & A. Tomlinson, eds., *Education, Sport and Leisure: Connections and Controversies*. Eastbourne: Chelsea School Research centre.

Armour, K.M., 2010. The physical education profession and its professional responsibility . . . or . . . why '12 weeks paid holiday' will never be enough. *Physical Education & Sport Pedagogy*, 15 (1), 1–13.

Atkins, R., 1991a. House of Commons Written Answers. 19 December 1991. Hansard.

Atkins, R., 1991b. House of Commons Debates. 27 November 1991. Hansard Columns 987–1015.

Atkinson, R. and Savage, S.P., 1994. The Conservatives and public policy. *In*: S.P. Savage, R. Atkinson and L. Robins, eds., *Public policy in Britain*. London: Macmillan.

Audit Commission, 1989. *Sport for whom?* London: HMSO.

Audit Commission, 2002. *Sport and recreation*. Wetherby: Audit Commission Publications.

Audit Commission, 2006. *Public sports and recreation services: Making them fit for the future*. Wetherby: Audit Commission Publications.

Audit Commission, 2008. *Background* [online]. Available from: http://www.audit-commission.gov.uk/cpa/guide/guidebackground.asp [accessed 14 August 2008].

Audit Commission, 2011. *Tough times: Councils' responses to a challenging financial climate*. London: Audit Commission.

Audit Scotland, 2008. *A performance overview of sport in Scotland*. Edinburgh: Audit Scotland.

Bache, I., 2003. Governing through governance: Education policy control under New Labour. *Political Studies*, 51 (2), 300–314.

Bailey R.P., 2005. Evaluating the relationship between physical education, sport and social inclusion. *Education Review*, 57 (1), 71–90.

Bairner, A., 2008. Still taking sides: Sport, leisure and identity. *In*: C. Coulter and M. Murray, eds., *Northern Ireland after the troubles: A society in transition*. Manchester: Manchester University Press.

Baker, C., 2011. *Partnership working for the promotion of sport and physical activity: An investigation into community sports networks in England*. Unpublished PhD thesis, University of Gloucestershire.

Ball, S.J., 2008. *The education debate*. Bristol: The Policy Press.

Barber, M., 2008. *Instruction to deliver: Fighting to transform Britain's public services*. York: Methuen.

Baumgartner, F.R. and Jones, B.D., 1993. *Agendas and instability in American politics*. Chicago: Chicago University Press.

Baumgartner, F.R. and Jones, B.D., eds., 2002. *Policy dynamics*. Chicago: Chicago University Press.

BBC, 2007. *Anger at lotto funds for Olympics* [online]. Available from: http://news.bbc.co.uk/1/hi/uk_politics/6456697.stm [accessed 17 December 2010].

BBC, 2009. *GAA school names 'not released'* 12 October [online]. Available from: http://news.bbc.co.uk/1/hi/northern_ireland/8302449.stm [accessed 12th January 2012].

Benson, A. and Henderson, S., 2005. UK leisure centres under Best Value: A strategic analysis. *International Journal of Public Sector Management*, 18 (3), 196–215.

Bergsgard, N.A., Houlihan, B., Mangset, P., Nødland, S.I. and Rommetwedt, H., 2007. *Sport policy: A comparative analysis of stability and change*. Oxford: Butterworth-Heinemann.

Berry, J., Brown, L., and McGreal, S., 2001. The planning system in Northern Ireland post-devolution. *European Planning Studies*, 9 (6), 781–791.

Biddle, S. and Foster, C., 2011. Health behaviour change through physical activity and sport. *In*: B. Houlihan. and M. Green, eds., *Routledge handbook of sports development*. London: Routledge.

Blair, T., 1994. *Speech to the Labour Party Annual Conference* [online]. Available at: http://keeptonyblairforpm.wordpress.com/1994-first-blair-speech-to-conference-as-party-leader/ [accessed 21 January 2010].

Blair, T., 1998. *The third way: Politics for the new century*. London: Fabian Society.

Bloyce, D. and Smith, A., 2009. *Sport policy and development: An introduction*. London: Routledge.

Bloyce, D., Smith, A., Mead, R. and Morris, J., 2008. 'Playing the game (plan)': A figurational analysis of organizational change in sports development in England. *European Sport Management Quarterly*, 8 (4), 359–378.

Bovaird, A.G. and Martin, S.J., 2003. Evaluating the local government modernisation agenda: 'Joined up' local government research. *Local Government Studies*, 29 (4), 17–30.

Brackenridge, C. and Telfer, H., 2011. Child protection and sport development. *In*: B. Houlihan and M. Green, eds., *Routledge handbook of sports development*. London: Routledge.

Bradbury, S., 2006. *Step into sport: Phase two research overview*. Loughborough: Institute of Youth Sport.

Bradley, J., 1998. *Sport, culture, politics and Scottish society*. Edinburgh: John Donald.

Brohm, J.M., 1978. *Sport: A prison of measured time*. London: Ink Links.

Burnham, J. and Pyper, R., 2008. *Britain's modernised civil service*. Basingstoke: Palgrave Macmillan.

Cabinet Office. *Modernizing Government*, 1999 (Cm. 4310, 1999). London: Stationery Office.

Cameron, D., 2010. *House of Commons debates*. 24 November 2010. Hansard Column 258–259.

Cameron, D., 2010. *Big Society speech* [online]. Available from: http://www.number10.gov.uk/news/big-society-speech/ [accessed 11 April 2011].

Campbell, D. and Vasagar, V., 2010. Olympians Darren Campbell and Denise Lewis join school sports protest. *The Guardian*, 7 December 2010.

Carmichael, P. and Osborne, R., 2003. The Northern Ireland civil service under direct rule and devolution. *International Review of Administrative Sciences*, 69 (2), 205–217.

Carrington, B. and McDonald, I., 2009. *Marxism, cultural studies and sport*. London: Routledge.

Carter, P., 2005a. *Review of national sport effort and resources*. London: DCMS.

Carter, P., 2005b. *Review of national sport effort and resources: Supporting evidence*. London: DCMS.

Central Council for Physical Recreation, 2008. *Getting the ball rolling: Sports contribution to the 2008–2011 public service agreements*. London: CCPR

Centre for Leisure Research, 1993. *Sport and Leisure Management, Compulsory Competitive Tendering National Information Survey Report*. London: Sports Council.

Centre for Social Justice, 2011. *More than a game: Harnessing the power of sport to transform the lives of disadvantaged young people*. London: Centre for Social Justice

Charlton, T., 2010. A new active sports partnership: Lancashire sport. *In*: M. Collins, ed., *Examining sports development*. London: Routledge.

Chitty, C., 2004. *Education policy in Britain*. Basingstoke: Palgrave Macmillan.

Chitty, C., 2008. *Education policy in Britain*. 2nd ed. Basingstoke: Palgrave Macmillan.

Chitty, C., 2011. A massive power grab from local communities: The real significance of the 2010 white paper and the 2011 Education Bill. *FORUM*, 53 (1), 11–14.

Coalter, F., 1995. Compulsory Competitive Tendering for sport and leisure management: A lost opportunity? *Managing Leisure*, 1 (1), 3–15.

Coalter, F., 2004. London 2012: A sustainable sporting legacy. *In*: A. Vigor and M. Mean, eds., *After the goldrush: A sustainable Olympics for London*. London: IPPR and Demos.

Coalter, F., 2007. *A wider social role for sport: Who's keeping the score?* Abingdon: Routledge.

Coalter, F., 2011. Sport development's contribution to social policy objectives: The difficult relationship between politics and evidence. *In* B. Houlihan and M. Green eds. *Routledge handbook of sport development*. Routledge: London.

Coalter, F., Long, J. and Duffield, B., 1986. *Rationale for public sector investment in leisure*. London: Sports Council/ESRC.

Cochrane, A., 2003. The new urban policy: Towards empowerment or incorporation? *In*: R. Imrie and M. Raco, eds., *Urban Renaissance? New Labour, Community and Urban Policy*. Bristol: UK: Policy Press, 223–234.

Coghlan, J.F. with Webb, I.M., 1990. *Sport and British politics since 1960*. London: Falmer Press.

Cohen, M., March, J. and Olsen, J., 1972. A garbage can model of organisational choice. *Administrative Science Quarterly*, 17, 1–25.

Collins, M.F., 1997. Does a new philosophy change the structures? Compulsory Competitive Tendering and local authority leisure services in Midland England. *Managing Leisure*, 2 (4), 204–216.

Collins, M.F., with Kay, T., 2002. *Sport and social exclusion*. London: Routledge.

Collins, M., 2008. Public policies on sport development: Can mass and elite sport hold together? *In*: V. Girginov, ed., *Management of sport development*. Oxford: Butterworth-Heinemann.

Collins, M., ed. 2010. *Examining sport development*, London: Routledge.

Collins, M.F. and Buller, J.R., 2000. Bridging the post-school institutional gap in sport: Evaluating champion coaching in Nottinghamshire. *Managing Leisure*, 5, 200–221.

Compass, 1999. *Sports participation in Europe*. London: Sport England.

Campbell, S., 2010. *Letter to Secretary of State for Education*. 29 October 2010.

Conservative Party, 2009. *Extending Opportunities: A Conservative Policy Paper on Sport*. London: Conservative Party.

Conservative Party, 2010a. *Invitation to join the government of Britain: The Conservative manifesto 2010*. London: Conservative Party.

Conservative Party, 2010b. *Conservative Sports Manifesto* [online]. Available from: http://www.conservatives.com/ [accessed 11 April 2011].

Cowell, R. and Martin, S.J., 2003. The joy of joining up: Modes of integrating the local government modernisation agenda. *Environment and Planning C: Government and Policy*, 21, 159–179.

Cox, E., 2010. *Five foundations of real localism*. Newcastle-upon-Tyne: Institute of Public Policy Research.

Crabbe, T., 2006. *'Going the distance': Impact, journeys and distance travelled. Third Interim National Positive Futures Case Study Research Report*. Manchester: Substance.

Daily Telegraph, 30 November 2007. *Sport England's Derek Mapp forced to quit* [online]. Available from: http://www.telegraph.co.uk/sport/olympics/2327112/Sport-Englands-Derek-Mapp-forced-to-quit.html [accessed 18 November 2011].

Davies, W., 2006. 'The governmentality of New Labour'. *Institute for Public Policy Research*, 13 (4), 249–256.

Davis Langdon Consultancy, 2003. *Condition and refurbishment of public sector sports facilities: Update of 1995 study*. London: Sport England.

DCMS/DfES, 2003. *Learning through PE and Sport*. Annesley: DfES Publications.

DCSF, 2008. *PE & sport strategy for young people* [online]. Available from: http://www.teachernet.gov.uk/docbank/index.cfm?id=12416 [accessed 31 September 2010].

Dean, H., 2004. The implications of Third Way social policy for inequality, social cohesion and citizenship. *In*: J. Lewis and R. Surender, eds., *Welfare state change: Towards a Third Way?* Oxford: Oxford University Press.

Dean., M., 2007. *Governing societies: Political perspectives on domestic and international rule*. Maidenhead: Open University Press.

Department for Children, Schools and Families (DCSF), 2007. *The children's plan: Building brighter futures*. London: DCSF.

Department for Children, Schools and Families (DCSF), 2008. *PE and sport strategy for young people*. Available from: https://www.education.gov.uk/publications/eOrderingDownload/PE_Sport_Strategy_leaflet_2008.pdf [accessed 16 July 2009].

Department for Culture, Media and Sport (DCMS), 1999. *Policy Action Team 10: The contribution of sport and the arts*. Report to the Social Exclusion Unit. London: DCMS.

Department for Culture, Media and Sport (DCMS), 2000. *A sporting future for all*. London: DCMS.

Department for Culture, Media and Sport (DCMS), 2001a. *Elite sport funding review* (chair, J. Cunningham). London: DCMS.

Department for Culture, Media and Sport (DCMS), 2001b. *Quinquennial review of sport England: Stage one*. London: DCMS.

Department for Culture, Media and Sport (DCMS), 2001c. *The government's plan for sport*. London: HMSO.

Department for Culture, Media and Sport (DCMS), 2004. *First 'Game Plan' delivery report*. London: DCMS.

Department for Culture, Media and Sport (DCMS), 2006. *Derek Mapp to chair Sport England* [online]. Available from: http://www.culture.gov.uk/reference_library/media_releases/2520.aspx [accessed 16 July 2008].

Department for Culture, Media and Sport (DCMS), 30 November 2007. Press Release. London: DCMS.

Department for Culture, Media and Sport (DCMS), 2008. *Playing to win: A new era for sport*. London: DCMS.

Department for Culture, Media and Sport (DCMS), 2010. *Plans for the legacy from the 2012 Olympic and Paralympic Games*. London: DCMS.

Department for Culture, Media and Sport (DCMS), 2011. *Business plan 2011–2015*. London: DCMS.

Department for Culture, Media and Sport (DCMS), 2012. *Creating a sporting habit for life: A new youth sport strategy*. London: DCMS.

Department for Culture, Media and Sport/Strategy Unit (DCMS/SU), 2002. *Game plan: A strategy for delivering government's sport and physical activity objectives*. London: DCMS/SU.

Department for Education, 2010. *A new approach for school sports—decentralising power, incentivising competition, trusting teachers* [online]. Available at: http://www.education.gov.uk/inthenews/pressnotices/a0071098/a-new-approach-for-school-sports-decentralising-power-incentivising-competition-trusting-teachers [accessed 21 December 2010].

Department for Education and Skills (DfES), 2001. *Schools: Achieving success*. London: DfES.

Department for Education and Skills (DfES), 2003. *Every child matters*. Cmnd, 5860. London: The Stationery Office.

Department for Education and Skills/Department of Culture, Media & Sport (DfES/DCMS), 2004. *High quality PE and sport for young people*. Annesley: DfES Publications.

Department for the Environment, Transport and the Regions (DETR), 1998a. *Modern local government: In touch with the people*. Cm 4014. London: The Stationery Office.

Department for the Environment, Transport and the Regions (DETR), 1998b. *Modernising local government: Improving local services through Best Value*, London: DETR.

Department for Transport, Local Government and the Regions (DLTR), 2001. *Strong local leadership—quality public services*. Cmnd 5237. London: The Stationery Office.

Department of Culture, Arts and Leisure (DCAL), 2009. *Sport matters: The Northern Ireland strategy for physical recreation 2009–2019*. Belfast: DCAL.

Department of Education and Science, 1991. *Sport and active recreation*. London: DES.

Department of Education, 2011. *Free schools: What are free schools?* [online]. Available from: http://www.education.gov.uk/b0061428/free-schools/what [accessed: 21 July 2011].

Department of Health, 1992. *The health of the nation*. London: DoH.

Department of Health, 1999. *Saving lives: Our healthier nation*. London: DoH.

Department of Health, 2002. *Securing our future health—taking a long term view (the Wanless Report)*. London: Department of Health.

Department of Health, 2004. *At least five a week: Evidence on the impact of physical activity and its relationship to health. A report from the Chief Medical Officer*. London: Department of Health.

Department of Health, 2005. *Choosing activity—a physical activity action plan*. London: DoH.

Department of Health, 2009. *Be active, be healthy: A plan for getting the nation moving.* London: Department of Health.

Department of National Heritage (DNH), 1995. *Sport: Raising the game.* London: DNH.

Department of National Heritage, 1996. *Sport: Raising the game: The first year report.* London: DNH.

Dery, D., 1999. Policy by the way: When policy is incidental to making other policies. *Journal of Public Policy*, 18 (2), 163–176.

DiMaggio, P., 1988. Interest and agency in institutional theory. *In*: L. Zucker, ed., *Institutional patterns and culture.* Cambridge, MA: Ballinger, 3–32.

Dobrowolsky, A., 2002. Rhetoric versus reality: The figure of the child and New Labour's strategic 'social investment state'. *Studies in Political Economy*, 69, 43–74.

Downe, J. and Martin, S., 2006. Joined up policy in practice? The coherence and impacts of the local government modernisation agenda. *Local Government Studies*, 32 (4), 465–488.

Downs, A., 1967. *Inside bureaucracy.* Boston, MA: Little, Brown.

Dryzek, J.S. and Dunleavy, P., 2009. *Theories of the democratic state.* Houndmills: Palgrave Macmillan.

English Sports Council, 1997. *England, the sporting nation: A strategy.* London: English Sports Council.

Enoch, N., 2010. Towards a contemporary national structure for youth sport in England. *In*: M. Collins, ed., *Examining Sports Development.* London: Routledge.

Entwistle, T., 2006. The distinctiveness of the Welsh partnership agenda. *International Journal of Public Sector Management*, 19 (3), 228–237.

Entwistle, T. and Laffin, M., 2005. The prehistory of the Best Value regime. *Local Government Studies*, 31 (2), 205–218.

Esping-Andersen, G., 1990. *The three worlds of welfare capitalism.* Cambridge: Polity Press.

Evans, G., 1995. The national lottery: Planning for leisure or pay up and play the game? *Leisure Studies*, 14 (3), 225–244.

Evans, J., Castle, F., Cooper, D., Glatter, R. and Woods, P.A., 2005. Collaboration: The big new idea for school improvement? *Journal of Education Policy*, 20 (2), 223–235.

Evans, J., Davies, B. and Bass D., 1999. More than a game: Physical culture, identity and citizenship in Wales. *In*: G. Jarvie, ed., *Sport in the making of Celtic culture.* Leicester: Leicester University Press.

Fairclough, N., 2000. *New Labour, new language?* London: Routledge.

Fielding, S., 2003. *The Labour party: Continuity and change in the making of New Labour.* Basingstoke: Macmillan.

Finlayson, A., 1999. 'Third way theory'. *The Political Quarterly*, 70 (3), 271–279.

Finlayson, A., 2003. *Making sense of New Labour.* London: Lawrence and Wishart.

Finn, G., 1994. Sporting symbols, sporting identities: Soccer and intergroup conflict in Scotland and Northern Ireland. *In*: I. Wood, ed., *Scotland and Ulster.* Edinburgh: Mercat Press.

Fischer, F., 2003. *Reframing public policy: Discursive politics and deliberative practices.* Oxford: Oxford University Press.

Flintoff, A., 2003. The school sport co-ordinator programme: Changing the role of the physical education teacher? *Sport, Education and Society*, 8 (2), 231–250.

Flintoff, A., 2008a. Targeting Mr average: Participation, gender equity and school sport partnerships. *Sport, Education and Society*, 13 (4), 393–411.

Flintoff A., 2008b. Physical education and school sport. *In*: K. Hylton & P. Bram-ham, eds., *Sports development: Policy, process and practice*. 2nd ed. Abingdon: Routledge.

Football Association, 2005. *Structural review of the Football Association*. London: The Football Association.

Freeden, M. 1999. The ideology of New Labour. *The Political Quarterly*, 70 (1), 42–51.

Friedman, M. and Friedman, R., 1962. *Capitalism and freedom*. Chicago: University of Chicago Press.

Gamble, A., 2010. New Labour and political change. *Parliamentary Affairs*, 63 (4), 639–652.

Garrett, R., 2004. The response of voluntary sports clubs to Sport England's lottery funding: Cases of compliance, change and resistance. *Managing Leisure*, 9 (1), 13–29.

Geddes, M., 2006. Partnership and the limits to local governance in England: Institutionalist analysis and neoliberalism. *International Journal of Urban and Regional Research*, 30 (1), 76–97.

Geddes, M. and Martin, S.J., 2000. The policy and politics of Best Value: Currents, cross-currents and undercurrents in the new regime. *Policy and Politics*, 29 (3), 377–394.

Gerhard, D., 1956. Periodisation in European history. *The American Historical Review*, 61 (4), 900–913.

Giddens, A., 1998. *The third way*. Cambridge: Polity.

Gilroy, S., 1995. Setting the boundaries: A critique of recent government initiatives affecting sport and leisure. *In*: L. Lawrence, E. Murdoch and S. Parker, eds., *Professional and developmental issues in leisure, sport and education*. Brighton: Leisure Studies Association.

Gilroy, S. and Clarke, G., 1997. Raising the game: Deconstructing the sporting text—from Major to Blair. *Pedagogy in Practice*, 3, 19–37.

Girginov, V. and Sandanski, I., 2011. Bulgaria. *In*: M. Nicholson, Russell Hoye & B. Houlihan, eds., *Participation in sport: International policy perspectives*. London: Routledge.

Giulianotti, R., ed., 2004. *Sport and modern social theorists*. Basingstoke: Palgrave Macmillan.

Giulianotti, R., 2005. Towards a critical anthropology of voice: The politics and poets of popular culture, Scotland and football. *Critique of Anthropology*, 25 (4), 339–359.

Glasner, P.E., 1977. *The sociology of secularisation*. London: Routledge and Kegan Paul.

Gove, M., 2010. *Letter to Baroness Sue Campbell* [online]. Available from: http:// media.education.gov.uk/assets/files/pdf/m/michael%20goves%20letter%20 to%20baroness%20sue%20campbell%20%20%2020%20october%202010. pdf [accessed 7 April 2011].

Green, A., 2010. Afterward: New Labour's legacy . . . The Con-Dems and Zombie Blairism. *In*: A. Green, ed., *Blair's educational legacy: Thirteen years of New Labour*. Basingstoke: Palgrave Macmillan.

Green, K., 2008. *Understanding physical education*. London: Sage.

Green, K., Smith, A. and Roberts, K., 2005. Young people and lifelong participation in sport and physical activity: A sociological perspective on contemporary physical education programmes in England and Wales. *Leisure Studies*, 24 (1), 27–43.

Green, M., 2004. Changing policy priorities for sport in England: The emergence of elite sport development as a key policy concern. *Leisure Studies*, 23 (4), 365–385.

Green, M., 2006. From "Sport for All" to not about sport at all? Interrogating sport policy interventions in the United Kingdom. *European Sport Management Quarterly*, 6 (3), 217–238.

Green, M., 2007. Governing under advanced liberalism: Sport policy and the social investment state. *Policy Sciences*, 40, 55–71.

Green, M., 2009. Podium or participation? Analysing policy priorities under changing modes of sport governance in the United Kingdom. *International Journal of Sport Policy*, 1 (2), 121–144.

Green, M. and Houlihan, B., 2004. Advocacy coalitions and elite sport policy change in Canada and the UK. *International Review for the Sociology of Sport*, 39 (4), 387–403.

Green, M. and Houlihan, B., 2005. *Elite sport development: Policy learning and political priorities*. London: Routledge.

Green, M. and Houlihan, B., 2006. Governmentality, modernisation and the "disciplining" of national sporting organisations: The cases of athletics in Australia and the United Kingdom. *Sociology of Sport Journal*, 23 (1), 47–71.

Greer, S., 2004. *Territorial politics and health policy*. Manchester: Manchester University Press.

Greer, S., 2006. The territorial bases of health policymaking in the UK after devolution. *In*: M. Keating and N. McEwen, eds., *Devolution and public policy*. Abingdon: Routledge.

Griggs, G. and Wheeler, K., 2007. 'Play up, play up and play the game': The implications of Every Child Matters within physical education and school sport. *Education, 3–13*, 35 (3), 273–282.

Guardian. 2006. Man on the inside who believes in outsiders, 15ᵗʰ September, p6.

Gunn, L., 1978. Why is implementation so difficult? *Management Services in Government*, 33, 169–176.

Hall, P.A., 1986. *Governing the economy: The politics of state intervention in Britain and France*. Cambridge: Polity Press.

Hall, S., 2007. Will life after Blair be different? *British Politics*, 2, 118–122.

Hamilton, B., 2001. *Creating a soccer strategy for Northern Ireland: Report from the advisory panel to the minister for culture, arts and leisure (chair B Hamilton)*. Belfast: DCAL.

Hardman, A.E. & Stensel, D.J., 2009. *Physical activity and health: The evidence explained*. 2nd ed. London: Routledge.

Hargreaves, J., 1986a. *Sport, power and culture*. Oxford: Polity Press.

Hargreaves, J., 1986b. The state and sport: Programmed and non-programmed intervention in Britain. *In*: L. Allison, ed., *The Politics of Sport*. Manchester: Manchester University Press.

Hargreaves, J., 1995. Gender, morality and the national physical education curriculum. *In*: L. Lawrence, E. Murdoch and S. Parker, eds., *Professional and Developmental Issues in Leisure, Sport and Education*. Brighton: Leisure Studies Association.

Harris, S., Mori, K. and Collins, M., 2009. Great Expectations: Voluntary Sports Clubs and Their Role in Delivering National Policy for English Sport, *Voluntas*, 20, 405–423.

Hart, S. and McInnes, H., 1993. The consultation document "Sport in the 90s— New Horizons". *In*: C. Brackenridge, ed., *Body matters: Leisure images and lifestyles*. Brighton: LSA.

Harvie, C., 1977. *Scotland and nationalism: Scottish society and politics*. London: George Allen and Unwin.

Hassan, G., 2011. Anatomy of a Scottish revolution: The potential for post-nationalist Scotland and the future of the United Kingdom. *The Political Quarterly*, 82 (3), 365–378.

Hay, C., Lister, M. and Marsh, D., eds. 2006. *The state: Theories and issues.* Houndmills: Palgrave Macmillan.

Haycock, D. and Smith, A., 2010. Inclusive physical education? A study of the management of national curriculum physical education and unplanned outcomes in England. *British Journal of Sociology of Education,* 31 (3), 291–305.

Health Development Agency, 2004. *The effectiveness of public health interventions for increasing physical activity among adults: A review of reviews.* Wetherby: HAD.

Health Education Authority/Sports Council, 1992. *Allied Dunbar national Fitness survey. A report on activity patterns and fitness levels: Main findings.* London: The Sports Council and the Health Education Authority.

Healthy Schools, 2006. *Physical activity* [online]. Available from: http://resources. healthyschools.gov.uk/v/32f5e04c-9d22–4d55–9f8d-9cbc00f37ae8 [accessed 31 September 2010].

Heffernan, R., 2001. *New Labour and Thatcherism: Political change in Britain.* Basingstoke: Palgrave.

Helm, T. and Asthana, A., 2010. Michael Gove's plan to slash sports funding in schools splits cabinet. *The Observer,* 21 November 2010.

Henry, I., 2001. *The politics of leisure policy.* 2nd ed. Houndmills: Palgrave.

Henry, I. and Bramham, P., 1993. Leisure policy in Britain. *In:* P. Bramham, I. Henry, H. Mommaas and H. van der Poel, eds., *Leisure Policies in Europe.* Wallingford: CAB International.

Her Majesty's Inspectorate, 1991. *Aspects of primary education: The teaching and learning of physical education.* London: HMI.

Her Majesty's Stationary Office (HMSO), 1998. *'The government's strategy', the government's annual report.* London: HMSO.

Hill, M., 2009. *The policy process.* 5th ed. London: Pearson Education.

Hills, J., 1998. *Thatcherism, New Labour and the welfare state.* Centre for Analysis of Social Exclusion [online]. Available from: http://sticerd.lse.ac.uk/dps/case/ cp/chapter13.pdf [accessed 15 July 2004].

HM Treasury (Gershon Report), 2004. *Releasing resources to the front line: Independent review of public sector efficiency.* London: HM Treasury.

Hodgson, L., 2004. Manufacturing civil society: Counting the cost. *Critical Social Policy,* 24 (2), 139–164.

Hogwood, B.W., 1987. *From crisis to complacency? Shaping public policy in Britain.* Oxford: Oxford University Press.

Holden, R., 2011. Never forget you're Welsh: The role of sport as a political device in post-devolution Wales. *Sport in Society,* 14 (2), 272–288.

Holt, R., 1989. *Sport and the British: A modern history.* Oxford: Oxford University Press.

Holt, R. and Mason, T., 2000. *Sport in Britain 1945–2000.* Oxford: Blackwell.

Holt, R. and Tomlinson, A., 1994. Sport and leisure. *In:* D. Kavanagh and A. Seldon, eds., *The Major effect.* London: Macmillan.

Home Office, 2003. *An evaluation of positive futures: The key elements.* London: Home Office.

Hood, C.C. and Margetts, H.Z., 2007. *The tools of government in the digital age.* Basingstoke: Palgrave Macmillan.

Horne, J., Tomlinson, A. and Whannel, G., 1999. *Understanding sport: An introduction to the sociological and critical analysis of sport.* London: E & FN Spon.

Houlihan, B., 1991. *The government and politics of sport.* London: Routledge.

Houlihan, B., 1997. *Sport, policy and politics: A comparative analysis.* London: Routledge.

Houlihan, B., 2000. Sporting excellence, schools and sports development: The politics of crowded policy spaces. *European Physical Education Review,* 6, 171–193.

Houlihan, B., 2002. Political involvement in sport, physical education and recreation. *In*: A. Laker, ed., *The sociology of sport and physical education: An introductory reader*. London: Routledge.

Houlihan, B., 2005. Public sector sport policy: Developing a framework for analysis. *International Review of the Sociology of Sport*, 40 (2), 163–185.

Houlihan, B., 2010. It's wrong to remove a child's sporting chance—schools do much more sport now than ten years ago. So why abandon a proven system? *The Times*, 29 November 2010.

Houlihan, B., 2012. Sport policy convergence: A framework for analysis. *European Sport Management Quarterly*, 12 (2), 111–135.

Houlihan, B. and Green, M., 2006. The changing status of school sport and physical education: Explaining policy change. *Sport, Education and Society*, 11 (1), 73–92.

Houlihan, B. and Groeneveld, M., 2011. Social capital, governance and sport. *In*: M. Groeneveld, B. Houlihan & F. Ohl, eds., *Social capital and governance in Europe*. New York: Routledge.

Houlihan, B. and Lindsey, I., 2008. Networks and Partnerships in Sport development. *In*: V. Girginov, ed., *Management of sport development*. Oxford: Butterworth-Heinemann.

Houlihan, B., Park, J.-W. and Yamamoto, M.Y., 2012. National elite sport policies in preparation for London 2012. *In*: V. Girginov, ed., *Bidding, delivering and engaging with the Olympics*. London: Routledge.

Houlihan, B. & White, A., 2002. *The Politics of Sports Development: Development of Sport or Development through Sport*. London: Routledge.

House of Commons, 1994. *Hansard report of debates*, 11 July 1994, Vol. 246 cc650–1. London: Her Majesty's Stationery Office.

House of Commons Committee of Public Accounts, 2006. *UK Sport: Supporting elite athletes*, 54th Report of Session 2005–06, HC 898. London: The Stationery Office.

Howlett, M. and Ramesh, M., 1995. *Studying public policy: Policy cycles and subsystems*. Toronto: Oxford University Press.

Howlett, M. and Ramesh,, M. 2003.(2nd edn.) *Studying public policy: Policy cycles and subsystems*. Toronto: Oxford University Press.

Hubbard, A., 2011. Team GB banking on foreign legion. *The Independent*, 10 July 2011.

Hunt, J., 2011. School games. Speech to the Sports College Conference, Telford, 9 February 2011.

Institute of Youth Sport (IYS), 2004. *Report on the 2004 National Survey of Specialist Sports Colleges*. Loughborough: Institute of Youth Sport.

Institute of Youth Sport (IYS), 2008.School Sport Partnerships: Summary of key findings. Loughborough: Institute of Youth Sport, Loughborough University.

Jarvie, G., 1991. *Highland games: The making of the myth*. Edinburgh: Edinburgh University Press.

Jarvie, G., 1993. Sport, nationalism and cultural identity. *In*: L. Allison, ed., *The changing politics of sport*. Manchester: Manchester University Press.

Jarvie, G. and Maguire, J., 1994. *Sport and leisure in social thought*. London: Routledge.

Jarvie, G. and Reid, I., 1999. Sport, nationalism and culture in Scotland. *The Sports Historian*, 19 (1), 97–124.

Jarvie, G. and Thomson, I., 1999. Sport, nationalism and the Scottish parliament. *Scottish Affairs*, 27 (Spring), 84–98.

Jessop, B., 1990. *State theory: Putting the capitalist state in its place*. Cambridge: Cambridge University Press.

John, P., 1998. *Analysing public policy*. London: Pinter.

Johnes, M., 2000. Eighty minute patriots? National identity and sport in modern Wales. *The International Journal of the History of Sport*, 17 (4), 93–110.

Johnes, M., 2005. *A history of sport in Wales*. Cardiff: University of Wales Press.

Jones, G. and Stewart, J., 2011. Reflections of the Localism Bill. *In*: J. Raine & C. State, eds., *The world will be your oyster? Perspectives from the Institute of Local Government Studies on the Localism Bill*. Birmingham: INLOGOV.

Kavanagh, D., 1994. A Major agenda? In D. Kavanagh & A. Seldon, eds., *The Major effect*. London: Macmillan.

Kay, A., 2005. A critique of the use of path dependency in policy studies. *Public Administration*, 83 (3), 553–571.

Kay, T. and Bradbury, S., 2008. Stepping into the community? The impact of youth sport volunteering on young people's social capital. *In*: M. Nicholson and R. Hoye, eds., *Sport and social capital*. Oxford: Butterworth-Hienemann.

Keating, M., 2006. Higher education in Scotland and England after devolution. *In*: M. Keating & N. McEwen, eds., *Devolution and public policy*. Abingdon: Routledge.

Kellas, J., 1990. The constitutional options for Scotland, *Parliamentary Affairs*, 43 (4), 426–434.

Kellas, J., 1991. *The politics of nationalism and ethnicity*. Basingstoke: Macmillan.

Kelly, L., 2011. 'Social inclusion' through sports-based interventions? *Critical Social Policy*, 31, 126–150.

Key, R., 1992. House of Commons debates. 30 October 1992. Hansard Columns 1245–1314

King, N., 2009. *Sport policy and governance: Local Perspectives*. Oxford: Butterworth-Heinemann.

King, N., 2011. Local government sport services: Where next? *Leisure Studies Association Newsletter*, 89, July 2011, 51–56.

Kingdon, J.W., 1984. *Agendas, alternatives and public policy*. Boston, Mass.: Little, Brown.

Kirk, D., 2004. Framing quality physical education: The elite sport model or sport education? *Physical Education & Sport Pedagogy*, 9 (2), 185–195.

Kisby, B., 2010. The big society: Power to the people? *The Political Quarterly*, 81 (4), 484–491.

Knight, Kavanagh & Page (KKP), 2005. *Active Sports / CSP Impact Study Year 3: Final Report*. Bury: KKP.

Knox, C., 1986. Political symbolism and leisure provision in Northern Ireland local government. *Local Government Studies*, 12 (5), 37–50.

Knox, C., 1987. Territorialism, leisure and community centres in Northern Ireland. *Leisure Studies*, 6 (3), 251–264.

Knox, C., 2010. *Devolution and the governance of Northern Ireland*. Manchester: Manchester University Press.

Kurunmäki, L. and Miller, P., 2006. Modernising government: The calculating self, hybridisation and performance measurement. *Financial Accountability and Management*, 22 (1), 87–106.

Laffin, M., 2008. Local government modernisation in England: A critical review of the LGMA evaluation studies. *Local Government Studies*, 34 (1), 109–125.

Lamont, N., 1991. House of Commons debates. 19 March 1991. Hansard Column 175.

Leach. S., 1995. The strange case of the local government review. *In*: J. Stewart & G. Stoker, eds., *Local government in the 1990s*. Basingstoke: Macmillan.

Le Grand, J., 2007. *The other invisible hand: Delivering public services through choice and competition*. Princeton, NJ: Princeton University Press.

Lentell, B., 1993. Sports development: Goodbye to community recreation? *In*: C. Brackenridge, ed., *Body matters: Leisure images and lifestyles*. Brighton: LSA.

Lentell, R., 2001. Customers' views of the results of managing quality through ISO 9002 and Investors in People in leisure services. *Managing Leisure*, 6 (1), 15–34.

Lewin, K., 1951. *Field theory in social science; selected theoretical papers*. D. Cartwright, ed. New York: Harper and Row.

Lewis, J., 2004. What is New Labour? Can it deliver on social policy?. *In:* J.Lewis and R. Surender, eds. *Welfare state change: Towards a third way*. Oxford: Oxford University Press.

Liberal Democrats, no date. *Sport and the Olympics: Policy briefing* [online]. Available from: http://www.libdems.org.uk/siteFiles/resources/PDF/Election%20 Policy/26%20-%20Sport_and_Olympics.pdf [accessed: 11 April 2011].

Liddle, J., 2007. Reflections on regeneration management skills research, *Public Money and Management*, 27 (3), 189–192.

Lindblom, C.E., 1977. *Politics and markets: The world's political-economic systems*. New York: Basic Books.

Lindeman, S. and Conway, S., 2010. Sport through education: A county strategy. In M. Collins, ed., *Examining sports development*. London: Routledge.

Lindsey, I., 2008. *Partnership and collaboration in sport: A Study in the context of the new opportunities for PE and sport programme in three English cities*. Unpublished PhD thesis, Loughborough University.

Lindsey, I., 2009. Collaboration in local sport services in England: Issues emerging from case studies of two local authority areas. *International Journal of Sport Policy*, 1 (1), 71–88.

Lindsey, I., 2010a. Governance of lottery sport programmes: National direction of local partnerships in the new opportunities for PE and sport programme. *Managing Leisure*, 15 (3), 198–213.

Lindsey, I., 2010b. *Improving partnership, increasing participation? A decentred study of a local sport and physical activity alliance*. Sport Policy Conference, University of Birmingham, 19 July 2010.

Lister, R., 2003. Investing in the citizen-workers of the future: Transformations in citizenship and the state under New Labour. *Social Policy and Administration*, 37, 427–443.

Llewellyn, N., 2001. The role of storytelling and narrative in a modernization initiative. *Local Government Studies*, 27 (4), 35–58.

London Evening Standard, 4 September 2008 [online]. Available from: http:// www.thisislondon.co.uk/standard/article-23550988-brown-is-throwing-away-britains-beijing-bounce.do [accessed 18 November 2011].

Loughborough Partnership, 2006. *School sport partnerships: Annual monitoring and evaluation report for 2005*. Loughborough: Institute of Youth Sport.

Loughborough Partnership, 2008a. *The impact of School Sport Partnerships on pupil attainment*. Loughborough: Institute of Youth Sport.

Loughborough Partnership, 2008b. *The impact of School Sport Partnerships on pupil attendance*. Loughborough: Institute of Youth Sport.

Loughborough Partnership, 2008c. *The impact of School Sport Partnerships on pupil behaviour*. Loughborough: Institute of Youth Sport.

Loughborough Partnership, 2008d. *Key findings from the School Sport Partnerships impact study*. Loughborough: Institute of Youth Sport

Loughlin, M., 1996. *Legality and locality*. Oxford: Clarendon Press.

Lowi, T.J., 1964. American business, public policy, case studies and political theory. *World Politics*, 16, 677–693.

Lowi, T.J., 1970. Decision-making vs. public policy: Towards an antidote for technocracy. *Public Administration Review*, 30, 314–325.

Lowi, T.J., 1972. Four systems of policy politics and choice. *Public Administration Review*, 32, 298–310.

Lowndes, V., 2004. Reformers or recidivists? Has local government really changed? *In*: G. Stoker & D. Wilson, eds., *British local government into the 21st century*. Basingstoke: Palgrave.

Lowndes, V. and Pratchett, L., 2012. Local Governance under the Coalition Government: Austerity, Localism and the 'Big Society', *Local Government Studies*, 38 (1), 21–40.

Lowndes, V. and Wilson, D., 2003. Balancing revisability and robustness? A new institutionalist perspective on local government modernisation. *Public Administration*, 81 (2), 275–298.

Mackintosh, C., 2011. An analysis of County Sport Partnerships in England: The fragility, challenges and complexity of partnership working in sports development. *International Journal of Sport Policy and Politics*, 3 (1), 45–64.

Major, J., 1994. Conservative central council meeting, held at Plymouth Pavilions, in Plymouth, on Saturday 26 March 1994.

Major, J., 1995. Introduction. *In*: Department of National Heritage, *Sport: raising the game*. London: DNH.

Major, J., 1999. *John Major: The autobiography*. London: HarperCollins.

Martin, S.J., 2000. Implementing Best Value: Local public services in transition. *Public Administration*, 78 (1), 209–227.

Martin, S.J., 2002. The modernisation of UK local government: Markets, managers, monitors and mixed fortunes. *Public Management Review*, 4 (3), 291–307.

McCarthy, M., 1989. Introduction: The boundaries of welfare. *In*: M. McCarthy, ed., *The new politics of welfare: An agenda for the 1990s?* London: Macmillan.

McDonald, I., 2000. 'Excellence and expedience? Olympism, power and contemporary sports policy in England'. *In*: M. Keech & G. McFee, eds., *Issues and values in sport and leisure cultures*. Oxford: Meyer & Meyer Sport, 83–100.

McDonald, I., 2005. Theorising partnerships: Governance, communicative action and sport policy. *Journal of Social Policy*, 34 (4), 579–600.

Midwinter, A., 2001. New Labour and the modernisation of British local government: A critique. *Financial Accountability and Management*, 17 (4), 311–320.

Miller, P. and Rose, N., 2008. *Governing the present*. Cambridge: Polity Press.

Mitchell, J., 2004. Scotland: Expectations, policy types and devolution. *In*: A. Trench, ed. *Has devolution made a difference? The state of the nations 2004*. Exeter: Imprint Books.

Monnington, T., 1993. *Politicians and sport: Uses and abuses. In*: L. Allison, ed., *The changing politics of sport*. Manchester: Manchester University Press.

Moore, P.G., 1997. The development of the UK National Lottery: 1992–96. *Journal of Royal Statistical Society*, 160 (2), 169–185.

Morgan, W.J., 1994. *Leftist theories of sport: A critique and reconstruction*. Chicago, Illinois: University of Illinois Press.

Moynihan, C., 1990. *Politics towards 2000. Sport development: Seminar report*. London: Sports Council.

Murdoch, E., 1993. Education, sport and leisure: Collapsing boundaries? *In*: G. McFee & A. Tomlinson, eds., *Education, sport and leisure: Connections and controversies*. Eastbourne: Chelsea School Research Centre.

Nairn, T., 1981. *The breakup of Britain: crisis and neo-nationalism* (2nd edn.), London: Verso.

National Assembly for Wales (Sport Policy Unit), 2003. *Climbing higher*. Cardiff: National Assembly for Wales.

National Assembly for Wales, 2007. *One Wales: A progressive agenda for the government of Wales*. Cardiff: National Assembly for Wales.

National Audit Office, 2005. *UK Sport: Supporting elite athletes*. London: The Stationery Office.

National Council for School Sport, 2005. *Schools competition developments: Bulletin.* 2 July 2005.

Nelson, L. and Henderson, S., 2005. Best Value and the market orientation of UK recreation centres. *Local Government Studies*, 31 (2), 237–257.

New Local Government Network, 2010. *The Decentralisation and Localism Bill: Pre⊠publication briefing* [online]. Available from: http://www.nlgn.org.uk/public/wp-content/uploads/NLGN-Briefing-on-the-Localism-Bill.pdf [accessed 30 June 2011].

Newman, J., 2001. *Modernizing governance: New Labour, policy and society.* London: Sage.

New Opportunities Fund, 2001. *Building for the tomorrow: Our vision for the new opportunities for PE and sport programme.* London: New Opportunities Fund.

Nichols, G., 1996. The Impact of Compulsory Competitive Tendering on planning in leisure departments. *Managing Leisure*, 1 (2), 105–114.

Nichols, G., 2007. *Sport and crime reduction : The role of sports in tackling youth crime.* London: Routledge.

Nichols, G. and Robinson, L., 2000. *The process of Best Value—further lessons from the leisure pilots.* Melton Mowbray: ISRM.

Nichols, G. and Taylor, P., 1995. The impact on local authority leisure provision of Compulsory Competitive Tendering, financial cuts and changing attitudes. *Local Government Studies*, 21 (4), 607–622.

Niskanen, W., 1971. *Bureaucracy and representative government.* Chicago: Aldine-Atherton.

Norman, J., 2010. *The Big Society: The anatomy of the new politics.* Buckingham: University of Buckingham Press.

Northern Ireland Executive, 2008. *Programme for government 2008–11*, Belfast: NI Executive.

Oakley, B. and Green, M., 2001. Still playing the game at arm's length? The selective re-investment in British sport, 1995–2000. *Managing Leisure*, 6 (2), 74–94.

Observer. 2005. The day Coe won gold. 10th July, p.3.

Observer, 2006. The ruinously expensive folly of this mad five-ring circus. 26th November, p31.

Offe, C., 1984. *Contradictions of the welfare state.* Cambridge, MA: MIT Press.

Office of the Deputy Prime Minister (ODPM), 2002. *Your region, your choice: Revitalising the English regions.* London: ODPM.

OFSTED, 1995. *Physical education and sport in schools: A survey of good practice.* London: HMSO.

OFSTED, 2006. *School sport partnerships: A survey of good practice.* London: HMSO.

O'Gorman, J., 2009. *Assessing external provider provision in schools.* European Sports Development Network Conference, Nottingham Trent University, 4–5 September 2009.

Paris, C., Gray, P. and Muir, J., 2003. Devolving housing policy and practice in Northern Ireland 1998–2002. *Housing Studies*, 18 (2), 159–175.

Parker, S., 2011. *Next localism: Five trends for the future of local government.* London: New Local Government Network.

Parrish, R., 2003. The birth of European Union sports law. *Entertainment Law*, 2 (2), 20–39.

Parsons, W., 1995. *Public policy: An introduction to the theory and practice of policy analysis.* Aldershot: Edward Elgar.

Paterson, L., 1994. *The autonomy of modern Scotland.* Edinburgh: Edinburgh University Press.

Penney, D. and Chandler, T., 2000. Physical education: What future(s)? *Sport Education & Society*, 5 (1), 71–87.

Penney, D. and Evans, J., 1999. *Politics, policy and practice in physical education.* London: Routledge.

Pickup, D., 1990. *Sport 2000. Sport development: Seminar report.* London: Sports Council.

Pickup, D., 1996. *Not another Messiah: An account of the Sports Council 1988– 93.* Edinburgh: The Pentland Press.

Pierre, J. and Peters, B.G., 2000. *Governance and the state.* Basingstoke: Palgrave Macmillan.

Pierson, P., 2001. Post-industrial pressures on the mature welfare states. *In*: P. Pierson, ed., *The new politics of the welfare state.* Oxford: Oxford University Press.

Polley, M., 1998. *Moving the goalposts: A history of sport and society since 1945.* London: Routledge.

Power, S. and Whitty, G., 1999. New Labour's education policy: First, second or third way? *Journal of Education Policy*, 14 (5), 535–546.

Pratchett, L., 2002. Local government: From modernisation to consolidation. *Parliamentary Affairs*, 55 (2), 331–346.

Pratchett, L. and Leach, S., 2003. Local government: Selectivity and diversity. *Parliamentary Affairs*, 56, 255–269.

Prior, D., 1995. Citizen's Charters. *In*: J. Stewart and G. Stoker, eds., *Local government in the 1990s.* Basingstoke: Macmillan.

Purnell, J., 2007. *Speech by James Purnell to the CCPR annual conference 2007* [online]. Available from: http://webarchive.nationalarchives.gov.uk/+/http:// www.culture.gov.uk/reference_library/minister_speeches/2056.aspx [accessed 18 November 2011].

Putnam, R.D., 1995. Bowling alone: America's declining social capital. *Journal of Democracy*, 6, 65–78.

Putnam, R.D., 2000. *Bowling alone: The collapse and revival of American community.* New York: Simon and Schuster.

Quick, S., Simon, A. and Thornton, A., 2010. *PE and sport survey 2009/10.* London: TNS-BMRB.

Raco, M., 2004. Governing from below—urban regions and the global economy. *Area*, 36, 89–91.

Raine, J.W., 2011. The Localism Bill: Introduction and overview. *In*: J. Raine & C. State, eds., *The world will be your oyster? Perspectives from the Institute of Local Government Studies on the Localism Bill.* Birmingham: INLOGOV.

Ravenscroft, N., 1998. The changing regulation of public leisure provision. *Leisure Studies*, 17 (2), 138–154.

Rawnsley, A., 2006. *The ruinously expensive folly of this mad five-ring circus.* Observer, 26 November. Available from: http://www.guardian.co.uk/commentisfree/2006/nov/26/comment.olympics2012 [accessed 18 December 2010].

Reid, G., 2003. Charitable trusts: Municipal leisure's 'third way'? *Managing Leisure*, 8 (4), 171–183.

Reid, G., 2007. Scottish political parties and leisure policy. *Scottish Affairs*, 59 (Spring), 68–91.

Revill, J., 2007. *U turn on sport for all pledge. Observer*, 25 November. Available from: http://www.guardian.co.uk/uk/2007/nov/25/olympics2012.london [accessed 18 December 2010].

Rhodes, R.A.W., 1994. The hollowing out of the state. *Political Quarterly*, 65, 138–151.

Richard Commission, 2003. *Evidence from the Welsh Sports Council*, 27 June [online]. Available from: http://www.richardcommission.gov.uk/content/template.asp?ID=/content/evidence/oral/sportscouncil/index-e.asp [accessed 5 May 2010].

Richard Commission, 2004. *Report of the Richard Commission on the powers and electoral arrangements of the National Assembly for Wales*. Cardiff: National Assembly for Wales.

Richards, D. and Smith, M.J., 2004. The 'Hybrid State': New Labour's response to the challenge of governance. *In*: S. Ludlam and M.J. Smith, eds., *Governing as New Labour*. Basingstoke: Palgrave.

Roberts, K., 1996. Young people, schools, sport and government policy. *Sport, Education and Society*, 1, 47–57.

Roberts, K., 2004. *The leisure industries*. Basingstoke: Palgrave Macmillan.

Robinson, L., 1999. Following the quality strategy: The reasons for the use of quality management in UK public leisure facilities. *Managing Leisure*, 4 (4), 201–217.

Robinson, L., 2004. *Managing public sport and leisure services*. London: Routledge.

Robinson, L. and Taylor, P., 2003. The performance of local authority sports halls and swimming pools in England. *Managing Leisure*, 8 (1), 1–16.

Robson, S. and McKenna, J., 2008. Sport and health. *In*: K. Hylton & P. Bramham, eds., *Sport development: Policy, process and practice*. London: Routledge.

Roche, M., 1993. Sport and community: Rhetoric and reality in the development of British sport policy. *In*: J.C. Binfield and J. Stevenson, eds., *Sport, culture and politics*. Sheffield: Sheffield Academic Press.

Rose, N., 1999. *Powers of freedom: Reframing political thought*. Cambridge: Cambridge University Press.

Rose, R., 1984. *Do parties matter?* Basingstoke: Macmillan.

Sabatier, P.A., 1998. The advocacy coalition framework: revisions and relevance for Europe, *Journal of European Public Policy*, 5 (1), 98–130.

Sabatier, P., ed., 1999. *Theories of the policy process*. Boulder, CO: Westview Press

Sabatier, P., ed., 2007. 2nd. Edn. *Theories of the policy process*. Boulder, CO: Westview Press.

Sabatier, P. and Jenkins-Smith, H., 1999. The advocacy coalition framework: An assessment. *In*: P. Sabatier, ed., *Theories of the policy process*. 1st ed. Boulder, CO: Westview Press.

Sabatier, P. and Weible, C., 2007. The advocacy coalition framework. *In*: P. Sabatier, ed., *Theories of the policy process*. Boulder, CO: Westview Press.

Scottish Executive, 2001. *Working together for Scotland: A programme for government*. Edinburgh: The Scottish Executive.

Scottish Executive, 2002. *Let's make Scotland more active: A strategy for physical activity*. Edinburgh: Scottish Executive.

Scottish Executive, 2007. *Reaching higher: Building on the success of Sport 21*. Edinburgh: Scottish Executive.

Scottish Government, 2010. *Delivering for Scotland: The government's programme for Scotland 2010–11*. Edinburgh: Scottish Government.

Scottish Parliament, 2002. *Sport in Scotland. Research Note, RN 00/92*, Edinburgh: Scottish Parliament.

Scottish Sports Council (**sport**scotland), 1998. *Sport 21: The national strategy for sport*, Edinburgh: The Scottish Sports Council.

Seldon, A., 1997. *Major: A political life*. London: Orion

Sharp, C., et al., 2003. *Playing for Success: An Evaluation of the Fourth Year*. Annesley: DfES Publications.

Shaw, E., 2004. The control freaks: New Labour and the party. *In*: S. Ludlam & M.J. Smith, eds., *Governing as New Labour*. Basingstoke: Palgrave.

Shirlow, P., 2001. Devolution in Northern Ireland/Ulster/the North/Six Counties: Delete as appropriate. *Regional Studies*, 35 (8), 743–752.

Simmons, R., 2003. *New leisure trusts*. Reading: Institute of Leisure and Amenity Management.

Simmons, R., 2004. A trend to trust? The rise of new leisure trusts in the UK. *Managing Leisure*, 9 (3), 159–177.

Simmons, R., 2008. Harnessing social enterprise for local public services: The case of new leisure trusts in the UK. *Public Policy and Administration*, 23, 278–301.

Sinclair, I., 2008. The Olympic scam. *London Review of Books*, 30 (12), 17–23.

Skelcher, C., 2004. The new governance of communicities. *In*: G. Stoker & D. Wilson, eds., *British local government into the 21st century*. Basingstoke: Palgrave.

Smith, A., 2011. *Back to the future?: Reflections on youth sport policy under the coalition government*. Paper presented at Edge Hill University, 1 June 2011.

Smith, J., 1988. Introduction. *In*: Sports Council. *Into the nineties: Sport in the community: A strategy for sport 1988–1993*. London: Sports Council.

Smith, A. & Leech, R., 2010. 'Evidence. What evidence?': Evidence-based policy making and School Sport Partnerships in North West England. *International Journal of Sport Policy,* 2 (3), 327–346.

Smith, A. and Waddington, I., 2004. Using "sport in the community schemes" to tackle crime and drug use among young people: Some policy issues and problems. *European Physical Education Review*, 10, 279–297.

Social Exclusion Unit/CMAP, 2002. *The Social Exclusion Unit's policy action team approach to policy development: The views of participants*. London: SEU/ CMAP.

Sport England, 1999a. *Investing in our future: Sport England lottery fund strategy 1999–2009*. London: Sport England.

Sport England, 1999b. *Survey of sports halls and swimming pools in England*, London: Sport England.

Sport England,1999c. *Best Value through sport: The value of sport to local authorities*. London: Sport England.

Sport England, 2000. *First Sport Action zones announced*. Press release, 17 January. London: Sport England.

Sport England, 2001. *Sport Action Zones: Report on the establishment of the first 12 zones*. London: Sport England.

Sport England, 2004a. *The framework for sport in England: Making England an active and successful sporting nation: A vision for 2020*. London: Sport England.

Sport England, 2004b. *DCMS/Sport England funding agreement: 2003–06*. London: Sport England.

Sport England, 2004c. *Participation in sport—results from the General Household Survey 2002*. Research briefing note. London: Sport England.

Sport England, 2005a. *Sport: Playing its part. The contribution of sport to healthier communities*. London: Sport England.

Sport England, 2005b. *Policy statement: The delivery system for sport in England*. London: Sport England.

Sport England, 2005c. *Sport playing its part: The contribution of sport to meeting the needs of children and young people*. London: Sport England.

Sport England, 2005d. *Sport playing its part: Executive summary*. London: Sport England.

Sport England, 2006a. *Jennie Price to be the new chief executive of Sport England* [online]. Available from: http://www.sportengland.org/news/press_releases/jennie_price_to_be_new_chief_executive_of_sport_england.htm [accessed 16 July 2008].

Sport England, 2006b. *Understanding the success factors in Sport Action Zones: Final report*. London: Sport England.

Sport England, 2007. *Community sports networks: Implementation and investment guidance*. London: Sport England.

Sport England, 2008. *Healthier communities: Improving health and reducing health inequalities through sport*. London: Sport England.

Sport England, 2010. *Annual report and accounts, 2009–10*. London: Sport England.

Sport England/UK Sport, 2004. *Moving On: A review of the need for change in athletics in the* UK (*The Foster Report*). London: Sport England/UK Sport.

Sport Northern Ireland, 2009a. *Corporate plan 2008–11*. Belfast: Sport Northern Ireland.

Sport Northern Ireland, 2009b. *Sport matters: The Northern Ireland strategy for sport and physical recreation 2009–2019*. Belfast: Sport Northern Ireland.

Sports Council, 1982. *Sport in the community: The next ten years*. London: Sports Council.

Sports Council, 1988. *Into the nineties: Sport in the community: A strategy for sport 1988–1993*. London: Sports Council.

Sports Council, 1991. *Sport in the nineties: New horizons*. London: Sports Council.

Sports Council, 1993a. *Young people and sport: Policy and frameworks for action*. London: Sports Council.

Sports Council, 1993b. *Sport in the 90s: New horizons*. London: Sports Council.

Sports Council, 1993c. *Women and sport. Policy frameworks for action*. London: Sports Council.

Sports Council, 1993d. *People with disabilities: Policy and current/planned action*. London: Sports Council.

Sports Council, 1994. *Black and ethnic minorities and sport: Policy and objectives*. London: Sports Council.

Sports Council (1996) *The Sports Council Annual Report 1995 / 96*. London: Sports Council.

sportscotland, no date. *Regional sporting partnerships: Consultation note*. Edinburgh: sportscotland.

Sproat, I., 1994. House of Commons debates 8 July 1994. Hansard Columns 584–592.

Sproat, I., 1995a. House of Commons debates 27 March 1995. Hansard Columns 682.

Sproat, I., 1995b. House of Commons debates 14 July 1995. Hansard Columns 800–803.

Sproat, I., 1995c. House of Commons debates 27 October 1995. Hansard Columns 1211–1282.

Sproat, I., 1996. House of Commons debates 7 June 1996. Hansard Columns 828.

Stevens, D. and Green, P., 2002. Explaining continuity and change in the transition from Compulsory Competitive Tendering to Best Value for sport and recreation management. *Managing Leisure*, 7 (2), 124–138.

Stewart, J., 2000. *The nature of British local government*. Basingstoke: Palgrave.

Stewart, J. and Stoker, G., 1995a. Introduction. *In*: J. Stewart & G. Stoker, eds., *Local government in the 1990s*. Basingstoke: Macmillan.

Stewart, J. and Stoker, G., 1995b. Fifteen years of local government restructuring 1979–1994: An evaluation. *In*: J. Stewart & G. Stoker, eds., *Local government in the 1990s*. Basingstoke: Macmillan.

Stoker, G., 2004. *Transforming local government: From Thatcher to New Labour*. Basingstoke: Palgrave.

Stoker, G., 2011. Was local governance such a good idea? A global comparative perspective. *Public Administration*, 89 (1), 15–31.

Stoker, G. and Wilson, D., 2004a. Introduction. *In*: G. Stoker & D. Wilson, eds., *British local government into the 21st century*. Basingstoke: Palgrave.

Stoker, G. and Wilson, D., 2004b. Conclusions: New Ways of being local government. *In*: G. Stoker & D. Wilson, eds., *British local government into the 21st century*. Basingstoke: Palgrave.

Stuart, G., 2010. House of Commons debates. 30 November 2010. Hansard Column 718–720

Sullivan, H., 2004. Community governance and local governance: A shoe that fits of the emperor's new clothes? *In*: G. Stoker & D. Wilson, eds., *British local government into the 21st century*. Basingstoke: Palgrave

Sullivan, H. and Gillanders, G., 2005. Stretched to the limit? The impact of local public service agreements on service improvements and central–local relations. *Local Government Studies*, 31 (5), 555–574.

Talbot, M., 1995. The politics of sport and physical education. *In*: S. Fleming, M. Talbot & A. Tomlinson, eds., *Policy and politics in sport, physical education and leisure: Themes and issues*. Brighton: Leisure Studies Association.

Taylor, A., 1997. 'Arm's length but hands-on': Mapping the new governance: The Department of National Heritage and cultural politics in Britain. *Public Administration*, 75, 441–466.

Taylor, P., 2011. *Torkildsen's sport and leisure management*. London: Routledge.

Taylor, R., 2006. *Major*. London: Haus Publishing.

Thelen, K. and Steinmo, S., 1992. Historical institutionalism in comparative politics.*In* S. Steinmo, K. Thelen and F. Longstreth *Historical institutionalism in comparative politics: State, society, and economy*. New York, Cambridge University Press.

Thomson, I., 2010. Sport in the devolved system: The Scottish experience. *In*: M. Collins, ed., *Examining sport development*. London: Routledge.

Thorburn, M., 2009. Physical education, the policy entrepreneur and comprehensive schooling: Can they exist in harmony? *Forum*, 51 (1), 101–106.

Tomlinson, S., 2001. *Education in a post-welfare society*. Buckingham: Open University Press.

Tonge, J., 2006. *Northern Ireland*. Cambridge: Polity Press.

Torkildsen, G., 2005. *Leisure and recreation management*. London: Routledge.

True, J.L., Jones, B.D. and Baumgartner, F.R., 2007. Punctuated-equilibrium theory: Explaining stability and change in public policymaking. *In*: P. Sabatier, ed., *Theories of the policy process*. Boulder, CO: Westview Press.

Tullock, G., 1965. *The politics of bureaucracy*. Washington, DC: Public Affairs Press.

UK Sport, 2003. *Funding agreement between the UK Sports Council and the DCMS for 2003–06*. London: UK Sport.

UK Sport, 2006a. '*No compromise*' [online]. Available from: http://www.uksport. gov.uk/pages/no_compromise/ [sccessed 6 June 2006].

UK Sport, 2006b. '*Olympic sport quick out of blocks with new funding*' (press release, July). London: UK Sport.

UK Sport, 2010. *Annual report, 2009–10*. London: UK Sport.

Universities of Leeds and Glamorgan and the London School of Hygiene and Tropical Medicine, 1998. *The health of the nation—a policy assessed*. London: Department of Health. (E copy only available: http://www.dh.gov.uk/en/Publicationsandstatistics/Publications/PublicationsPolicyAndGuidance/DH_4121577 Accessed 10.05.2012)

Van den Berg, A. and Janoski, T., 2005. Conflict theories in political sociology. *In*: T. Janoski, R. Alford, M.A. Hicks & M.A. Schwartz, eds., *The handbook of political sociology*. Cambridge: Cambridge University Press.

Vigor, A., Mean, M. and Tims, C., 2004. *After the gold rush: A sustainable Olympics for London.* London: IPPR/Demos.

Wales Audit Office, 2007. *Increasing physical activity.* Cardiff: Wales Audit Office.

Ward, N. and Lowe, P., 2007. 'Blairite modernization and countryside policy'. *The Political Quarterly,* 78 (3), 412–421.

Weible, C.M., 2007. An advocacy coalition framework approach to stakeholder analysis: Understanding the political context of California marine protected area policy. *Journal of Public Administration Research and Theory,* 17 (1), 95–117.

Welsh Assembly Government, 2006. *Climbing higher—next steps.* Cardiff: WAG.

Welsh Office/Sports Council for Wales, 1995, *Young people and sport in Wales.* Cardiff: The Welsh Office

Welsh Office/Sports Council for Wales, 1996, *Young people and sport in Wales: Moving on.* Cardiff: The Welsh Office

Wharton Consulting, 2009. *Welsh Assembly government: Performance and excellence sport review, final report.* Harrogate: Wharton Consulting.

White, J., 1999. Managing the lottery: Evaluation of the first four years and lessons for local authorities. *Managing Leisure,* 4, 78–93.

Whitty, G., 2010. *Evaluating 'Blair's educational legacy?': Some comments on the special issue of Oxford Review of Education.* Abingdon: Routledge.

Wilding, P., 1997. The welfare state and the conservatives. *Political Studies,* 45 (4), 716–726.

Wilson , D., 2003. Unravelling control freakery: Redefining central-local government relations. *British Journal of Politics and International Relations,* 5 (3), 317–346.

Wilson, D., 2004. New patterns of central-local relations. *In*: G. Stoker & D. Wilson, eds., *British local government into the 21st century.* Basingstoke: Palgrave.

Wilson, D. and Game, C., 1994. *Local government in the United Kingdom.* Basingstoke : Macmillan

Wincott, D., 2005. Reshaping public space? Devolution and policy change in British early years childhood education and care. *Regional and Federal Studies,* 15 (4), 453–470.

Young, H., 1994a. The prime minister. *In*: D. Kavanagh & A. Seldon, eds., *The Major effect.* London: Macmillan.

Young, K., 1994b. Local government. *In*: D. Kavanagh & A. Seldon, eds., *The Major effect.* London: Macmillan.

Zahariadis, N., 2003. *Ambiguity and choice in public policy: Political decision making in modern democracies.* Washington, DC: Georgetown University Press.

Zahariadis, N., 2007. Multiple streams framework: Structure, limitations, prospects. In P.A. Sabatier, ed. Theories of the policy process, 2nd. Edn. Boulder Col.: Westview Press.

Zheng, J., 2011. *An investigation of the UK squad's performance in the five most recent summer Olympic Games and the correlation between performance and government financial support.* Unpublished MSc dissertation. Loughborough University.

Index